51370410 7

CN00920213

Please return this item
by the last date shown.
Items can be renewed online at
inderby.org.uk/libraries

RELENTLESS

ALISTAIR BROWNLEE

RELENTLESS

SECRETS OF THE SPORTING ELITE

WRITTEN WITH DUNCAN CRAIG

HarperCollins*Publishers*

HarperCollins*Publishers*
1 London Bridge Street
London SE1 9GF

www.harpercollins.co.uk

HarperCollins*Publishers*
1st Floor, Watermarque Building, Ringsend Road
Dublin 4, Ireland

First published by HarperCollins in 2021

1 3 5 7 9 10 8 6 4 2

A catalogue record of this book is
available from the British Library

HB ISBN 978-0-00-829528-8
PB ISBN 978-0-00-840815-2

www.fsc.org FSC™ C007454

This book is produced from independently certified FSC™ paper
to ensure responsible forest management.

For more information visit: www.harpercollins.co.uk/green

To Mum and Dad
Thank you for making me endlessly curious

CONTENTS

INTRODUCTION

Want to know the best thing about being a double Olympic gold medallist?

The free kit's great. The golden postbox? That was pretty cool. Never having to buy a round in your local? What Yorkshireman wouldn't enjoy that? Then there's the fan mail – mostly via social media these days, though some people are still refreshingly old school; the marriage proposals (awkward); and the proposals of a rather less wholesome nature (even more so). The sponsorship deals have certainly made my day-to-day life as an athlete a lot easier. And I've loved playing a part in giving thousands of young people a chance to experience triathlon.

But, for a sports obsessive such as myself, there's one perk that beats all others: the access gold medals give you to the sporting elite. Those surprisingly weighty discs are like a currency recognised throughout the sporting world (not that I walk around with them, you understand). The immortals past and present, those setting the pace or leading their fields – all suddenly seem happy for you to chew the fat with them pretty much as equals, even when you feel far from it.

It helps that my sport, triathlon, has exploded in popularity in recent years. Seemingly every sportsman and woman I bump into these days is into their tri, or at the very least reaping the benefits of running, cycling or swimming in one form or another. It used to be that golf was every sportsperson's second sport. For many years, in certain sports, it was drinking. Times have changed.

I wasn't about to squander this privileged access. I'm bewildered by fans who queue up to meet their sporting heroes and want only selfies. I want more. I want to sit them down and pick their brains, to find out what it is that makes them tick – and goes on doing so. That's so much more interesting to me than a gurning photo for a few social media likes.

And what fascinates me more than anything are those who don't just win, but dominate. Those who don't shrink on the highest stage, but grow on it. Athletes and sportspeople who through their achievements expand the very parameters of what is thought possible.

I've never shared the British appreciation for the underdog. Anyone can run hot, lightning can strike, rogue caps can get awarded. But what of those who do it week in, week out; World Cup after World Cup; grand slam after grand slam; season after season; Olympic cycle after Olympic cycle? Those who refuse to bow to despondency or triumphalism, to boredom, to distraction, to adulation or to enrichment (not a problem for triathletes, I can assure you)?

A sporting career, like life, is finite and over quicker than you might imagine. To stay at the top for 10, 15, sometimes even 20 years – that takes a special calibre of person. Does it actually get easier, given the funding, the support, the seeding, the experience? For sure. But it also gets exponentially harder due to the target on your back, age tapping at the window, and the event or sport you call your own changing almost beyond recognition with the passing of years.

I've achieved – but I'm no expert in what it takes to achieve. Really, I'm an expert in just one thing: what works for me. And therein lies my curiosity. I want to understand what it takes – in the words of Seb Coe about his old friend, the decathlete Daley Thompson – 'to grip your event by the throat and make it your own'. I love that phrase. Any sportsperson would. Choking the life out of it. A dogged, white-knuckled refusal to relinquish.

How do these people do it? What can I learn from them? And, crucially, what do such people share – physiologically, behaviourally and psychologically? These are the questions I've always longed to ask. And one day it suddenly hit home: now I'm in a position to do so.

So that's what I've done here: England's two most inspirational cricketers of the past century; the leading try scorer in Welsh rugby; the lynchpin of Sir Alex Ferguson's all-conquering Manchester United reign; one of England's greatest-ever goal scorers; the fastest female marathoner of all time; a multiple Formula One winner who battled through more than 200 Grands Prix and went front-wing to front-wing with arguably the strongest grid ever assembled; a four-time Tour de France winner; the champion jockey who battered himself into submission to fuel his addiction to winning; the man with one of the best Ryder Cup records in golf; the world's most astonishing endurance athlete; the dazzlingly articulate captain of a team that rewrote the book on teamwork; the most distinctive sprinter, and two of the most dominant swimmers in history; the fastest cyclist of all time; and the most naturally gifted snooker player of this or any generation.

Mavericks and monomaniacs, show-offs and introverts, team players and individual stars – the diversity of characters I've met and spoken to is striking. In fact these sporting superstars only really share one thing: they are all, in Seb's words, bona fide 'grippers'. Some have trained with me. Others have hung out with me. All have indulged me, and I'm pretty sure you're going to want to hear what they have to say.

To this list I've added a cast of supporting characters: World Cup coaches; the world's leading experts in human performance and exercise physiology; surviving relatives of athletes who were once unstoppable competitive forces; a multiple world champion turned motivational speaker and high-performance consultant; athletes whose roles in epic sporting moments were limited to a brief cameo; and a professor heading up groundbreaking research into the well-being and welfare of elite athletes.

All these characters provide the context, clarity and colour as I explore themes around performance that have fascinated me from a time before I could articulate them: decision-making, focus, innovation, motivation, conditioning, adaptability, superstition, belief, aura, ruthlessness, passion – and that biggie, the one us athletes never like to dwell too much upon ... luck.

I remember attending a dinner at my old school, Bradford Grammar, around eight years ago. On my table was Adrian Moorhouse MBE, who triumphed in the 100m breaststroke at the 1988 Seoul Olympics. A rather self-important Old Bradfordian was quizzing me about how I could possibly continue to train intensively, hour after hour, day after day, year after year, four-year cycle after four-year cycle.

Before I could come up with a response, Moorhouse stepped in. 'If you can answer the question of why you do it, then you're in the wrong game.' It was a neat line, and it seemed to satisfy the old buffer. Thanks, Adrian. But you know what? The further I've progressed in sport and the older I've got, the more I've realised that I *want* to be able to answer that question: why and how I do what I do – and whether it's the same for others.

There are a couple of common misconceptions regarding motivation. People tend to think that it's a binary force for sportspeople – you've either got it or you haven't – and that it comes from a single, unwavering, inexhaustible source, with your career dying when it's snuffed out. I've always found it far more enigmatic than that; the wronged man nursing a burning injustice only works in the movies (though we'll meet several sportspeople for whom being written off early in their careers, either physically or in some other way, provided the bedrock to their success).

For me, the internal fire of motivation has to be selectively deployed. And it can be drawn from multiple sources. Glory, financial gain, fear of failure, the desire to impress, anger, mastery of the process, jealousy, rage, love of the great outdoors, silencing of doubt (both external and internal) – these are sources I've tapped into at some point to aid my performance, sometimes all during the same day.

Over my career, I've learned not to judge someone's source of motivation in a 'mine is more intrinsic and authentic than yours' sort of way, but simply to respect the varied wells from which high achievers draw their reserves. If hate gets you over the line – and do dig out footage of the final game of the Andre Agassi vs Boris Becker US Open semi-final in 1995 if you want to see how effective channelled rage can be (Agassi was nursing a sense of burning injustice after a perceived Becker slight) – then great. 'Just written the other side's team talk' is an expression the media like to use in such situations. For all the finely tuned preparation, it can sometimes be forgotten that sport is played by humans.

By the same token, those of us who compete understand that leaping over a bar, kicking a ball over some posts, or – for me – swimming, cycling and running around a course are highly contrived forms of behaviour that have little or nothing to do with real life. And yet we must believe, with every fibre of our being, that the two are inextricably linked. That sport is life, and therefore failure is death (Bill Shankly put it best), and that everything else around us – family, friends, other people, other interests – matters less at that moment. Only then can we begin to scale the heights of training and performance to compete with the world's best. Cognitive dissonance, I believe they call it. Or as Welsh and Lions rugby legend Shane Williams, who we'll meet in a future chapter, once put it, a sort of temporary insanity.

Of course, for some, cognitive dissonance isn't required. I had a comfortable middle-class upbringing in Yorkshire, leaving Bradford Grammar with four As at A level and studying medicine at Cambridge until I chose to leave to focus on being an athlete. The breadline and the finishing line were unlikely to ever be linked in my life. Siya Kolisi, the inspirational captain of the South African rugby team that swept to World Cup glory in Japan in 2019, grew up in a township outside Port Elizabeth, was raised by a grandparent and often trained on an empty stomach.

Undisputed middleweight boxing champion Claressa Shields faced similar early adversity. She endured an unimaginably tough upbringing in Flint, Michigan; she was introduced to boxing by her father, who spent many of her early years in jail. Although we both did the double in London 2012 and Rio 2016, any other similarities between us on the surface would be hard to find.

But this book is not a study of what breeds success: nature versus nurture; the effects of calendar bias in the formative years; the 10,000 hours rule of Malcolm Gladwell's excellent *Outliers*. Enthralling stuff, all of it, but that path is well trodden. I want to shift the focus onwards and upwards, to the territory that lies *beyond* achievement. Multiple grand slams rather than occasional tournament wins. Not just a single Tour de France victory, but a drive to win more than any rider in history. What are the motivating factors in this? Hunger? Insatiable competitiveness? Greed? Habit? Fear?

You won't be surprised to learn which camp, as a well-grounded Yorkshire lad, I lean towards in the perspiration vs inspiration debate. There's a cracking anecdote I first heard as a schoolboy about the legendary Seb Coe–Steve Ovett rivalry. You'll have heard it, I'm sure. Coe, the story goes, went training one Christmas morning, desperate to grab an advantage over his great middle-distance rival. But, once showered and changed and sitting down to Christmas dinner, he became beset by worry. What if Ovett were training twice that day? So he went out again that evening. Years later, when the two had become friends, Coe felt compelled to share the story.

'So you only trained twice that day,' was Ovett's response.

Almost certainly apocryphal. Or is it? We're a crazy bunch, us athletes, and gluttons for punishment. But as I've progressed in my career I've come to realise something quite surprising: while hard work is the foundation of success, in and of itself it's largely pointless. I've heard boasts of training the most, of training the least, and of pretty much everything in between. The boast of 2021 is who trains the cleverest. You can 'bury yourself', to use the endurance terminology – training until your muscles burn, your eyes bulge and your ear-drums are fit to burst – but unless you're training smart, it's worthless. Worse, it can be counterproductive.

I've known many contemporaries blessed with more extravagant physical gifts than me. And yet I'm a double Olympic champion. Why? I like to think that 'purposeful practice' – something about which the journalist, author and speaker

Matthew Syed has written in detail – has much to do with it. We'll look at this, and to what extent it rings true for the sporting greats.

All manner of themes feed into the question of the sources of success: teachability, innovation, adaptability. Not seeing yourself as the finished article and opening yourself up to advances in sports science, one might imagine, would be great qualities in top-flight sport. Psychologists speak of having a 'growth mindset' in contrast to a fixed one, and of the ability to view yourself as a work in progress rather than a finished article. But, as I can attest, an athlete is almost completely surrounded by input: from coaches, managers, agents, family, friends, fans, -ologists, the media. Unless you can filter, and at times silence this near-constant 'noise', you will quickly become overwhelmed.

Former chess prodigy Josh Waitzkin – whose 2007 book *The Art of Learning: An Inner Journey to Optimal Performance* is something I've turned to again and again during my career – has a theory that you are better off focusing hard on a small range of skills than risking spreading yourself too thinly. Mastery in one skill, he reasons, translates to mastery in others. 'Work on your weaknesses,' we all grow up being told. But do the elite really do this, and risk their USP being neglected? Or do they maximise that strength – the Agassi return, Megan Rapinoe's shooting from outside the box, Shields and her power punches – draw their confidence from this and rely on the trickle-down effect?

As hateful as injury is, at least it punctuates the periods of endless preparation. I train for an average of 1,500 hours a year. That's roughly four hours a day, every day. Take it from me, maintaining intensity and consistency throughout those long weeks and months is not easy. So it's not enough for the practice to be purposeful; it also needs to be creative.

Kílian Jornet, the great Catalan endurance athlete who broke into the public consciousness with his twin speed ascents of Mount Everest in 2017, has built a career out of reinventing himself. Ski mountaineering; ultramarathons; sky races; chasing FKTs (fastest known times) on the world's biggest summits; fell running. He follows his whims and, endlessly inspired and motivated, is constantly achieving. It's a defence against mental, but also physical, burnout, as the load on muscle groups is shared around. There's no stagnation. We'll hear from Kílian in a later chapter.

Any discussion of elite performance in sport has to consider pressure. How are champions affected by it? How do they conquer it? Is it even desirable to conquer it? Riding over the Serpentine Bridge in Hyde Park with my brother Jonny before the Olympic triathlon final in 2012, we were hit by a wall of noise. It was like nothing either of us had experienced before and I'm fairly confident ever will again. And it was only the warm-up. I could have been daunted, but the words of my running coach and mentor, Malcolm, from five years before (as I was preparing for the World Junior Championships) came back to me: 'Pressure is a privilege,' I could hear him saying in his understated way.

It's a much-used phrase – tennis great Billie Jean King wrote a book with this as the title. But, at the time, I'd never heard it before. It became my mantra and, on that day, what could have been a terrifyingly inhibiting factor became a cool tailwind driving me onwards to gold: the privilege of incredible, hair-raising support.

This makes it sound easy, but handling pressure and expectation is of course anything but. The list of top-class performers who have wilted in their glare is long and distinguished. Opening Test batsmen (my respect for whom has grown enormously with this project) who succumb and are never the same again; boxers who quit on their stools; elite tennis players who double-fault their way through multiple championship points then tailspin to a crushing defeat.

Few have witnessed sporting pressure close up like Donna Fraser. The British 400m runner was training partners with Cathy Freeman in the summer that preceded that crazy night in Sydney in 2000 when the Australian athlete carried the expectation of both her nation and her Aboriginal people on her bodysuited shoulders. Did Freeman win in spite of this pressure, or because of it? Fraser, who finished just a few yards back in that Olympic final, with a front-row seat to one of the most highly charged sporting moments of recent decades, offers her insight.

What else? Well, we'll certainly take time to consider the role of ruthlessness among leading sports stars. To what lengths would you go to win? Four kilometres from the finish in the Olympic final in Rio in 2016, Jonny and I were out in front together – clear of the field but locked in an unspoken battle for gold. It was hot and we were both feeling the effects of the punishing pace we'd imposed during the cycling stage to open up the field.

Jonny was first to break the silence. 'Relax,' he said, between deep intakes of breath. My ears pricked up. It was just one word. But, knowing him as I do, it was far more than that. It was a tell. He was struggling. 'Go, go, go!' something inside me screamed, and I did – cranking up the pace, kicking on, and embracing the agony because, whatever hell I was suffering, I knew with the certainty of a thousand training runs that Jonny was feeling it just that little bit more.

We're brothers. We've trained together for years. He's been instrumental in getting me to where I am today. Without our rivalry I'd be half the athlete. Yet here I was, preying on his weakness. Do I regret it? Not at all. I like to think he'd have done the same. And that's the ruthlessness I believe is an essential component in all champions – in the arena of competition but, just as importantly, in their daily life, too.

The Wimbledon winner clearing out their support team, without sentiment, in pursuit of that extra 1 per cent. The jockey missing the birth of a child to chase winners in a second-tier jump meet. The boxer parting with the promoter who brought her to the big time. Whatever shape or form ruthlessness takes, it must surely be a central component. Elite sport, someone once told me, is not the place to make friends.

And no study of sporting mastery would be complete without an assessment of what I see as perhaps the two biggest determiners of sustained sporting success: passion and luck. The more passion you have, the more prepared you are to act with conviction. And the more conviction you have in a decision, the more passionate you will be about it. It's self-perpetuating.

In footballer Steven Gerrard's autobiography *My Story*, he summed it up in pyromaniacal terms: 'If Gérard [Houllier] had left me out for the Ipswich game I would have set fire to his office. I hate being rested. Hate it. Even if I know it is for my own good. I'm a nightmare, kicking up a stink, turning the air blue. Play me! Being deprived of football is like being starved of air. I live and breathe the game. Missing one minute of one match feels like death.'

Hyperbole aside, that's a pretty articulate illustration of what I'm talking about. What is pressure, form, performance anxiety and the like, measured against such all-consuming passion for what you do? And I'm not sure this can be manufactured. That passion isn't always for the most obvious things, too. For a footballer, it might be training drills but not fitness work; or the thought of a backs-against-the-wall relegation battle but not trying to break in to the top three. I've definitely encountered endurance athletes with a deep, intense love for six-hour training days – but not for putting the resulting fitness into racing. The swimming great Ian Thorpe, for all his victories, always made clear it was the training that he truly loved.

Sportspeople like to believe that practice makes you lucky, and practising more makes you luckier. I wouldn't dispute that, but nor would I pretend that I'm anything approaching the master of my destiny. The uncontrollables are never far away. Those injuries, of course. But also the punctures. The crashes. The scandals. The geo-political fluctuations. The global health crises.

Ask Vanderlei Cordeiro de Lima, attacked by an unhinged spectator while leading the 2004 Olympic marathon in Athens and limping home in third place. Ask tennis star Monica Seles, stabbed by a mad fan when at the peak of her powers and her rivalry with Steffi Graf. Or ask Eddy Merckx, punched by a spectator in the 1975 Tour de France on his way to the summit of the Puy de Dôme, denying him a shot at a record sixth victory.

Sergey Bubka raised the bar, literally, in the men's pole vault 35 times in his career but had a modest Olympic record. Injury, disqualification, boycotts – all contributed. Two months before the 1984 Los Angeles Games, to which Russia refused to send a team, he vaulted 12cm higher than the height that would claim gold. Yet the record books don't show context, they just show records, something I'll discuss with the great Michael Johnson in the final chapter.

But while luck (and whether your country invades Afghanistan) is out of your control, how you greet its fleeting appearances, or infuriating desertions – without getting all Kiplingesque about it – really isn't. Josh Waitzkin talks about the way momentum can work both ways, the 'deadly pattern' of error begetting error, and how the 'downward spiral' can be stopped by a simple act of mental resetting. How often over the years have we seen the likes of Roger Federer or Steffi Graf or Alastair Cook regard an error with a sort of detached curiosity, mentally give a little shrug, then continue with the business of dismantling, or thwarting, their opponents?

To what extent is there a correlation between this fiendishly difficult trick, and protracted sporting accomplishment? Ronnie O'Sullivan, who has struggled more than almost anyone with this, is particularly enlightening on the subject, as we'll see.

I think back to receiving my second consecutive gold medal in Rio in 2016. Podiums are awkward places at the best of times, but this was on a different level. It was stiflingly hot, and I was shattered, physically and emotionally, from the strain and strategising of the race a few hours earlier. The months of preparation and expectation, training and fine-tuning, had taken a huge toll.

The pressure was gone and I was dizzy with relief. But I don't think that entirely explained the nagging discomfort I felt as the medal was hung from my neck. It was something more instinctive: I simply didn't know what to feel. 'Beyond my wildest dreams' is a cliché that many a sportsperson turns to at such moments. In this instance, it was apt. My dreams (wild and, mostly, not) only extended so far.

Children grow up wanting to play for their country, not collect 100 caps. To conquer Mount Everest, rather than tackle it twice in a week. And my Everest moment had come four years earlier on that unforgettable day in London 2012 when the home crowds stood 20 deep around the Serpentine, and Hyde Park seemed to pulsate with partisan energy: Olympic glory.

But now I was a double Olympic champion, and the first man to successfully defend an Olympic triathlon title. I'd joined an elite club of back-to-back gold medallists. And yet I felt … entirely normal: Al, the down-to-earth Yorkshireman who loves nothing more than haring round the lanes and trails of the Yorkshire Dales; whose friends call him 'thin fat lad'; who probably drinks one too many pints of Yorkshire bitter for someone practising a sport that's built on the finest of margins (the pitfalls of having, until a couple of years ago, a pub a few yards from my house).

Given the obstacles I'd faced, and the field I'd beaten, I was perhaps prouder of this gold than the one four years earlier: the personal battle to come back from surgery on my ankle 10 months before; the hurdles I'd had to deal with along the way; the unfamiliar climate Jonny and myself had needed to over-come (Yorkshire is decidedly un-Rio at the best of times). Above all, the knowledge that backing up victory is so much harder than achieving it first time around. And yet.

'Don't cry, you big softie,' I whispered to Jonny as the anthem started. It was the identical, admittedly lame, comment I'd made to my brother at the equivalent moment four years earlier in London. How's that for consistency? Jonny flashed me the sort of withering look that only siblings can. Same old Al. Yes, whatever a sports 'star' was meant to look like, I was pretty sure I wasn't it.

Someone once said to me (and I think it was a compliment): 'You're so normal, and when I see what you've achieved, it makes me think that perhaps anyone could.' It's an intriguing prospect, isn't it? I don't think anyone is naïve enough to think that talent and sporting success follow a neatly proportionate ascending scale. Hard work; decision-making; focus; pressure management; motivation; versatility; teachability. Weave all these together into the optimum mix and have you actually got what's misleadingly known as talent? There are plenty of intangibles there – but not unreachables.

If we as sportsmen and women are guilty of a distorted outlook, then surely fans, myself included, are equally so. We use the tag of genius all too easily. We're hardwired to do so.

Watch Usain Bolt in full flow, as I did on the night of my Rio victory when I sneaked into the Estádio do Maracanã for the 200m final, or Ben Stokes's 135 not out at Headingley in 2019 to square the Ashes, or Katie Ledecky smashing yet another world record in the pool, and you'll hear talk of these sorts of feats 'inspiring the next generation'.

When I watch such performances, inspired is the last thing I feel. I feel disbelieving. I feel awestruck. I feel intimidated. I feel privileged. But I don't feel inspired. So what happens when you start to poke around behind the performances, to see what they're built on, and the common themes that perhaps link dominance across all sports? That, I think, is where true inspiration can be found.

Because the danger of not just revering champions but putting them on a different plane or pedestal is that you render them, and their achievements, untouchable. Look at these people as a different breed, and that level becomes inaccessible to you.

This book, indeed my career, is the antidote to that. My imposter syndrome when around these people got me thinking: what if everyone feels a bit like this? Cyclist Victoria Pendleton, winner of two Olympic golds and nine world titles, was once asked what she felt set her apart. 'I don't see myself as having anything different or exceptional from the next person,' she responded. 'I just have an ability to focus.'

Over the coming pages, I'll search for other examples of elite sporting careers that – once we drill down and put our hero-worshipping tendencies aside – may actually be built on equally prosaic foundations. I'm not trying to break the sporting equivalent of the magician's code here. I simply have an inkling that, just maybe, others at the top of their sports might be more human than we think.

Sure, you can't 'polish a turd', as England's greatest batsman will tell me in memorable terms. But equally, in the coming pages, we'll meet crushingly dominant figures in their respective fields who have blatantly suboptimal physiologies or rate themselves as little more than average in terms of talent. Are they falling into the sportsperson's trap of insincere self-deprecation? You'll have to make up your own minds.

A few caveats. If you're a hardcore triathlete with 6 per cent body fat and perhaps an Ironman M-dot tattoo on each calf, you may be disappointed with what you read here. Event-specific insight or training tips is not what this is about. Nor is it a thinly disguised rehashing of my career to date. I've included my own observations, where relevant, but have done so sparingly. Take it from me: I'm the least interesting person here.

No, this book is all about transcending triathlon to look at the wider sporting world. Is it just me, or does it feel like we're living in a mini golden age? Everywhere you look, in men's and women's sport, it seems like records are being broken, compelling personalities unearthed, landmarks achieved, nail-biting drama played out, standards raised. Innovation, and the sort of characters we'll be meeting over the coming pages, are driving this.

What's particularly pleasing is how many sports fans are also now competitors in their own right. The growth in mass sporting events, particularly, in my lifetime is nothing short of remarkable. Strava, the social network for athletes, is used by 73 million people worldwide, with 2 million new athletes having joined the platform every month during 2020. As of December 2020, 9 million people in the UK – 13 per cent of the population – were using it.

Maybe it's optimistic, but I like to think that much of the insight I've gathered here is scalable and applicable to any level of competition, as well as to the non-sporting world. Its relatability has struck me at every step of the process: optimising performance is surely as important for an individual in a classroom, boardroom or office as it is in an Olympic final. Who hasn't had their pride knocked in a business meeting, then watched the rest of the meeting, if not their day, unravel from there? Perhaps the same people who would berate controversial Australian tennis player Nick Kyrgios for imploding off the back of a disputed line call. 'If I were him, I'd behave differently.' Well, you are him in a way. We all are. Our courts are just different shapes and our matches of different durations.

Without getting all self-help about it, I think that understanding sporting dominance not only enables you to understand success, or mastery in life, but helps you down that path. For what is sport but 'life in fast-forward', in the words of Simon Barnes, one of my favourite sports journalists.

While I've tried to cast the net wide and get out of my comfort zone (horse racing, for one, was a crash course), the book is unashamedly Anglocentric and skewed towards sports to which I have a close affinity (there are multiple runners, three cyclists and no American footballers, for example). So please don't write in. Sport is an imperfect enterprise, just like writing about it. At every stage of the way, I've sought to incorporate characters and stories that move the narrative on and exemplify the themes we're exploring.

There'll be too much jargon and sports science for some (I've got a degree in sports science and physiology, so I might have got carried away in places), but not enough for others. We'll explore metacognition and counterphobia, stress buffering and cognitive dissonance theory, extrinsic and intrinsic motivation, performance affiliation, perception of effort and transcranial direct-current stimulation. We'll talk about heart-rate variability, the autonomic nervous system and the central governor model, as well as associative and dissociative cognitive strategies and thermal regulation. If it's overly geeky in places, I apologise, but you won't struggle. It's all logical stuff and I've strived for clarity at all times.

So what have I learned? Well, that this writing thing is bloody hard and that interviewing is a real skill (I'll never be grumpy and monosyllabic in interviews again*). Most of all I've learned that sport, this thing I've been lucky enough to devote my entire life to, is even more fascinating and rewarding than I ever believed possible.

A final confession: one of the key motivations for writing this book is a selfish one. This summer, barring injury, I'll hopefully be competing in my fourth Olympics – and going for my third consecutive gold. As my old running coach, mentor and advisor Malcolm once told me (on the day it was announced that London would host the Olympics seven years hence), 'You can win Olympic gold – but never believe you can win by more than a stride.'

It was a great thing to tell a 17-year-old, perhaps the best piece of qualified advice I've ever received. The implication was clear: work your arse off, as the margins are tiny (just ask Moorhouse, who won by 1/100th of a second in Seoul). And if they're tiny, then what I've learned and absorbed in researching and writing this book could prove crucial. Consider this my attempt to lengthen that stride.

My four-year quest to understand sporting mastery has taken me around the world to rub shoulders with some of the greatest athletes, and most innovative thinkers, to ever draw breath. From Kona to Cork, West Yorkshire to Western

---

* Probably not true.

Australia, I've burned the candle at both ends, writing up interviews and crunching down paragraphs, occasionally skipping training, and zealously chasing down those I felt might contribute to my understanding.

As I embarked on this project, there was one name at the top of my list: one of the most compelling sporting characters of this or any generation – and one of the most complex. And it's with him that we begin.

I

RISK-TAKING, SELF-SABOTAGE AND THE MYTH OF GENIUS

'I think he's overdone that slightly ... has he?'

John Virgo is commentating on a first-round match at the Embassy World Championship in Sheffield's Crucible Theatre in 1997. It's between Mick Price and a fresh-faced young player with a black waistcoat, neat bow tie, slicked-back 90s curtains and the hint of a swagger. The young man came to the table and potted a long, difficult red while the applause for the preceding safety shot was still trickling around the hall. He followed this with five quick reds and blacks – 10 balls in total – but now the alignment appears just a little off.

'Can he force the cue ball into that cluster?'

Barely has Virgo finished his sentence than the player has cannoned the white off the black and split the reds into a perfect configuration. 'He can,' Virgo says, impressed. More balls are sunk. Black, red, black, red. The player, if anything, is picking up speed. He criss-crosses back and forth at the bottom of the table like a perfectionist waiter setting a table. An exact placement here. A little flourish there. Several more balls are sunk, straight down the throat of the hole, the white stunned, or spinning off at a crazy angle to come to rest where the player already waits, cue cocked.

'This is amazing,' says Virgo's co-commentator Dennis Taylor as the score ticks up to 57. Price sits in his chair, trying to concentrate on his cue, his shoes, his water. He doesn't want to watch what's happening but, like the rest of the Crucible, he can't take his eyes off his opponent: 21-year-old Ronnie O'Sullivan.

'Well, one more red and the frame is safe,' says Virgo, as the score reaches 72. He pauses. 'But Ronnie's got other things on his mind, and so does everyone in the audience.'

As O'Sullivan reaches 80, Taylor's thoughts turn to reflected glory: 'Listen, John, I know you've commentated on a maximum before, I have never. I'm starting to get a bit excited here.' He's not alone. Everyone watching is aware that something special is unfolding, an 'I was there' moment. With every ball that's potted, the tension mounts. The only person apparently not affected by it is O'Sullivan himself. His economy of movement is striking. At one point he glances up at the crowd as he walks around the bottom of the table to the spot where he knows, with complete confidence, that the white will come to rest. There's almost a smirk on his face. It seems to say, 'Stick around – this could be good.'

In all my time watching and participating in sport, I don't think I've ever seen someone more in their element. I've watched this clip dozens of times, so I know with certainty what's going to happen. But it's almost as if that certainty existed even then. Ronnie was doing something that – in snooker terms – was, and still is, almost beyond comprehension. And he was making it look like a foregone conclusion.

That something was the fastest-ever maximum clearance. A 100mph 147. The minimum maximum. Every red followed by a black – the highest-scoring ball on the table – then the colours in regulation order. No mistakes. No room for error. No breathing space. The maximum is the toughest task in the game. The hundreds of permutations revealed by every shot. The chess-like complexity. The horrible claustrophobia of those reds orbiting the all-important black.

It's also, in the sense of a wider match, largely pointless. A maximum doesn't win you any more than one frame; but it can easily lose you one. Far better (i.e. safer) to release the pressure by switching to a more open pink or blue to keep your break going. But where's the fun in that? The 147 is snooker's showboating – the chipped penalty, the reverse dunk or the through-the-legs baseline shot, something that players give back to fans. And Ronnie, as the decades that follow are to show, is all about the fans.

'There's the no small matter of £147,000 on offer this year for a maximum break,' says Taylor. Only it is a small matter, at least as far as O'Sullivan appears to believe. He ups the pace, looking like someone clearing balls in a provincial pool hall after a five-minute warning. The final three reds bring up the century. It has taken four minutes.

The crowd are now struggling to contain themselves. 'Come on, Ronnie!' Down goes the black, the white bounces off the bottom cushion, then the side, then begins its long journey up the table to come to a halt with a neat angle on the yellow. Massive applause. Twenty-six seconds later, the table is empty.

As I say, I've seen this clip dozens of times over the years, and its impact never lessens. On that evening of 21 April 1997, O'Sullivan's virtuoso performance lasted 5 minutes, 20 seconds. Fifteen reds, fifteen blacks, all the colours. He averaged just under nine seconds a shot. No one, not even the 'Rocket' (as O'Sullivan was to become known), has come close to matching that.

'I can't see that record ever being beaten,' Dennis Taylor said subsequently, having broken his 147 commentary duck in spectacular fashion. To give you a sense of how quick it was, when a shaven-headed O'Sullivan played his nemesis – and antithesis – Peter Ebdon in a horribly taut encounter in 2005 (Ronnie was in full erratic mood that night, even standing on his chair to assess shots over Ebdon's shoulder), Ebdon needed the same amount of time to build a break of … 12. Little wonder that Ronnie feigned falling asleep.

Yes, the 1997 147 was a piece of astonishing skill. Outrageous audacity. Total mastery of the game and the occasion. But don't you dare call it genius.

'I absolutely fucking hate it.'

It's a damp October night 21 years later and I'm sitting with Ronnie in the kitchen of his mum's house in Chigwell, Essex. Those thick, arched eyebrows are bushier, there are flecks of grey in his sideburns, and, in a pair of dark trousers and a low-hanging T-shirt, he's leaner than I can ever recall seeing him – a product of the strict exercise and dietary routine he follows these days.

We've spent the past couple of hours chatting, laughing, gorging on his mum's (exceptional) lasagne. And now I've put it to Ronnie that, just maybe, the 'genius' tag pisses him off. The BBC compared him to Mozart. Shaun Murphy, the 2005 world champion and a career Triple Crown winner, said: 'Any time you get to play Ronnie O'Sullivan it's a dream come true because you get to find out just where you are in relation to the greatest player that's ever picked up a snooker cue. He really is an absolute genius on the table.' Jimmy White once said: 'Anyone who had held a cue before knew he was a genius.' According to Judd Trump, the 2019 world champion, 'Ronnie is just a genius, really. Easily the best player that has ever played.' Stephen Hendry, Ronnie's inspiration, rival and one-time adversary, merely called him 'the best player that I've ever seen'.

Genius comes up so regularly – and it clearly infuriates him. 'I still hate it now,' says Ronnie. 'Whenever people mention it, I go, "Listen, you go and speak to anyone on the snooker tour, or who's practised in the same club as me – ask them how hard I work." Because all this genius tale – I ain't no genius. I was never the best junior. I was never the best amateur. I was talented. I worked really hard. I wanted it. Not that I wanted it 'cos I wanted it. I wanted it 'cos I loved competing. I loved the game. I was fascinated. Y'know what I'm saying?'

Ronnie speaks as he pots. Straight and quick.

'So I don't buy that genius thing. Because I've seen geniuses: Alex Higgins was a genius. Jimmy White was bordering on genius. Me, I was never a genius. I was always more of a Stephen Hendry, Steve Davis type of player. But I had a quick brain. I kind of attack the ball.' (He'd later tell fellow pro Tony Drago that, during the famous maximum, he felt that if he'd slowed down to think, he'd have missed.) 'So a lot of people went, "Oh, it's easy for him, it's all right for him," but the hours and practice that were put in, people don't see. They think, "He just has to turn up."'

I'm intrigued as to what he thinks separates the good from the very best. He points to something that resonates with me – something I've tried to focus on in my career, particularly on the biggest stages. The ability to up the ante when the ante is already at its highest. Pressing your opponent, or opponents, when they're most vulnerable. Sport as foot-on-the-jugular combat.

'See, with snooker there's an element of skill,' he says, sitting back in his armchair, with a long line of trophies on the mantelpiece behind. 'You have to be skilful. It's not a physical sport. But skill? That'll only take you so far. The very, very best have the skill, but they also have the courage and that killer instinct. I always believe the greatest take risks. So it's all right being a percentage player, and that's very good, but the greatest players, come that moment, they take on the shot, or grab the game by the scruff of the neck, kind of make it happen.'

He references his extraordinary World Championship semi-final against Hendry in 2002, won by the Scotsman 17–13. To some people (with apologies to 2019's Trump–Higgins world final), it is the highest-quality match in the history of the sport. With echoes of that Agassi–Becker semi-final in 1995, Hendry was playing angry that day; O'Sullivan, in an interview before the match, had spoken of sending Hendry home to his 'sad, little life in Scotland'. It got to 12–12, then the Scot blew him away.

'I was always kind of an aggressive player but it wasn't until I played Stephen Hendry in that semi-final that I really … got it. I got to the final session with us attacking each other, and I'd got my nose in front, and I thought, "I'll just try and play a bit careful here." And Hendry just got more and more and more aggressive. That was the biggest lesson for me: that if I ever wanted to achieve anything like he'd achieved, in them situations I had to make it happen rather than wait for someone to make a mistake. He taught me why he was so successful.'

I suggest that it's easy to take that risk as an underdog, less so when you're on top. At my first Olympics, in Beijing in 2008, I was an unknown 20-year-old student. Free from pressure or expectation, I was able to race my own race, take chances. I went off hard, was second out of the water, and I attacked repeatedly on the bike and in the run. With just 3km to go, I was leading the Olympic final. Then, as I said at the time, 'the wings came off'. I came 12th. In the years that followed, that anonymity – the freedom of the underdog – was a luxury I was never to enjoy again.

'Yeah, that's what I'm saying,' Ronnie agrees, leaning forward in his chair. 'Hendry never done it in a "Oh, I got nothing to lose" way. It was done 'cos he'd been in that situation many times before, he was experienced at it, and he knew how to kill someone. He knew what he had to do to get over the line and I kind of thought, "OK, what do I wanna be?" I wanna be Stephen Hendry, taking risks, might fuck up, but I know that the ball's absolutely in my court. Go out all guns blazing!'

Ronnie looks serious for a moment. 'Hendry was the greatest player I'd ever seen, you know. He made me feel … uncomfortable. No other player made me feel uncomfortable, and you do that with your shot selection. There was times when I first played him that I'd think, "Yeah, go on, mate, go for that. You'll never get it." Then, after about three or four years, I'd think, "Oh fucking hell, he's gonna pot it." They was such high-risk shots to the average player. Not even to the average player. To most top players. But to him it was like a bread-and-butter shot. And I thought, "Fucking hell, this is what makes him so good." And if I wanna be so good, I've gotta kind of find something.'

I'd been apprehensive about sitting down with Ronnie. Most people who try to get to grips with him end up getting under his skin. We've met before, with his well-publicised conversion to running giving us plenty to talk about. But this is our first in-depth chat, and I know Ronnie doesn't always respond well to interview-type scenarios. And where do you start? You know it's almost impossible to ask something that over a 25-year career hasn't been asked before. Eventually, his answers become almost a caricature of themselves. Like me, he has better things to do than answer other people's questions. Also, like me, he has ways of avoiding doing so.

He famously adopted a robotic voice while being interviewed by former player Neal Foulds for ITV Sport after his win over Chinese teenager Yan Bingtao at the World Grand

Prix in Preston in February 2017. 'Yes ... it resonates ... very much ... for me ... when I come ... here to the Preston ... Guild ... Hall.' Funny to watch, excruciating to be a part of. Foulds, to his credit, wrapped up the encounter with: 'You played a bit like a robot tonight, Ronnie. Well done.' Several months after we meet, O'Sullivan adopts a parody Aussie drawl in an interview with BBC Lancashire Sport at the Players Championship after reaching the quarter-finals. He's boycotted interviews, gone mute in others, zoned out or got fired up. Yep, Ronnie's unpredictable all right.

Controversy has followed him throughout his career. Success and scandal: the two Ronnies. There's been the smashing of cues. The swiping of the balls in frustration, an automatic concession. The self-sabotage of maximums on the final ball in protest at the size of the financial incentive offered by the tournament. The fines. The shoulder barges. The disciplinary letters. The criticism of refs. The picking of fights with photographers. Playing shoeless. The mental-health battles. The public meltdowns. The visit to the Priory. The abuse of venues and of press officers. So rich and consistent has been the controversy, you almost forget about his extraordinary dominance of his sport. It's like Roger Federer and Nick Kyrgios rolled into one. But he's never been less than box office. In my taxi on the way to his house, I reflect that I don't think I've watched snooker to watch the game itself. Just to watch Ronnie.

Then, of course, there's the playing left-handed thing. In a notorious match with Alain Robidoux in 1996, Ronnie so enraged the Canadian by playing with his 'wrong' hand that Robidoux went on playing long after he needed snookers to win the frame and then refused to shake Ronnie's hand at the end. It was uncomfortable to watch. But there's another way to look at this, as commentator Clive Everton did. 'Ronnie sometimes plays a series of shots left-handed when he doesn't need to, as if to shake something up inside him,' said Everton, while commentating on one of his matches. 'I think the word "genius" should be used sparingly, but I think he is [one]. Geniuses see things differently from the rest of the world.'

Geniuses see things differently from the rest of the world.

I fully understand Ronnie's frustration with the 'genius' tag. In sport it has come to mean someone preternaturally gifted; someone presented with a wholly formed talent that they can exploit or squander. It robs you of both credit for your success and excuses when you fail. Barry Hearn, snooker supremo and vocal critic of O'Sullivan, put it with stinging succinctness: 'His biggest strength is what God gave him. His biggest weakness is Ronnie O'Sullivan himself.'

But if defined as the ability to see things differently, to think creatively and with imagination, to not just look for the needle in the haystack but – as Einstein once said of himself when asked what separated him from others – to go on looking for *all* the possible needles, then Ronnie's left-handed exploits, and indeed Ronnie himself, start to make a lot more sense.

Snooker is a game of absolutes. There may be a million permutations, but all are governed by physics, by angles. The balls are stationary (not for long, in Ronnie's case). Being able to play with both hands, and to a championship standard, vastly increases your options: the cueing angles; the body positions; the shot selection. Far from showboating – and I'm not saying Ronnie hasn't deployed the skill in this way at times in his career – is this not something that multiplies Ronnie's ways of winning matches? He simply had the imagination to recognise this and – again, through countless hours at the practice table – refine it and make it a weapon.

'Some people can only play one way,' he tells me. 'If you can play that shot two, three, four ways, against certain opponents you have to play, it's nice to have that. I like to be creative in a game. Sometimes I can go, "Well, that's the shot to play but, no, I wanna play this shot."'

Studies over the years have shown that, purely in terms of their imaginations, very young children far outperform adults in the genius stakes. Education kicks in, traditional perspectives are applied; we start focusing on what to think rather than how to think and thereby practise reproductive rather than productive thinking. Asked what half of 13 is, to use that often-cited example, adults usually conclude that it's six and a half rather than, say, '1' or '3'. Or 'THIR' or 'TEEN'.

O'Sullivan has never seemed to succumb to the traditional mindset. Could the near-miracles he has performed on the snooker table be attributed to his tendency to continually ask one simple question: why? 'Why do we play this way?' 'Why can't I do this?' 'Why should I pot this final ball for a maximum just because I can?' These are not questions you feel Peter Ebdon was overly burdened with.

This free thinking has proven invaluable in the latest, golden period of Ronnie's career, when directed in the service of reinvention. The 2017/18 season saw him score a career-high 74 centuries. He tells me he's had to reinvent himself 'four, maybe five times' because of new players coming through with fresh ideas and new techniques. He talks of the fear of coming up against a rising star, thinking you've got them beat, and then them hitting you with a multiple-frame burst and loading the pressure back on you. 'You kind of get over the line, but you think, "Fucking hell, I've not had that done to me before,"' he says.

'So I've had to change my technique. Hendry didn't wanna change his game, he was like, "Nah, I'm staying the same." Steve Davis didn't wanna change his game; probably didn't feel like he could. When you see new talent coming through and they do things better and they're more aggressive and they've got 15 years on you, it can send the shivers down you 'cos they haven't got the scars either. So I've kind of had to go, "Well, you're doing all right because you're reinventing yourself. You're in the lion's den all the time with these young kids, and you're kind of having a go." So I think what Hendry didn't do, I kind of have. I'm adapting. Which is fun.'

It's a lovely house, his mum's. Homely. Ronnie Jr, O'Sullivan's 12-year-old son, is running around – he drags himself away from Fortnite on the computer to join us for some dinner – and the house is full of memories and mementoes, of both the normal and exceptional. This has been his mum's house since they moved in as a family when Ronnie was 16, he explains. I almost ask to see his room. Is it as he left it as a 22-year-old when he moved out, already a sporting icon?

I want to ask Ronnie about confidence – that vital yet intangible component of any sporting success. At times over the years, such as with his record 147, he's appeared like he's built of nothing else. At other times, he can resemble one of the most brittle characters in any sporting arena.

Let's deal with the former first.

'It must be a hell of a feeling,' I suggest, 'when you – of all people – are in the zone, Ronnie.'

He smiles widely. 'Yeah, I absolutely love it. I always think to myself, if I didn't play snooker and I didn't have them tournaments to look forward to, how fucking normal is my life going to become. I'm not denying there's stress, pressure, but when you're going to the Crucible and then you get a bit of form and you're fucking flying and you know you're flying and you think, "There's no amount of money in the world that can put anyone in this situation." This is like a god. It's amazing – 99.9 per cent of people will never have this, know what I mean?'

It's great to hear, in a climate of cautious sporting self-deprecation, genuine candour about the joys of total, crushing dominance.

'I think I've reached a skill level … there's been times when I've played tournaments where I've thought it can't get any better than that. I know it can't. I mean, from start to finish. My mate said to me that, for an opponent, it's like a train with no brakes. It's coming at you, you know it's coming at you, it ain't gonna stop, no matter what you do. I knew, no matter what they done, I'd have an answer and more. Do you see what I'm saying?'

I do – at least to a lesser degree. For me, it was the three or four years following Beijing and culminating in London. On the start line, no matter the race, or the level, I was certain that there was only one person who stood between me and victory. Myself. And opponents seemed to feel this, too. My agent tells a story of me arriving at a World Triathlon Series event to find a queue of my fellow competitors waiting to register. I just walked to the front. No one complained. I'm not an arrogant man, I'd submit. This was just a mindset, built on dominance and absolute focus. It's a wonderful feeling – but it never lasts.

'Nah,' Ronnie agrees. 'You have, like, little moments of it, but then there's other moments where you just gotta hang in there. You still might win, but you think, "Fucking hell, how have I won that by hanging in there?" I'm a feelings sort of player. I can lose a match, but if I felt good, I can come off feeling like I've enjoyed it. But I've won tournaments before and thought, "I hated that, because I played shit, performed shit, I didn't get no satisfaction out of that."'

The hanging in there is a relatively new string to Ronnie's bow, helped by his alliance with sports psychologist Steve Peters, which began in 2011. For many years, he was 'hit or miss', he tells me. Win a tournament or exit in the first round.

Then the penny dropped. 'Whenever the World Championship come up, I thought, "17 days – you can't be hit and miss." To win the world title, it's not always the best player that wins; it's the player that's the most consistent. And I knew that. And I knew that I could play brilliant for 14 days but have a stinker of a day, and then my whole tournament would be fucked up. So I knew I had to iron that out – and to do that I had to work really hard at going against the grain, and not doing what comes natural to me. I had to work on technical stuff.'

For years, he truly believed he would never win the World Championship. 'And then when I won it once [in 2001] I was like, "Ahhh, big monkey off my back." And then I never thought I'd win it two, three, four times. By some miracle I've managed to win it five times [he would go on to win his sixth in 2020, the oldest world champion in more than 40 years], but I never thought I had the type of game that was suited to win a tournament.'

Now, he says, he's learned not to overanalyse. And to keep putting himself in the frame. 'The last six years I've become more hit than miss, and I put that down to working with Steve. Some days I'll be having a shit day, whereas before I'd go, "Oh, it's a shit day, I just wanna get out of here." Now I'm thinking, "It's a shit day, but I'll stick in this match." 'Cos tomorrow could be a good day. Since I've done that, I've been much more consistent with my results and become a different player.'

Talking to Ronnie, I realise he's almost nothing like the player – or the man – I had in my mind when I first started following him years ago. I explain that self-belief, for me, is something of a fallacy. You can't truly believe you're going to win until you start winning. Or that's as I've found it. Ronnie nods.

'I've always had no belief. When I was younger I had faith in my game. And then over the years I kind of lost this because, as an amateur, you can get away with one or two mistakes, but at the highest level I found that, making mistakes, I could get picked off. It was only when the match would start that my belief would increase and increase.' He talks about listening to Mike Tyson being interviewed ahead of a big fight, initially fearing his opponent, his size, his punching power. Then, as the fight got nearer, the confidence would build, until the boxer was walking into the ring thinking, 'I'm gonna take his head off.'

'I'm like that,' says Ronnie. 'When the moment comes, I kind of find my confidence.'

I qualified for my first Olympics out of the blue at a race in Madrid in June 2008. At the time, it was the best performance of my career and probably the minimum required for me to get the nod from the selectors. A childhood dream realised. As the following three months passed by, I noticed a subtle change in my psyche: from happy to get in the team, to thinking maybe I could get a top 20 finish, to readjusting my goal to a top 10. By the time I stood on the swelteringly hot start line above a reservoir near Beijing, I was convinced I could win. This despite it being my first senior championship race, and the first time I had lined up next to many of the athletes I had looked up to for the past decade. In reality I had no chance of victory, but I was willing to give it a go. That 12th place, having been leading with just over 3km to go, came with the crucial realisation of how close I was to the very best.

Ronnie takes another sip of his tea. Then he tells me something startling. 'There have been parts of my career where I've been in the dressing room, and I've gone, "I can't go out there, I've got stage fright." I'm 15–10 up, in the final session of the World Championship, and I've got stage fright.' He pauses. 'And then I play three of the best frames I've ever played.'

He adds: 'I wish I wasn't like that because it puts you off wanting to perform; it puts you off wanting to go through it.

But it's kind of what you do. I think some people thrive on living on the edge a little bit, or having that bit of anxiety.'

Something I see as essential, and believe all great sporting achievers need, is role models. Mentors. Sometimes directly, sometimes from afar. Sometimes a father; sometimes, as in the case of AP McCoy and Richard Dunwoody, a rival. For Ronnie, it was Steve Davis, whom he'd painstakingly modelled himself on as a youngster: his waistcoat, his shoes, even the way Davis – then the best British player – walked around the table. Then, as a 17-year-old prodigy, ranked 57, Ronnie defeated Davis in the quarter-finals of the 1993 Royal Liver Assurance UK Championship at the Guild Hall, Preston, and went on to beat Hendry in the final.

The other big mentor and motivator for Ronnie, of course, was his father. Sport is littered with overbearing, inspiring or controlling parents, influences both positive and destructive. Mine are comparatively normal: both doctors, a mum who swam and a father who ran. Endlessly supportive, they'd take Jonny and me to two different training sessions most days, before school and after. For the best part of 10 years, weekends for them were mostly spent on the motorway driving us to a triathlon, cross-country or fell race.

Ronnie's dad, also called Ronnie, was sentenced to 18 years in prison for murder after a fight in a nightclub. He was an enormous presence, both for an adoring son and in his own right: a raconteur and a character brimming with passion. When Ronnie became the youngest winner of a ranking event aged 17, he took his trophy to Gartree Prison in Leicestershire to show to his dad. The media were all over the story, pinching themselves at being handed something so remarkable. 'We had two and a half hours of laughing and joking,' Ronnie said at the time. 'At the end of it, Dad just said, "Go and get another trophy."'

A throwaway comment? Certainly, but also one imbued with significance. The character who had forged him, sacrificed so much for him, kept him in check, given him a kick up the arse when he needed it and filled him with a will to win (Ronnie once said: 'He's hungry. I'm not hungry – I'm laid-back.') had simultaneously disappeared from his life and eclipsed it. And now he'd made a request that Ronnie had no option but to deliver on.

I ask Ronnie about him. He looks thoughtful. Then he says: 'He was such an idol of mine, and I looked up to him so much. I dunno, it was a weird thing 'cos I felt that, if I didn't become successful in my career, what impact would that have on him? So I kind of felt more pressure to succeed so that he would feel like he wasn't to blame, that he could get on with serving his time. 'Cos I didn't want him to fucking kill himself, seeing me implode and that, going on drink or drugs like some nutcase, and make him think, "Oh no, I'm responsible and that." He might not have thought that, but it was in my head, and I thought I want my dad to come home one day, so I've gotta hold up my end of the bargain.

'So that was a motivation in itself, and whenever I saw him he said, "Every time you're on TV it's like a visit for me." So I thought, how can I give up a sport that is like a visit to him? The most important thing to them inmates in there is their visits. That's what they look forward to. They have a shower, shave. How can you deprive someone of that, especially your dad? So that was more pressure than the actual game.'

It's sobering to listen to. I wonder how few elite sportspeople will understand these conflicting emotions. I certainly don't, though I sympathise. Motivation, such a complex beast, will pop up again and again in this book. His is both potent and destructive. Would Ronnie have been the player he is without this defining experience (his father wasn't released until

2010)? Probably not. Would he have had fewer demons, been happier? Who's to say?

He tells me he lost probably six years, from when he was around 19 all the way to 25, 'coming to terms with Dad'. 'I just kind of went off the rails a bit. I was still competing but I wasn't getting the best out of myself. I think my dad going away, I lost that person who kept me on the straight and narrow. I remember coming home from a tournament and, like I said, I was never the most confident. But he instilled his confidence in me. He made me feel like I could go and do it. So without having him around, I kind of lost that confidence.

'I think if he hadn't have gone away, I probably wouldn't have gone missing for six years. I could possibly have had seven, eight world titles, maybe. I'd like to think I'd have broken all of Stephen Hendry's records. But looking back at my career, I think I'm happy. I don't need to prove myself. I play for the right reasons – for the love of the sport.'

And the fans, of course? He agrees. 'If someone's paid money to be there they're expecting to see good quality; I've gotta deliver. I might not always deliver, but I need to put the work in to go there and go, "Right, if I have a stinker, I don't feel so bad, because I put the work in." But if I go and have a stinker and I don't put the work in, I don't feel good about taking people's money or their time. I wanna give them the best night. It's like performance pride. They've invested in me. I've gotta put my bit in.'

He tells me that he still loves going down the club and putting on a performance, even if there are only a few people there to watch. These people possibly can't make 100 breaks, but they love the game so much, perhaps even more than him. 'And when I'm playing there's about seven or eight of them standing there for like three or four hours and they're like, "This is fucking unbelievable," he says. 'I know I'm playing shots that they, you know ... But to see it up live is different to watching it on the TV, so I kind of get a buzz, that they love the sport, they appreciate it.'

He gives me a nod. 'It's like you. Someone like a young triathlete watching you train and running probably is in awe. Or someone watching Federer play tennis or Messi or anyone who's great at what they do – when someone comes along that loves that sport, gets to watch the best there is at what they're doing, you know you're giving them a special bit of entertainment. So I get a buzz out of that. Would I get that from anything else? Probably not.'

It's getting late. I need to go, and I'm conscious of having used up so much of his time. This dad of three – on home turf, his mum next door and his young son in the next room – is in a good place. The personality traits that have driven him – the relentless perfectionism, the insatiable thirst for improvement, the questing mind and that boundless creativity – seem in balance. A lot to handle. But with Steve Peters in his corner, he's calmer, and he's got his family and his record to fall back on. Experience, too. One forgets, but dominance can – and I emphasise *can* – be self-perpetuating. Ronnie has played nearly 12,000 frames in his professional career. Yes, the young players have fewer scars. But they also don't have that enormous stockpile to fall back on.

I depart, full of lasagne and tea, enthused and encouraged. Ronnie – generous to the end – is anxious to ensure I've got everything I want. It feels like I've got far more than that.

Later, poring over the notes of our conversation, the following quote jumps out. 'Momentum's the key. For me, that's my strongest asset. Once I get momentum, I take my opponent to a place where he don't feel comfortable, and once he ain't comfortable, I'm picking up on it and that's when I go for the throat. I think all the greatest sportspeople that I've looked at

– Messi, Federer, Phelps, Bolt, Michael Johnson … they all go: "You know what, fuck it – the gun goes and I'm gone, mate. Catch me if you can. Catch me if you can!" That's the sportsman I want to be. I'm out of the blocks, you gotta worry about me, mate. I ain't worrying about you. I know what I'm capable of.'

A couple of months after our meeting, Ronnie becomes, statistically, the greatest player ever, winning his 19th Triple Crown event at the UK Championship at the Barbican Centre in York – surpassing Hendry's record. Then, on 10 March 2019, in the process of wrapping up the Players Championship in Preston, he becomes the first player to make 1,000 professional centuries (Hendry, his old rival, is the next highest on 775).

The red to get him to the landmark century? Potted with his left hand.

2

THE SCIENCE OF SUFFERING

It's the morning of 25 May 2018. Chris Froome wakes and sends a message first to his wife, then to his long-time coach, the Australian Tim Kerrison. After a torrid three weeks, the world's greatest cyclist is lying fourth in the Giro d'Italia, more than three minutes adrift. With just two meaningful stages to go, his dream of holding all three grand tours – cycling's biggest stage races – simultaneously is slipping away.

But he has a plan. A lunatic plan. And he's looking for some sounding boards. What if, on that day's 185km mountain stage from Venaria Reale to Bardonecchia, he attempts what no cyclist has pulled off in a grand tour in a generation and goes for a solo breakaway 80km from the finish?

His two biggest rivals, compatriot and surprise leader Simon Yates of Mitchelton–Scott, and Dutchman Tom Dumoulin of Team Sunweb, are beginning to feel the strain. He reasons that if his Team Sky teammates can soften up the peloton with some hard riding on the hairpins at the base of the climb up the Colle delle Finestre, then he might just be able to stage an ambush. An ambush that he would need to back up with 80km of the toughest riding of his life: three climbs – starting with the 2,178m Finestre, one of the fiercest in the Alps, with an average gradient of 9.1 per cent and large stretches of gravel – and two flying-by-the-seat-of-his-pants descents. All tackled solo, without a domestique (support rider) in sight and with legs heavy with fatigue from the preceding weeks of racing.

He would, in effect, be turning this most exacting of mountain stages into a do-or-die time trial. 'I knew it would take something absolutely crazy to turn the race upside down,' Froome would later say. Kerrison's response is telling. He cautions his star rider that what he is proposing entails the mother of all struggles. But, crucially, he does not say no. He knows that no other cyclist in the world – perhaps in history – is more suited to such sustained, self-imposed suffering.

What followed over the next 5 hours, 12 minutes and 26 seconds of racing has passed into cycling folklore. Lance Armstrong, on his maligned but often astute podcast 'The Move', called it 'one of the most monumental rides that we will ever see'. I said much the same watching at home in a break between long training rides that suddenly didn't seem quite so brutal.

The 'Sky train', the nickname given to the team's highly organised unit of riders, duly attacked at the foot of the Finestre, lifting the pace at the front and stretching out the peloton. Yates was dropped. Froome then powered off the front, with a 16-second burst during which he averaged, according to Team Sky data later released, 603 watts. That effort would have a fresh me on the ropes. On gruelling slopes, with three weeks of racing in the legs and three mountains to conquer, the power stats are mind-boggling.

By the top of the Finestre, 25 torturous minutes of grey slopes, thick snowbanks and uneven track later, his lead was 42 seconds over his four closest pursuers, headed by Dumoulin. Descending with courage and skill – if not quite that piston-legged, jack-rabbit style he pioneered on the Col de Peyresourde in the 2016 Tour de France – Froome's lead grew to one minute and 52 seconds at the foot of the penultimate climb, up to Sestriere.

By the time he reached the finish line at Bardonecchia (1,908m), punching the air with an arm that appeared even more fragile than normal after the rigours of the stage, it was a full three minutes. In grand tour terms, when multiple weeks' work can come down to an aggregate of a few tens of seconds' lead, that's a considerable margin. He had destroyed his rivals, overturned the leaderboard and reclaimed the pink jersey, the *maglia rosa*, which he would retain all the way to Rome. The win gained him entry to the most prestigious of all elite cycling clubs: only two other cyclists – Eddy Merckx (who did something similar on Stage 17 of the 1969 Tour de France) and Bernard Hinault – had held all three 'majors' in cycling. Yates, the overnight leader, finished 38 minutes back, broken and tearful, having endured – thanks to Froome – 'the hardest day of my life'.

And they say Chris Froome is boring.

It's nearly a year later, in May 2019, that I finally catch up with Chris. As the peloton have so often found, it's no easy task. He's in my neck of the woods, Leeds, racing in the Tour de Yorkshire – and my home county has just given him one of its old-fashioned welcomes. All day long it has hosed down with rain, the wind gusting as he and the other riders tackled the race's penultimate stage, a 132km coastal stretch from Bridlington to Scarborough via the North York Moors, Robin Hood's Bay and Whitby.

Froome is competing in new colours. Revered/reviled Team Sky has transformed into Team Ineos, funded by British industrialist and financier Jim Ratcliffe's millions. After a choreographed unveiling of the crimson and black kit a few days earlier, this is Ineos's first outing. But Froome is not out to win the race. He's here more for the conditioning – and with one eye on the bigger prize: reclaiming his Tour de France crown from the 2018 winner, his teammate Welshman Geraint Thomas.

Thomas's win – breaking a run of three consecutive tour victories for Froome, and four in five years – had been a surprise. But not if you looked at Froome's schedule coming into that race, culminating in his extraordinary effort at the dénouement of the Giro, little more than a month before the start of the 2018 Tour in the Bay of Biscay. 'Burning the candle at both ends,' was Froome's characteristically understated assessment, as if he'd been putting in a few late nights in the office.

We meet in a quiet corner off the lobby of the Thorpe Park Hotel in Leeds. In the build-up to this I have checked, and rechecked, several times that he's happy to meet; were it me, midway through a training camp or after a hard day's competition, I'd be in lock-down mode. Focused, unresponsive. It's a welcome surprise, therefore – and to his immense credit – that he agrees to see me.

Froome is alone rather than with a PR or team representative. With the doping controversies and the lingering resentment towards the so-called Team Sky machine, Froome has been accompanied by a bodyguard for a number of years now. But here, in Yorkshire, he's among friends. He's taller than I pictured, maybe 6ft 2in, with a soft handshake and a firm gaze. As we speak, we're interrupted regularly by fans coming over to request photos, or explain how much their sons or daughters adore cycling. Others simply want to relay their admiration.

I'm one of them. I've followed Froome since he broke into cycling's upper echelons, relatively late in his career, with his second place in the sapping heat of the Vuelta a España, his favourite grand tour, in 2011 (he was later promoted to winner after Spanish rider Juan José Cobo was stripped of the title for doping violations). Then, as an over-performing domestique for Bradley Wiggins when the more established rider and prodigious Olympian became Britain's first Tour de France winner in 2012. Froome's performance in that race – he came second – and the manner of his riding left no one in doubt that a major figure in cycling had arrived.

Unlike Wiggins, with his lamb chops and mic drops, his podium tomfoolery and golden throne posing, or Slovak rider Peter Sagan, with his one-liners and one-handed wheelies, Froome is strikingly low-key off the bike. The uninitiated lament an apparent lack of charisma. The ignorant question his patriotism (he was born in Kenya, to a British father and half-British mother, was educated in South Africa and lives in Monaco). But I find him the most fascinating of characters.

He's the model of the quiet assassin. See him off the bike, and you wouldn't look twice; with his tightly cropped hair, slender frame and Zen-like calm, he might seem more like the general manager of a provincial hotel with perhaps a penchant for yoga rather than a sporting great.

Yet on a bike, he's an animal: a warrior, a remorseless bully and a sadist (he's to tell me about the pleasure he derives from the pain in fellow riders' eyes when he's competing, pain he's so often causing). In the most respectful of senses, he's a machine. Watching the grand tours at home, with those front-on cameras, you can't always get a handle on just what prodigious power he generates from that super-slim frame. Then you see some aerial footage of one of his breakaways and it's like watching a bullet fired from the peloton. Sure, he's ungainly (many commentators have picked over his gangly, unorthodox style). But he's never less than brutally effective.

Grand tour racing is uniquely demanding: pulverising distances, relentless, three-week schedules, a variable surface. Heat, cold, rain. Mechanicals, TV motorbikes crashing or stopping in front of you, thousands of (often inebriated) spectators lining the route intent on their five seconds of fancy-dress fame or on whispering (phlegm-spattered) sweet nothings in your ear. These events can sometimes resemble less a race, more a demonic computer game with challenges popping up from all quarters at any moment. One slip-up and you're out. Game over. Return to start.

And through the maelstrom Froome has always endured, and with equanimity. His focus – which I'm itching to ask him about – is borderline cyborgian. He's been shoved, punched (he got his own back with a Colombian fan in 2016), spat at, and had urine and multiple doping allegations thrown at him. When his bike was totalled in the 2016 Tour de France in a pile-up caused by a TV motorbike having to take evasive action from encroaching fans, he famously started running up Mont Ventoux in his cleated cycling shoes rather than wait for his (stranded) support team to arrive with a replacement bike. There was more than a hint of the Terminator. He. Just. Won't. Die.

Indeed, for a character parodied as robotic, there's plenty of non-conformity, even audacity, when you bother to look. That Giro-winning solo feat; the Mont Ventoux run; the Col de Peyresourde break in 2016, followed by that crazy 80kph descent, body folded round his handlebars and top tube like some sort of novelty bike accessory.

But what I like, and respect, most about him – as one sportsman to another – is that everything he does, and doesn't do, seems geared towards cycling success. The calm he radiates when out of the saddle (why exert yourself unnecessarily?). The thick skin (essential). The refusal to succumb to pained introspection. The uncontroversial interviews (unnecessary attention is a distraction). The lack of triumphalism (who would risk displeasing the cycling gods when the next horror fall may only be moments away?).

And the training. Above all, the training. 'Deserve success' is the most rudimentary of sporting phrases. It's one that governs the professional life of the man sitting in front of me – and to a degree that seems to outstrip almost all the sports-people I know, including myself.

Chris Froome stirs his tea, and considers my question. I've asked about the gap between his racing and non-racing selves. Pretty decent opener, I thought. So often, I've been on the other side of the interview divide, inwardly cursing the unimaginative question or tensing up when confronted by a really profound one. I don't think this is either, but it's a start and I'm eager to hear his answer.

'I know my parents always brought me up to be polite and well-mannered and all the rest of it,' he says eventually. 'But when I'm on the bike … all of that just goes out the window. I think you've got to have an element of … "arrogance" is not the right word – single-mindedness. Everything else goes, and you're there to do one job – and that's to ride your bike fast.'

Froome speaks slowly, his words measured. The pauses are long and considered. He doesn't go in for the funny aside, but nor does he seem to be reverting to stock answers, the inter-view persona that is constructed by anyone in top-flight sport as a form of self-preservation. But I'm treading carefully. I don't want the shutters to come down.

I ask about the benefits, or not, that come with being a major player, even the biggest name, in the field. When you're winning in a sport, everything – everyone – changes. Dominate for a sustained period and that dynamic can change still further. Is this always a negative, or can it be used to your advantage? He answers with reference to the Tour de France.

'When you pull on that yellow jersey it feels like you've got a massive target on your back – 100 per cent,' he says. 'You do become the person to beat and you stand out like a sore thumb. But at the same time, having that jersey does buy you a little bit of moving space in the bunch; you find gaps open up where they weren't previously there. It has a level of respect that comes with it, for a good reason – as it's so hard to get it on your shoulders.'

He pauses, then adds: 'I tend to go well under pressure. I enjoy it. I find pressure … puts me into the zone. I'm able to block out pretty much everything around me. When I feel pressure, it forces me into this state of mind where I become so single-minded. Everything is about focusing on what I need to do. I've had my best results when I've been under pressure.'

So he's not just coping with pressure, but harnessing it. He's using it as a tool – turning a potential negative into a potentially decisive positive. Some actually seek it out. British fighter Tyson Fury's ring entrances are legendary, but even he excelled himself in Las Vegas in February 2020 before his world title bout against the American Deontay Wilder. He was carried to the ring on a throne, wearing a crown. Fittingly, the most regal performance of his turbulent career followed.

I nudge my conversation with Chris onto the subject of suffering, something I associate so much with cycling. It's only a third of what I do, by definition, but some of my hardest triathlon moments have been on the bike, working hard at the front, pushing out the watts, trying to make a race-shaping break – particularly in recent years, having stepped up to tackle long-course races. On my Ironman World Championship début in Kona, Hawaii, in 2019, my split for the hot and humid 180km stage was just under 4 hours 20 minutes. In an

Olympic triathlon, the *entire* race is over in around 1 hour 45 minutes. And, as we've seen, grand tour stages can be far longer than that, and with much more punishing gradients.

So, Chris, is your ability to suffer in some way greater than that of those around you? Can you bury yourself just that little bit more? He looks thoughtful once more. 'How do you measure suffering? I definitely feel, and I often get told by other people, that it seems as if I suffer more than others and I can just sit there and take it. I think the truth is that I hate suffering. I hate being on the receiving end of it. There's no better feeling than knowing you're suffering less than other people. You're hurting, but if you see that it's too much for other people then you get such a kick out of it. I'm very much like that.'

He continues in his distinctive accent, with the slight hint of clipped South African vowels. 'When I'm not at my best it motivates me to go home and train harder. To do absolutely everything right to make sure that when the next sufferfest comes round, I can be on the other side of that and can be pushing on while other people can't.'

Another selfie-hunter apologetically interrupts. 'Sure, let's do it,' says Froome to them, with a thin but genuine smile, then he picks up where he left off. 'The interesting thing is that you find another gear when you're on the positive side of that suffering rather than when someone is dishing it out to you. It's hugely psychological. If you can feel like it's on your terms, rather than someone else's, then you're always going to be in a better state. At least that's true for me.'

The parameters of performance, particularly in our shared fields of endurance sport, have always fascinated me. To what extent are they set by physiological or psychological limitations? There's a theory that will be familiar to anyone who has ever studied sports science, and first put forward by a professor from the University of Cape Town named Tim Noakes, of a 'central governor'. Noakes argued that this 'governor' acts like an off-switch, triggered by the brain on a subconscious level when the body encroaches too far into the red zone. This was, in Noakes's mind, pre-emptive. Essentially, the brain will not let you run or cycle, say, to the point of collapse.

I've been sceptical about this theory since competing in the London leg of the World Triathlon Series more than a decade ago. I went into the 2010 event with my confidence sky-high after winning my previous six World Series events and, a few weeks before, the European Championships. It was a muggy, oppressive summer's day in Hyde Park. The crowds were large due to Olympic fever (the countdown to the 2012 London Games was already underway).

Into the final stages of the race, I was at the front in a group of three with Jonny and my main competitor, Javier Gomez. I wasn't feeling great, but as an athlete you learn that you also need to perform when you're feeling suboptimal. My resolve hardened – I wouldn't, couldn't, lose this race. In the early days on the local chain gang when I was a scrawny lad desperately trying not to get dropped, I would pick a spot on the bike in front of me to focus on – usually the rear brake caliper – and I'd tell myself that the only thing in the world that mattered at that moment was not letting that spot get any further away. It's a tactic I've used many times since and here I did the same, zoning in on a spot on the back of Gomez's tri suit, shutting out the stinging in my legs and the burning in my chest.

Then everything went black.

I woke up on a bed in the medical tent covered in ice, wires coming from all kinds of places and with about 20 people standing over me looking worried. Only months later did I pluck up the courage to watch the footage: eyes rolled back, grey skin, swaying sideways and stumbling forward down the finishing straight. Monty Python would call it the Ministry of Silly Runs. It was the same fate that would befall Jonny six years later, in Cozumel, Mexico, when I helped him the final couple of hundred metres to the finish in a desperate bid to win Sports Personality of the Year (sorry, I mean, out of concern). 'When he cracked, he went big,' said the rather excitable American commentator on the footage of my collapse in Hyde Park.

In the days after my collapse in London in 2010, I sat up reading about Noakes and the central governor, mainly because I was intrigued by what had happened, but also because I couldn't sleep for days as my body was so out of kilter. I didn't know it at the time but I'd done some significant damage to myself, probably by the 'denaturing' (destroying the molecular make-up) of proteins in my cell walls. I had managed to push through the warning signals, past the restrictions of the central governor, to the point at which my body effectively overheated and homeostasis was disrupted. So what had happened?

My interest in the subject – as it applies to me and also to elite cyclists such as Chris Froome, who spend their entire careers tiptoeing around the edges of human performance – led me to get in touch with Samuele Marcora. Marcora is a brilliantly enthusiastic sports physiologist and one of the world's leading thinkers on human endurance. Specifically, the psychological tricks that might be used to hijack our systems and improve performance.

One of his most notable experiments, conducted by his University of Kent Endurance Research Group and published in 2014 in the journal *Frontiers in Human Neuroscience*, saw subliminal images and words flashed up on screens watched by two groups of equally talented cyclists engaged in 'time to exhaustion' (TTE) stationary bike trials. TTE is used in thousands of sports science studies as a way to determine someone's capacity for exercise on a given day. The subject has to exercise at a set intensity for as long as they can manage. It's different from purely physiological markers such as VO_2 max or lactic threshold because, on some level, the subject's motivation plays a part.

Marcora's research found that those subjects who were shown happy faces or positive affirmations such as 'go' or 'lively' (rather than 'toil' or 'sleep') performed markedly better. Skirting over the paucity of happy faces and positive affirmations Chris Froome is faced with in a typical Tour de France these days, it's a significant finding.

I spoke to Marcora the day after winning my début Ironman event, in Cork, Ireland. He turned out to be equally sceptical about the central governor, even admitting that he uses video of my (non) performance in 2010 in lectures to show the weaknesses of the theory. I'm flattered. Sort of.

In recent years, he has developed a 'psychobiological model' of human effort regulation, emphasising the importance of the role of the conscious and subconscious mind – with the former, in his opinion, being the more critical.

'This is exactly what happened to you,' he told me. 'The body is trying to govern you, to keep your temperature within a healthy range. One of the ways it does this is by generating the sensation of what we call "thermal discomfort". It's uncomfortable, unpleasant. Most people in that situation would stop running, and possibly go and find a place with air conditioning and a pina colada and relax, right? The problem in your situation is that you had a competing goal – which was to win at all costs. And the problem is that both motivations act on the same physiological system. These two goals compete – and something has to give.'

Marcora's model is about how the conscious mind integrates with the physiological signals given off during effort. He labels this 'perception of effort'. In my case the conscious perception of effort was enormous and I knew it. It was simply that the extreme motivation of the situation made me 'deal' with it.

I think one of the key things about perception of effort is how it is intrinsically linked to motivation. Obvious, in a way. If I were asked to pedal at 400 watts for as long as I could in a lab, I'd be saying that it was horrendous after 10 minutes or so. Asked to do it in a race, I'd probably be 40 minutes in and still not really thinking about it. But it goes further than this. 'If you do something that you're not invested in, your motivation will be reduced, and your perception of effort will be higher,' Marcora told me. 'So you have both less motivation *and* a reduced aptitude towards the task. So it becomes like a self-fulfilling prophecy.'

He continued: 'The main determinants of perception of effort at a given output – power and speed – are current fitness level and state of fatigue. Furthermore, the other side of the bidirectional relationship between perception of effort and self-efficacy is stronger: perception of effort is one of the main determinants of self-efficacy. In other words, the harder cycling, running, swimming feels, the less confident you are that you can sustain that speed for the rest of the race. I believe that pacing decisions during endurance races – and thus the speed you sustain over the race – are primarily based on this kind of self-efficacy.'

Chris Froome set out on his audacious breakaway at the foot of the Colle delle Finestre on a pre-determined strategy that he had shaped. He was confident, he knew his preparation had been painstaking, he knew this was his final, best and only shot at victory. He was highly motivated. This will have had a material impact on his level of discomfort and thus on his performance.

This is one facet of what Froome means by suffering on his own terms. Another is the difference between trying to keep up with the other top-level climbers on a climb and them trying to keep up with him. There are endurance athletes out there who are superhuman when setting their own pace and making others uncomfortable but who crumble as soon as they are the ones playing catch-up – and vice versa. Real champions can probably get the most out of themselves in both scenarios.

Marcora called my way of ignoring all physiological pain in the middle of a race and zoning in on a point in front of me 'response inhibition', which is in itself an effortful process to maintain. It makes me wonder whether the best conscious input into perception of effort is focus or distraction (i.e. staying in the moment or trying to blank everything out). This was the subject of one of the most famous and earliest studies of sports psychology, by Morgan and Pollock in 1977. Studying marathon runners, they found that dissociative thoughts – 'Let's focus on anything but the pain of running', essentially – tended to be used by lower-level runners. Faster athletes were more likely to use associative thought processes to focus on the task.

'It's true usually that if you don't pay attention to your pain and you try to ignore it, it makes you stronger because your perception of effort should be reduced,' said Marcora when we discussed this. 'But the problem is that, in order to pace yourself properly, you need to listen to your bodily feelings, you need that association, otherwise you may go too fast or too slow – then pay for it later with a very high perception of effort too early.' Sounds familiar.

* * *

Still with me? Good. So is Froome.

The rider looks up as his Ineos teammate Chris Lawless walks past. 'Well done, today,' he says to the less-experienced rider. The next day, Lawless would go on to win the Tour de Yorkshire, the first Briton to do so, with a strong ride on the last stage to Leeds. The key moment? A decisive final break on an old favourite climb of mine, the Chevin, just outside Otley (renamed, amusingly, the Côte de Chevin for the purposes of the race). With Lawless appearing to struggle, this would be led by none other than team captain Froome.

The man in front of me is unarguably an extraordinary athlete. It's fair to say that I've reached some extremely high levels of fitness over the course of my career. Froome, while obviously less versatile, is another step up. Lab testing that Team Sky submitted their star rider to in 2015 in a bid to silence critics (given cycling's doping history, extraordinary feats tend to be viewed not just with admiration) produced some eye-catching readings. His power output in watts per kilogram was, quite literally, off the chart. His GE, or gross efficiency – a measure of biomechanics in the saddle – was superior to many other riders. He performed equally strongly in hot conditions (two tests were done at the GSK Human Performance Laboratory, at room temperature and hotter conditions), with his high surface-area-to-body-mass ratio (he's tall for a bike rider) enabling him to dissipate heat well. And his VO_2 max – a measure of cardiovascular fitness and aerobic endurance based on the maximum amount of oxygen that an individual can utilise during intense exercise – was clocked at 89.5ml/kg/min, ludicrously high. Mid-70s for international-standard endurance athletes is not uncommon. The highest-ever reading is nearly 97.

But fitness and optimal physiology are not enough in isolation, as we've seen. The conscious mind steering the ship is just as key. And I want to learn more about some of the mental processes that Froome deploys to cope with the physical torment of elite cycling. Australian rider Adam Hansen, who held the record for competing in the most consecutive grand tours with a run of 20, once said he 'had no idea' quite how much suffering was involved in cycling and said it placed extraordinary demands on what we can most simply call riders' self-talk.

Froome's self-talk has to be truly outstanding. That focus, that self-control. Or does he have some other tricks? 'For me, what's been really helpful is visualisation,' he answers. 'Particularly when I've been able to go and recon certain summit finishes or really key moments of the race. Once I've seen it, I can then visualise how I'd like it to go in the race. I think about that so much that come race day I just make sure I re-enact that little video clip I've had in my mind, almost regardless of how my legs are feeling. You've got this thing stuck in your mind saying you *have* to do this at this moment.'

I'm amazed. Is he visualising things right down to a specific tree on the side of the road?

'Pretty much.' He gives me an example from Stage 8 of the 2013 Tour de France, a 195km rollercoaster stage from Castres to the lofty Pyrenean ski resort of Ax 3 Domaines. 'I always remember the first mountain-top finish. I went there a month and a half before the race to see that stage and, when I did, I decided that this is going to be the perfect, perfect place: 6km or 7km to go, so quite far from the finish. But it was just a perfect piece of road. And I figured it was there that I was going to attack.

'I can remember getting there in the race and because I'd played this so many times in my mind it felt so easy at that point. And I think I rode away and put a minute into second place, which formed the foundation to go and win that Tour de France.' Left in his wake on that day were two-time Tour winner Alberto Contador, Alejandro Valverde and Nairo Quintana.

Judging from the previous couple of days of racing in Yorkshire, which I've been watching, Froome looks fresh. But going into the 2018 Tour de France, he was burnt out. Marcora's other significant research area is the effect of mental fatigue on performance. In a 2010 study, he compared endurance performance with and without mental fatigue, discovering that time to exhaustion was significantly shorter in a mentally fatigued state – without seeing any change in physiological data.

Furthermore, there was a marked increase in perception of effort. In short, being mentally fatigued makes a given level of exercise feel harder than it should, and therefore makes it harder to reach the highest levels of intensities. Throughout my career, I've always known the importance of feeling mentally fresh in the days before a big event but I've never understood why.

Marcora concluded that being mentally fatigued had a similar effect on endurance performance as doing 100 drop-jumps – a plyometric exercise in which you drop from a small platform then spring up. The underlying mechanisms of muscle fatigue and mental fatigue are totally different, but the final effect – that exertion feels harder, and your performance is therefore impaired – is exactly the same.

The holy grail for an athlete is to be able to operate at a high intensity automatically, effortlessly – not in a physiological sense but mentally. Marcora believes that this could be a key factor at the very highest levels of sport, particularly endurance sport, helping a few select individuals gain a crucial marginal gain over their opponents.

The principle is this: if you're able to make a particular speed one that you can maintain without much conscious mental effort, or with less than somebody else at the same kind of physiological strain, then you don't have to exert so much attention and inhibitory control, so you will have an advantage in terms of perception of effort and mental fatigue. Marcora says this may be something genetic – 'because your brain is wired slightly differently to lesser athletes' – but also, crucially, something that can be achieved through practice.

What Marcora is saying is that we could, and should, be training our brains alongside our bodies. In BET, or brain endurance training, tests funded by the Ministry of Defence, Marcora made some fascinating discoveries. A group given mentally fatiguing tasks at the same time as performing time to exhaustion (TTE) tests showed similar increases in VO_2 max over a 12-week period to the control group – but could ride for significantly longer in the TTE test by the end.

Other studies, notably one with Red Bull athletes in Santa Monica in May 2014, have tried to assess the endurance-boosting potential of something called transcranial direct-current stimulation – essentially altering the way the brain processes physiological distress signals during endurance tasks in a bid to boost performance.

'When you're talking about the very elite where there are such small differences,' Marcora had told me, 'it's not about fitness. I was a consultant for a professional [cycling] team for many years. Everyone in the team was like 75 VO_2 max. That wasn't what made the difference, right? It was something else that makes you a champion.'

By repeatedly taking himself to the darkest of places mentally, Froome is acclimatising himself to extreme suffering in the way a mountaineer might acclimatise themselves to altitude. Not just for the fitness benefits, but to train his brain to adjust more quickly come the race, so that he can endure higher speeds or steeper gradients with lower conscious mental effort.

He suffers, if you like, so as not to suffer.

'I have to go all in and push the boundaries as far as I can in my preparation,' says Froome, softly. 'I don't think I'd be comfortable going into the race if I hadn't. I don't think I could go into a race like the Tour knowing that I'd not done *everything* to be ready. I'm an all or nothing kind of person.'

Like Ronnie O'Sullivan, Froome doesn't always receive the plaudits for the amount of training he puts in to achieve his success, particularly given the team nature of grand tour cycling. 'He's a natural.' 'It's easier for him.' 'He can't fail with the best team around him.' He bristles at this. 'It's just not accurate,' he says. 'You don't just have this ability and you're able to win the Tour de France. That view almost negates everything you've done to be there. Like any other sportsperson at the top of their sport you have to work extremely hard, especially in cycling, to be there. I get that a lot of the time it's meant as a compliment when people give me that [natural] label but it does negate all that hard work, the hours and the sacrifices that go into reaching peak condition. Sure there's got to be a level of natural ability, VO_2 max or whatever. But there's no other way to put it – you need the dogged hard work to push the limits.'

Before he goes, I want to ask him about Tim Kerrison, his Australian coach with a rowing and swimming background. A mentor, a guiding hand, someone who can make an athlete click, is a huge piece in the puzzle that comprises an elite sportsperson. Froome doesn't hold back with his praise. 'Working with Tim is such a privilege. I don't think I've ever met a human being like him – his mind is like an intellectual's. It's incredible how his mind works. As an inspiration for me, he's head and shoulders above anyone else.'

One of Froome's urine samples from the Vuelta a Españã in September 2017 got picked up as a potential adverse analytical finding (AAF). He was found to have twice the permitted levels of 1,000 ng/ml of salbutamol, an asthma medication, in his system, and Kerrison was one of the most vocal of his supporters. Many, including David Lappartient, the president of the UCI (Union Cycliste Internationale, cycling's world governing body), and rival rider Tom Dumoulin, called on Froome to step away from cycling until his case was resolved. Froome carried on, insisting he'd done nothing wrong, saying he did not exceed the limit of eight puffs per 12 hours or 16 puffs per 24 hours, and vehemently pleading his innocence. Potential AAFs are normally kept confidential while anti-doping bodies work out whether or not they occurred for suspicious reasons. But not in Froome's case.

It took until July 2018, the week of the Tour de France that Froome lost to teammate Geraint Thomas, for the UCI to announce that they were dropping the case against Froome – saying they were satisfied that the higher dose of salbutamol found in his urine 'did not constitute an actual adverse analytical finding'. Froome called it 'an important moment for cycling'.

Kerrison is not surprised that questions are asked about performances such as Froome's storming Giro breakaway in 2018. As spectacular an aberration as it was, he sees it as part of a wider raising of the performance bar, with average peloton speeds rising and summit times falling. 'We are nowhere near the limits of human performance,' he said in an interview after Froome's Giro success.

That's an exciting prospect for any athlete, one supported by records being broken across the spectrum of endurance sport. On the same day that I was slogging my way round the World Ironman Championship course in October 2019, Eliud

Kipchoge lit up Vienna with his sub-two-hour marathon-length run. A day later, Kenya's Brigid Kosgei smashed Paula Radcliffe's 16-year women's marathon world record, running 2.14.04 in Chicago. Seven of the 10 fastest women's marathons have come in the past two years, while the top five quickest for men have all been achieved in just over a year.

Froome finishes his tea and politely explains that he has to go. He has a Chevin breakaway to visualise for the next day and I've got the Tour de Yorkshire highlights to catch up on.

One thing we've not really discussed is luck – such an integral part of sporting success and, particularly, given the variables and hyper-dynamic nature of the sport, cycling success. But I only think of it on the way home in the car.

A month later, while out on a recon stage for the Critérium du Dauphiné race, in south-east France, it deserts him spectacularly. Froome sustains multiple fractures after a high-speed horror crash. He fractures his neck, sternum, hip, femur and elbow, as well as losing four pints of blood – and his shot at a record-equalling fifth Tour de France win in 2019. The cause? Removing a hand from the handlebars of his time trial bike to blow his nose on a descent.

He's back in the saddle indecently quickly (as early as the following month he's posting videos of himself training one-legged on a stationary bike) and at the time of writing is targeting that Tour de France record. But Froome is now in his mid-30s, and no one has won the Tour after their 35th birthday in almost a century.

Chris Froome has beaten pretty much everyone and everything in his career. Could he beat the onset of time? You wouldn't bet against it.

3

THE PAWN, THE GOAL KING AND THE POWER OF CONSISTENCY

'If you can assemble a team of 11 talented players who concentrate intently during training sessions, take care of their diet and bodies, get enough sleep and show up on time, then you are almost halfway to winning a trophy.'

Sir Alex Ferguson, *Leading*

It's mid-morning in a nondescript coffee shop in the White Rose shopping centre in Leeds. Shoppers are coming and going, struggling with armfuls of bags, ordering complicated coffee combinations, gearing up for further retail assaults.

Sitting in a corner, sipping a filter coffee and talking with intelligence, candour and a soft Irish accent, is one of the greatest footballers of the modern era. Signed by Sir Alex Ferguson for £625,000 from Oldham in 1990, Denis Irwin went on to win 19 trophies over a dozen years at Manchester United, including seven Premier League titles, three FA Cups and that extraordinary injury-time Champions League victory in 1999 at Camp Nou.

For Irwin's final Manchester United game on 12 May 2002, Fergie – a man not exactly given to gratuitous shows of emotion – awarded him the captain's armband. It was to be far from the last accolade he gave the Corkman. When pushed to name his greatest-ever Manchester United XI after his reign at Old Trafford came to an end, Fergie would commit to only one name: his stunningly reliable and consistent full-back.

Just consider that: Cantona, Beckham, Robson, Keane, Giggs, Ronaldo. And the gaffer plumps for Irwin. Pundit Alan Hansen was of a similar opinion. He once said that if you were picking the best full-backs in Premier League history, the spots were nailed down: 'Denis Irwin at right back and Denis Irwin at left back.'

Dressed in a plain polo shirt, the man himself looks fit, lean and at least a decade younger than his 53 years. He runs a bit, he tells me. Does some gym work. Just a week before we meet, he turned out at Old Trafford for a corporate game with sponsors Aeroflot against a media team, something he does a bit of these days with a few other former stars such as Andy Cole. 'Still got it,' one of his opponents on the day would tell me. 'No one could get near him.'

Sitting here, he attracts not a second glance, even when the waitress comes over to offer us another drink. Hiding in plain sight – how very Denis Irwin.

Where to begin? There's so much I want to quiz him about, but I'm most interested in how he coped with the unrelenting pressure and scrutiny of playing for the biggest club in the world during its most successful era. During the 1990s and early 2000s, big names came to Old Trafford and big names swiftly departed, unable to hold down a place or incurring the wrath of their irascible Scottish manager. But of those who couldn't stick the course, most left because they buckled under the pressure of playing for the world's biggest club. Not Irwin. He just kept on delivering, week in, week out.

'I used to love it,' he says with a smile. 'Particularly those big games. Liverpool. Leeds. The atmosphere was electric. I've taken penalties at Liverpool and it didn't bother me at all. I think it was just in my make-up.' He gives me some insight into a football dressing room before a game. Some players bouncing around, unable to sit still. Those who need to juggle a ball, or who spend most of the time in the toilet. Irwin would just sit there and read the match-day programme. 'I just concentrated on my job, on what was in front of me, and I felt fine with all that, so it wasn't a problem for me.'

He scratches his chin and looks around. 'I don't think you can get to the very highest level, and certainly not stay there a long time, if you can't handle the pressure. You see players on their way up that you think are fantastic footballers, but there's something stopping them from kicking on – and it's usually that. They just don't want to be exposed to it, day in and day out.'

I've certainly seen, first hand, how pre-event pressure can burrow its way into the consciousness of even the toughest competitors, compromising (sometimes destroying) months of preparation. I've always preferred to twist it the other way: applying pressure to myself in the months building up to competition, believing in the process and doing everything humanly possible to deliver myself to that start line in optimum mental and physical condition. At that point, the old cliché goes, there's little you can do about it. Which means, at least relatively speaking, you can relax.

Before the 2012 Olympics I was strangely calm. Jonny's twitchier than I am ahead of big races, but prior to this one I remember we were both at least able to have a good laugh at one point. There's always more faffing around before an

Olympics race than at any other event. Everyone was pacing around in the start tent, nervous as hell. I definitely think some athletes do way too much stretching and warming up ahead of races; my thought is always that I want to save every last reserve of energy I've got. Give me a programme to read every day of the week.

I've heard sport scientists talk about the optimum off-the-shelf pre-race strategy, and gurus evangelise about the importance of individualism. In truth, I'm not sure anyone knows. I'm not sure I've found the perfect formula, but I suspect the right thing to do before a race is at the same time scientific, individual, specific to the day and very, very subjective.

An approach that has worked for one race doesn't necessarily work the week after. In an 'open environment' sport such as triathlon, there are plenty of factors you can't control – the weather, the course, different pre-race hoops to jump through. But to an extent, even the most controllable of events, such as those held on the hallowed tables of the Crucible perhaps, have significant differences between matches – travel, the quality of sleep the night before and just the general feel on the day. Making sure my equipment is all prepared, and being physically and mentally fresh, are the most important things for me. How I get to that point can vary from race to race.

You're each given a plastic box to put your kit in and I remember, in 2012, Slovak triathlete Richard Varga turned his over, went to sit on it and fell straight through the box. Jonny and I cracked up, as Varga jumped up and then started trying to frantically inspect his wetsuit for rips. We were, in hindsight, the only ones laughing. Telling? Difficult to say.

In this age of footballers chopping and changing clubs seemingly on a whim, Irwin's dozen years at Old Trafford seem remarkable. He was 36 when he left, and still hungry enough to join Wolves, the club he supported as a child, help get them promoted, then play a final top-flight season before, as he puts it, 'my legs kind of went'. The lack of serious injuries (seven weeks out with a medial-ligament issue was about his longest absence) certainly helped. But the credit for his longevity he's customarily keen to pass on – to Ferguson.

'You need a manager who pushes you all the time, and Ferguson was that. Obviously you should be up for every game the same, though it's quite hard to do that when you play 600, 700, 800 games. But our manager demanded you be on it, every game, and he'd let you know that. I think that kept everybody up. For my entire 12 years at Manchester United, there was no comfort zone.'

Irwin pauses. 'As hard as he was, he was very, very fair. People thought, to see him, "Oh, I'd hate to work for Ferguson." But he was perfect for me, exactly what I needed. All I did was work my hardest and try to play football, and all he demanded was that. I wasn't bothered if I was under the radar. I just got on with my job. And the full-back is not the biggest position on a football field – it's almost like a pawn on a chessboard. But if I could do my job to the best of my ability, I was happy with that.'

This work ethic was allied to a talent for dodging the lime-light; the Rebel County lad was the model conformist. During the glory years, at the end of the period of legendary Premier League excess at Old Trafford, Irwin's idea of cutting loose was to overdo the computer chess. 'If you didn't go out at night, if you didn't drink, you were in Ferguson's good books,' he says, taking a sip of his coffee. 'If you looked at part of your job being to rest up big time, then as long as you did that, he was delighted. And obviously you needed to perform on a Saturday. Do that and you'd be a long way down the road in his trust, and I was.'

He points to a number of his teammates at Old Trafford who had similarly long careers with Manchester United: 10, 11, 12 years – the likes of Roy Keane, Brian McClair, Gary Pallister, Gary Neville, David Beckham. Ryan Giggs managed 23 years. Why did he think this was?

'Because when you got there you wanted to stay there. It was such a great place to play, such a great environment to work in. You had a chance of winning things. You knew you were at the very top of club football in the world, on top of Real Madrid and Barcelona as well. I didn't want to go anywhere else. You just kept working because there were young lads coming through who wanted your place.'

Psychologists have flooded into sport in recent years. I've never really gone there, backing my ability to apply my learning and experience to maximise my performance and being wary of overcomplicating the process. 'Classic Yorkshireman,' as a shrink would probably put it. Many fellow athletes whom I respect feel differently.

Attending a sponsor's day before the London Games, when I was still a young lad of 22, I got chatting to Sir Chris Hoy about the role of psychology, and psychologists, in our profession. I trod carefully because I was aware of his work with Dr Steve Peters, who has helped a string of high-profile sportspeople including, as we've heard, Ronnie O'Sullivan. Hoy was frank about his reasons: he said he might not necessarily need it, but since he spent his whole life trying to maximise every last element, from nutrition to training, it made sense that he addressed psychology, too.

Irwin shares my view but, as we chat, it becomes apparent that he saw Ferguson as a sort of prototype sports psychologist. 'I think everybody would say this: Ferguson knew how to handle people. For people who could handle it, like myself, he'd give us a rollicking from time to time. For a lad like Eric

[Cantona], he needed to look after him sometimes. His man-management was second to none. He came across as this tough, tough Scotsman, but away from that, if you wanted a day off to be with the family, he'd be perfect with that. That's what was best about him. People skills, all day long.'

Warming to his subject, he says: 'I was talking to Brian McClair recently, very much of the same era as me. The manager brought him down from Scotland in 1986 and he was there till about 1997. And Brian was remembering that, sometimes, on a Saturday, the manager after a game would have a go at you even if you'd won two or three–nil. Or he'd be great with you if you'd played really well and we'd lost two or three down. You'd always go back into training on Monday and want to fight your knackers off for him.

'He had this ability to get everything together and everybody going in the same direction. And it's not easy, because you've only got 11 players that are going to play; you've got three, four or five subs coming on every now and again, and there's probably another six or seven very unhappy. But he just knew he needed them at some point so he kept everybody in the mix. Hell of a balancing act.'

And he didn't shirk the big calls, did he? 'Yeah, he made plenty of tough decisions. He left Robbo [Bryan Robson] out of the '94 FA Cup Final squad. Completely. Down at Wembley. This was Mr Manchester United through the 1980s, remember. He left Brucie [Steve Bruce] out of the 1996 FA Cup Final squad, and he'd been there since 1987. You know, he moved them on. He moved *me* on. It was just part of his job.

'I think you have to have that something in you to succeed. I wouldn't call it nastiness, but that little bit of difference, that little bit of … edge that just gets you there in the end.' I'd call it ruthlessness, and I believe it's one of the key components of any champion mentality.

Irwin has mentioned the C-word, and as a member of a family of fervent Leeds United fans, I'm obliged to follow up: Cantona, the flamboyant Frenchman who lit up (and, at times, tarnished) the earliest years of the Premier League.

Irwin played an unwitting part in one of the best/worst signings in football history, depending on which side of the Pennines you're from. His wife Jackie is from the Leeds area – we've met here today so she can do a bit of shopping before the pair of them drop in on Irwin's in-laws – and he began his career at Elland Road. There followed a successful loan spell with Oldham, where he caught Fergie's eye. But in 1992, with Leeds champions, managing director Bill Fotherby called up Old Trafford to ask about the possibility of bringing Irwin back to the club. Chairman Martin Edwards and Fergie said no chance, but they then called back to make a counter-offer for Cantona, already a cult figure at Leeds, despite being largely peripheral.

The deal was done on the quick, my mother's heart was broken (I was only four at the time, so not overly concerned with the transfer market), and the struggling Manchester United went into overdrive, winning four titles in five years.

I ask Irwin about it. He says Ferguson never told him about either the enquiry or the immediate knock-back. 'It wasn't until somebody brought a book out, 15 years later, that I heard,' he says. 'I was probably better off not knowing. I think my wife probably would've been happy to come back here but my career would've been totally different. I've never really thought about it until now.'

He looks pensive, then adds: 'You always like to think your career is in your control. But it's not, because particularly through the 1980s and early 1990s, pre-Bosman ruling, it was the clubs that ruled the footballers, that could tell them when to go and when not to go.'

Sure, but I feel obliged to point out that Ferguson – swayed by Irwin's professionalism and reliability – wouldn't contemplate selling him. In those terms, you might argue that Irwin was in total control of his career.

The arrival of Cantona had a galvanising effect, and the mercurial Frenchman and the monastic Irishman formed an unlikely bond. Watch Manchester United's 4–1 thrashing of Tottenham in January 1992 and you'll see what amounts to the Irwin-and-Cantona show. The first goal is a pinpoint cross from Irwin, and a looping Cantona header. For the second, Cantona dinks an audacious chip over the last line of defence for Irwin to smash it in. Commentator John Motson can barely control himself. Cantona 'is playing a game of his own', he gasps.

Of all the top players of that era, it was Cantona above all who seemed to exhibit a God-given talent. Collar up, nonchalantly strutting around the pitch, occasionally deigning to intervene to win a match. The very model of what England's Australian rugby union coach Eddie Jones likes to call a 'Test-match animal'.

But chatting to Irwin, I realise that I had Cantona all wrong. Yes, he had an ego the size of the Yorkshire Dales. Yes, he was volatile. But this was underpinned by a ferocious work ethic. 'Eric had great ability, a lot more than the majority of us. But you'd be surprised how hard he worked,' recalls Irwin. 'We used to finish a training session, and some would go off to the gym, and others would mess about. He brought a culture of working a little bit after, of working on finishing, shooting, crossing, things like that. We used to stay out quite a bit and just join in. Eric brought that to the young lads, and they learned an awful lot.'

Arrogance, confidence and self-belief. It's a fine line. Cantona wasn't short of any of those but, as Irwin explains: 'He looked after himself, he did everything right. You must have some talent to get to a level, and then you've got to develop this and keep pushing yourself. The best ones are the ones who can do it all the time, find a way of doing it – because in a 10- or 15-year career in any sport, you're gonna have dips.'

He stirs his coffee. 'You'll always have one or two – the same in any environment, probably in yours too – who don't train as hard as they should, and it often catches up with them in the end. I didn't work with Ronaldo, but I've seen him in training. He was given a mega amount of talent, the highest ability of anybody I've seen. But he worked as hard as anybody on a training field; you know, set pieces, in the gym looking after himself, trying to be as powerful as anything. Gary Neville and Phil Neville were two very, very talented footballers. If you'd ask anybody, they'd say Philip Neville was the more talented, but Gary just had a work ethic that would drive him to be the best he possibly could be.'

The relationship between talent and success is one we'll explore at length in the coming pages. But, before we part, Irwin adds something that has stayed with me: too much ability can actually be a negative. 'The thing that I've seen most is players between 16 and 18 who've got mega ability or who can run like the wind, but when they get to 18, people catch them up a little bit, and they have to use their head a little bit more. And because they've got away with it between, say, 10 and 18, and not used their head because they're pure pace, for example, they're the ones that struggle the most. You see a lot of that.

'There's always players that you think are going to make it who don't for some reason, and it's usually within their make-up. When you get in with the big boys, you've got to keep learning and you've got to keep trying to push yourself – because otherwise somebody will overtake you.'

We settle up (Irwin won't hear of me paying), and as we get up to leave, a young lad of around 10 comes over and asks if he can have a selfie. With me. I'm self-conscious about such things at the best of times, but particularly given the company I'm in. I agree, but take a nervous look at Irwin as the boy holds up his smartphone. Irwin is unfazed. Perhaps the boy would have had a different target if he'd made that Leeds transfer all those years ago.

Driving home, I reflect on how speaking to Irwin – pleasant, direct, uncomplicated – left me with the sense that being a pivotal player during one of the greatest periods of club dominance in the world's biggest sport was actually, well, rather straightforward.

But as any sportsperson knows, the hard part is making it look easy.

'They say centre-forwards will always drive the fastest cars, because they're the ones under the most pressure. They've got to deliver week in, week out. They get paid the highest amount of money – and rightly so.'

Flicking through the notes of our interview, this comment from Irwin jumped out. It was a typically attention-deflecting line, perhaps a bit tongue in cheek, but almost certainly grounded in truth. The ball may not be clattering into your stumps or thudding off a poorly positioned pad, but with every failure, every score-less match, the pressure on a striker mounts as surely as it does on an opening batsman in cricket. Goal drought – the two most dreaded words in a striker's lexicon.

We all remember the goal celebrations, particularly the good ones (Peter Crouch's robot, Gazza's dentist's chair and Ryan Giggs's shirt-twirling lap of Villa Park in 1999 are among my favourites – though I fear, as a player, I'd probably have settled for a straight raised arm, à la Alan Shearer); few get to see the agonies that follow the succession of fluffed chances that extend a barren run, however.

That's pressure, particularly in a sport with as vociferous and tribal a following as football. So what is it like to live under this all your career? Are those fast cars worth it?

There were a number of defining footballing moments in my childhood. One was me kicking the ball so hard at Jonny in the nets (two jumpers) during a game of beach football that it broke his middle finger. He tried to pretend it was an easy save for days until it swelled up so much he couldn't use a knife and fork. Another, England's run to the semi-finals of Euro 96. But the biggest stage is the World Cup and the biggest moment for me was a goal in a knock-out match between England and Argentina in Saint-Étienne, two years later at that tournament in France.

I won't walk you through it; I could never do it justice. John Motson called it a 'Maradona moment'. Fellow commentator Jon Champion later said of the goal: 'It took us out of the humdrum to the doors of the land of fantasy.' That, without the eloquence, is how I remember it as a 10-year-old school-boy, watching it – like much of the rest of the country – from the edge of the living-room sofa. It was, to use modern foot-balling parlance, a 'worldie'.

The goal came to nought. David Beckham was sent off, the match was tied after extra-time and England lost the game on penalties, a nasty affliction they suffered for many years that's only just showing signs of healing up. But here was a moment that caught the imagination, not least because it was provided by a kid of 18 – exactly half the age of Denis Irwin when he made his final appearance for Manchester United.

Michael Owen, off the back of the tournament, became the highest-paid teenager in the history of British football (Denis was right about the money) and his career accelerated from there like Owen himself given half a yard of space. He won back-to-back Golden Boots, the prize given to the highest goal-scorer in the Premier League. He won a treble of trophies in 2001 with Liverpool. He won the Ballon d'Or for best player in Europe, the first Englishman to do so in 20 years. He was feted by Pelé. And he went on to score 118 goals in 216 Premier League appearances for Liverpool and 40 goals for his country in just 89 appearances.

But taking him back to that day, how exactly was he able to score a goal like that, in a moment like that, at an age like that? And I don't mean technically.

Owen's in no doubt: self-belief. He breaks it down for me. 'Genetically, we've all got what we're given, you know. Some people have got a big pair of lungs; some, loads of fast-twitch muscle fibres. You're born with that and you're not going to be able to change that. Not really. After that, you've got to make the absolute best of what you've been given. The decisions you make, what you do with that frame, your determination, how courageous you are … And that's all in the mind – it's all between the ears.

'So, in my case, I had masses of power; real speed in short bursts. I was not a good long-distance runner. I was only 5ft 8in, and 11 and a half stone, but I had a massive dollop of self-belief. That's what made me get better results than possibly I should have done, if you just looked at me in a physical sense. If you typed "ideal footballer" into a computer you'd probably come out with Cristiano Ronaldo. But what got me to the top of my game was that self-belief.'

I agree, I tell him. Confidence is key.

He pulls me up on this – they're not the same thing in his book. 'Confidence comes and goes,' he says. 'If you rely on confidence too much, then you are flimsy. You'll play well for three games and go missing for 10.' He likens it to a pint glass.

Some players have a glass that's full with 50 per cent confidence, 50 per cent self-belief. They might be able to perform as well as someone who's 90 per cent self-belief and 10 per cent confidence – a ratio Owen says he had as a player. But not consistently. Poor form, an unlucky break, injury, press or fan criticism – then they 'go missing', as he puts it. But not those with the self-belief.

'The great players, the likes of Messi and Ronaldo or whoever, I don't even think confidence is a factor. They could miss 100 chances and still believe they're the best player in the world. So it's like their pint glass is totally full.'

I've never really broken it down like this in my own mind. Confidence as something fleeting; self-belief more deeply ingrained. It would be interesting to apply the pint-glass test to some of the characters we meet in this book. Ian Botham in his pomp? His pint glass, somewhat aptly, would have been spilling over.

I wonder where Owen thinks this self-belief comes from, and where it came from with him. Does this tie in to the mantra of 'deserving to win': putting the extra-long hours in and going further than anyone else, all the time adding extra substance to those foundations of self-belief?

But you surely have to start with something, and something substantial at that. Or do you? 'I think there's lots of places self-belief can come from,' Owen responds. 'Mine was nurtured almost from being a kid: from my dad, in the main, but also the coaches I worked with. If you're talented at something, then it's far easier to have a good opinion of yourself, and therefore gain self-belief. If you've got no ability whatsoever, you're just going to end up being delusional.'

'But,' he adds, 'I think being delusional can help. Because you have to have a better opinion of yourself to then develop and get better.' Owen uses the example of boxers in their final years. 'You see the press conferences, and they genuinely think that they can make a comeback at 50 years of age. And I don't doubt that they believe that, but they're obviously delusional. If you don't think like that, you'll never have been great in the first place, in my opinion. If you just think, "Oh, I'm at my limit now. I've scored two goals in the last three games," then that is the ceiling you've set and that will always be the ceiling. You won't be able to get better. But if you always think, "Well, no, I'm even better," then ...'

Owen always thought he was better. He struggled throughout his career with hamstring injuries (his stats are all the more dazzling when you consider this) that threatened to defuse his explosive pace. But missing games, not being able to always operate effectively, the goals drying up as a result, long periods of recuperation ... these things barely made an impact psychologically.

In the wrong hands, it occurs to me, such boundless self-belief could be interpreted as arrogance. It often is. In terms of an unwavering confidence in their respective qualities, Michael Owen and South Africa-born Kevin Pietersen – Alastair Cook's long-time teammate (and *bête noire*) in the England cricket team – are perfectly aligned. But the manifestation of this was so very different. Both had colossal self-regard, but only Pietersen faced continued accusations of arrogance, which ultimately seemed to contribute to a shortening of his spectacular international cricketing career. Owen's was more internal. Real self-belief, it occurs to me, is expressed externally as modesty.

He explains a few of the ways in which this inner belief was gradually, but effectively, established during his formative years, to the point where he could do what he did on that night in Saint-Étienne – at an age when others his age would have been fretting about their exams or overdoing it down the pub.

His father – former Everton striker Terry, whom Owen clearly reveres in the same way as Ronnie O'Sullivan does his father – would strictly ration his praise for the young Michael. But he knew the power of a little nod of approval at a key moment ('My heart would melt,' Owen tells me). Even when Owen was smashing age-group records, there was never any discussion about the glory and success that so clearly lay ahead. 'It was never, "You're gonna be this or you're gonna be that" or "If you continue like this, you can win the Premier League, or win the Ballon d'Or." That was all a by-product. It was more, "How good a footballer can you be?"'

We're back to focusing on the process rather than the outcome – and making the mastery of that process the end goal rather than setting arbitrary targets. 'One day you could play for England, son,' rather loses its resonance when that's been achieved, after all. Challenge someone to be the best they possibly can be, and the heights are limitless. It's what developmental psychologist types would refer to as a 'growth mindset'.

But remember to give them plenty of nods of encouragement. Terry Owen seems to have played a masterful game of carrot and stick. Steak and stick, too, as Owen recalls. 'I'm one of five children, and was fourth in the line,' he says. 'We had no money at all, but Dad on a Tuesday would go to the butcher's and buy a piece of steak. And everyone else would have beans on toast, but it was, "We gotta build Michael up for when he's a footballer, he's still slight." Things like that plant seeds in your mind, make you think, "Oh, I'm a bit different."'

They also, I'm guessing, place enormous expectation and responsibility onto young shoulders. But is that necessarily a bad thing? Owen nods. 'I'd think, "Oh god, the pressure's on me." But I realised, you either shirk it, or you take on that responsibility.' You need courage to do that. It's a word that Owen uses a lot. Others have alluded to it – in Chapter 11, Stuart Lancaster will speak about the enduring admiration he has for anyone who can line up in the bowels of a colosseum of world sport and step out to play, but he is at least in part referring to the physical confrontation of rugby.

But courage isn't just about standing your ground when a 24st French prop is charging at you, or when a West Indian quick is bowling 99mph bouncers at your head. It's about psychological courage – to try to become the best, to continue to subject yourself to the appalling pressure of top-flight sport.

Owen is now happily retired. He hung up his boots in 2013, 16 years after scoring on his Liverpool début. He's now a pundit, and mentors thoroughbreds, both footballing and equine. Like Denis Irwin, like many of my interviewees, he enjoyed a distinguished career. How did he stay motivated, and how did the source of this motivation change?

He talks about the diminishing returns in terms of the euphoria, even the excitement of victory, and how your relationship to this can change. As a keen racehorse owner, he's spent plenty of time with AP McCoy, the godfather of long sporting careers. 'If anyone thinks after 20 years of continually beating the best in the business, AP was driving up to Scotland on a 600-mile round-trip to ride a winner because that made him feel really excited, they're sadly mistaken,' Owen says.

'I think that when you've been the best, and when you continue to be the best for a long period of time, the fun of being the best is not really fun any more. So you go through a cycle: in my case, the excitement of getting there, of scoring goals, people talking about you. And then you're winning trophies, honours, you get the Ballon d'Or. And then you go through the other side of the cycle: you're getting worse, and now it becomes a fear that drives you on.'

He explains what he means. 'I won two Golden Boots back to back. All of a sudden, I believed that's my trophy. And to see Ruud van Nistelrooy or Thierry Henry or whoever coming in, and me thinking they're gonna take my mantle ... enjoyment didn't spur me on – it was fear of somebody being better than me. And that's totally the opposite to when I first got into the team.

'So I think everyone in sport goes through a cycle of what drives them to be the best. Someone like a Tony McCoy, or Phil Taylor in darts – I think the fear of somebody being better than them has probably driven them to stay on top for many, many years, as opposed to the pure pleasure of doing something they've done a million times.'

It feeds in to something I believe that people who are successful are really good at: resetting their boundaries, their targets, their benchmarks for success, their motivations for striving for it. Something we're finding again and again is that sport is far from being the last resort for those at the bottom of the class, as I've often heard it said. Particularly in its upper echelons, sport is rather a collection of, and breeding ground for, the highly intelligent.

There's sport-specific intelligence, of course. To listen to Owen, a great player himself, express his awe for the footballing brains of some of those he played with is thrilling – 'the Paul Scholeses of this world, the Steven Gerrards, Wayne Rooneys, the Ryan Giggses – by the time you've thought it, they've already done it. The ball is already there because they saw it two or three seconds before everyone else.' But I believe it's broader than that, and certainly broader than academic intelligence. This is about having the mental faculties to moderate your own psychology. Metacognition, essentially – thinking about thinking.

In one sense it's a concept with which we're already all familiar. How many times do we say something along the lines of, 'I failed at X, but at least I learned Y.' The issue I've always had with this sentiment is that it easily becomes a justification for sub-optimal performance. But, really, how often have we actually isolated the failure and worked out which decisions really caused it? I decided during that race in Hyde Park to push on, but in the end it led to me blowing up. What caused me to make that decision? What was going on at the time? Fatigue? Anxiety? A compromised mental state? It follows that only with this kind of objective analysis can you make an informed decision as to whether a call was a correct one – or if you'd make a different one next time.

A meta-cognitive approach allows you to modulate and improve your decision-making processes, but also to imagine scenarios. Froome spoke about visualisation. With the world's best rugby players we'll learn about what's known as 'chunking'. Nothing to do with front-row forwards; it's about good decisions stemming from the ability to group up experience and knowledge into chunks to be effectively deployed in a split second. The interesting question is whether that well of experience can be augmented by imagined situations, stored somewhere in the mind ready to use if required. Can these scenarios be built up in a classroom environment? Probably, to an extent.

The role of luck in the careers of the very successful is expressed repeatedly in my conversations in this book. But Owen resists the idea, believing that, given their self-belief and quality, certain players will always rise to the biggest occasions. He uses the example of Gerrard, his Liverpool and England teammate.

The 2005 European Cup final is known as the 'Miracle of Istanbul' for Liverpool's improbable comeback from 3–0 down against AC Milan at half-time. The catalyst for that was captain

Steven Gerrard. What's often forgotten is that they were minutes from elimination from the tournament way back in the group stage, until Gerrard scored an 86th-minute wonder goal against Greek team Olympiacos (worth a look again, as much for Andy Gray's 'Oh, ya beauty!' commentary).

Owen says: 'You know there are just certain people that you can set your clock by, that you can rely on when the pressure is at its absolute peak. You just know they're going to perform. Big-game players, we call them. It's strange – put them in a friendly, and they're so-so. They can turn it on and off or whatever. But put them in a big final, or a game when you need a crucial goal, and you know that they'll be the difference. So I hesitate to say it's luck. Things go right occasionally for most, but they go right most of the time for the big players. They come to the fore.'

We talk about the nature of team sport – well, he does; it's largely a blind spot for me. He's interested in the comparatively controllable world of what I do. My performance regularly correlates to my degree of success. In football, and countless other team sports, you can play a blinder and be let down by others. Did that play on his mind?

He tells me that he's never known any different. Although he never ran on to a pitch actively hoping a teammate didn't let him down, trust is a big factor: that they have prepared as meticulously as you have; that they're as motivated as you; that they haven't been out on the piss the night before.

'It's a fascinating dynamic, the individual side in a team sport,' he says. 'Football is a team sport, but the centre-half can't do what I can do: the instinct to be in a certain position, and then to deliver in the heat of the moment. But I can't do what the defenders are doing: pre-empting something, thinking, "Right, if he misses this, I've gotta cover that." I'm a totally different animal to a defender, to a goalkeeper. Cricket's the same. Yes, it's a team sport, but is it really a team sport when the batsman is facing the bowler? It's very much individual – individuals within a team having that mindset to get their job done.'

And what of the benefits of a team dynamic, everyone pulling together for a common cause? That must be quite some feeling. Owen agrees. 'You can almost get extra powers, an extra performance out of yourself, because you want to have gone that extra mile for your mate because you know he'd do anything for you. In an individual sport, I suppose you're only letting yourself down. In triathlon, you've got a team around you, I understand that. But if you wanted to quit halfway through, you could. No one's gonna stop you. In a team environment, you'd literally just get dragged along.' Particularly if Gerrard was playing.

'You're in the trenches and everyone is in there with you. We're a team and we're gonna live and die as a team. I suppose you're very vulnerable in that respect but, you know, when one unit of people are all pulling in the same direction, it's a great thing.'

It certainly is, and it's something we're going to look at in the next chapter through the eyes of a couple of masterful team players who achieved spectacular success on the world sporting stage.

Lurking in the footnotes of Owen's extraordinary career is a brief and overlooked spell playing for Manchester United. Seven years after Denis Irwin made his emotional farewell, Alex Ferguson (still there, remarkably) made an approach for the one-time Liverpool favourite. It wasn't a box-office signing, more a pay-as-you-play marriage of convenience. But Ferguson had always admired Owen, and knew a big-game player when he saw one.

It wasn't the most productive of partnerships, yielding only a handful of goals in total. But there was one marvellous high left for this most likeable and humble of *galácticos*. A game at Old Trafford against Manchester City in the late summer of 2009 – and the autumn of Michael Owen's career. It had sweeping attacks, goalkeeping howlers, frenzied goal-mouth clearances, wonder goals. A classic derby.

And then, with the scores locked at 3–3 deep into injury time, up pops a substitute, drawing on all the experience of his stellar career, and his boundless self-belief, to score his first goal at Old Trafford and send Ferguson skipping down the touchline in delight. Owen.

As someone once said: 'There are certain people you can set your clock by.'

4

THE POSTMAN, THE TALISWOMAN AND THE POTENCY OF TEAMWORK

If there's one international sports star who makes Michael Owen look like a late developer, it's Alex Danson. The captain of the Great Britain women's hockey team and star of their engrossing gold medal-winning run at the 2016 Olympics in Rio was just 16 when she won her first cap. The following year, she played, and scored, in a World Cup. What took you so long, Michael?

That was 18 years ago. In the intervening years she made an incredible 306 appearances for England and Great Britain – in hockey, the two are separate entities – scoring 115 goals. Brave ones, skilful ones, outrageous ones. The reverse-stick beauty she bagged against the USA at the 2018 World Cup on her 200th England cap to equal the England and GB scoring record, with a mazy run followed by an unerring, cross-goal strike, is uncannily like Owen's defining moment. And like him, her career was grounded in belief drawn from unwavering focus and dedication.

I've met Alex a number of times before. Out in Rio, in the wake of our respective successes, we shared a drink or two at some of the Olympic after-parties. She was quietly spoken, intense and committed to a degree that would stand out even in a city swarming with the world's best athletes. I'm now eager to chat to her again and explore some of the themes we've been teasing out with my interviewees – she seems to embody so many of the qualities that I think drive sustained success in sport. But I'm nervous about doing so after all she's been through in the past two years.

Immediately after that World Cup in 2018, she went on holiday to Kenya with her then boyfriend. While there, Alex suffered a freak brain injury when she threw her head back to laugh at a joke and cracked it on a brick wall. Months of treatment, brain scans and rehabilitation followed – at her lowest point she could barely speak or tolerate noise or light of any sort. It wasn't until January 2020 that she felt sufficiently restored to tentatively return to the national training centre at Bisham Abbey.

In August 2019, her triathlete sister Claire was paralysed in a collision with a tractor while riding her bike. I've never had the pleasure of meeting Claire, who had won the 30–34 age category at the European Championships a few months before. Claire was lucky to survive this appalling accident – Alex and the family were told to prepare for the worst – but she's shown incredible resilience to battle back and was almost immediately contemplating a Paralympic career. Her wonderfully frank and inspiring Instagram posts documenting her adaptation to these life-changing injuries are a reminder to all of us in sport not to take anything for granted.

Despite everything, Alex is delighted to chat, and we hook up in early 2020 – with Claire's plight seeming to add resonance to almost everything she says. We speak about her early years, when Alex would beg a local school to let her practise on their astro pitch because her school didn't have one. How she'd go running before class to try to raise her beep-test scores. Then, when she was a little older, the way that she'd avoid risky holidays (ironically) – anything too far away or potentially hazardous – in case they'd affect her hockey, and how she'd turn down social plans that might keep her out late before training the next day. But this was a work ethic grounded in enjoyment.

'Working hard, for me, definitely changed over my career,' she tells me, simply. 'I just always found ways to do more, because I enjoyed it – I enjoyed the challenge. I always based my athletic career on making good decisions around what made me a better hockey player. I knew if I ever made a World Cup team or a Commonwealth team or an Olympic team, I wanted to make sure that, whatever happened, I would have zero regrets. I remember always thinking, I must work harder, sometimes probably to my detriment. I've had times in my career when I've overtrained, or perhaps haven't had the right balance. But having experienced the last 16 months, which have been incredibly challenging, I'm so proud about how I lived my career, the manner in which it consumed me, and the performances and teams I've been part of.'

Particularly that 2016 GB team. Their journey to gold captured the public imagination like few other stories at the Rio Olympics. It was an unbeaten run to a thrilling final against the reigning champions, Holland, that was watched by an audience of nearly 10 million in the UK and that was settled by a penalty shoot-out. There were so many endearing sub-plots – goalkeeper Maddie Hinch consulting her little black book of notes before her penalty-saving heroics; the Richardson-Walshes, Kate and Helen, the first same-sex couple to win an Olympic gold; posts struck; goalmouth scrambles. It had everything.

But it was the story behind the journey, and the team, that I found most interesting. This was a victory for player-led, value-driven, ego-free, ultra-fastidious teamwork. Like the

England World Cup-winning rugby team in 2003, here was a team assembled over a number of years, motivated by both the striving for success and the need to atone for disappointment – just two years earlier, England had come 11th in the World Cup in the Netherlands – and that was peaking at exactly the right time. Several high-profile names departed in the wake of the success, including captain Kate Richardson-Walsh, who vacated the role that Alex took over.

There were leadership groups, buddy groups and core values underpinned by collectively agreed behaviours. It was progressive, it was enlightened, it was meticulous and it was inclusive. In an interview after the tournament, Kate recalled meetings of the pre-tournament, 31-strong training squad: 'In that room we had 31 brilliant minds, 31 sets of ideas – we needed to hear all those points of view,' she said. This was cognitive diversity before it became a buzz phrase in sport and business.

The team's physical and technical preparation were also superlative. Ahead of London 2012, where the team had rallied after an agonising semi-final defeat to win bronze, they'd pushed hard for centralised contracts that would enable full-time preparation and training. Now they had the dieticians, the psychologists, the tailored fitness programmes and the video analysis to study opposition patterns of play. Everything they needed, in fact. They weren't about to squander it.

Alex recognised it for the opportunity it was. 'For me, the challenge throughout my career was trying to be successful at an Olympic Games,' she says. 'And that was the goal for all of us. I was involved in two Games before. In 2012 we had success, won a bronze medal, and in Beijing in 2008 we were unsuccessful. But it was all a process; some of us played together that entire time.

'The challenge of playing hockey is that it's a team game. The skill in winning in our sport is everybody having an equal value and doing a job that makes us collectively excellent. And that takes years: to understand what your role or super-strength is; to understand what the person next to you offers, so that when the shit hits the fan, you know what you can access, and what they can access. It takes years to form a culture.

'When we went to Rio, were we the greatest set of individuals? Absolutely not. Were we the most prepared and diligent, the best team? Yes. I'd never want to sound arrogant but I had utter belief in what the team had evolved to be. We almost dissected everything that you need for a winning team, hand-picked everything that we needed, and brought it together. As it played out and we began to win, it was almost like, "Oh my goodness it works!"'

We talk about affiliation, particularly performance affiliation – the idea of a close bond forming as a result of everyone doing their job effectively on the pitch. When you're a professional athlete, you can't handpick who you play with – you play with the most talented individuals, and they may or may not be the individuals with whom you would form a social bond. But when you're driven to be winners, you're so performance affiliated that it brings you together as a group. 'We saw each other at our best and at our worst, and that was OK,' says Alex. 'And we understood what each other was going to bring to the team and what perhaps they wouldn't. So we knew where to look, and what to ask for, when we needed it.

'Because we were so driven towards success in Rio, and it was culture driven, it brought a whole group of very different personalities together.' She smiles. 'And, yeah, we had a great time – but you could argue that it's easy to have fun when you're winning!'

It's such a fine line, though, as we've seen. Winning has a self-perpetuating dynamic, but so does losing. I wonder how that culture would have stood up to, say, underperformance and defeat? Many a team at a big tournament has started to turn on itself, to mutiny even (French teams have made something of a habit of it over the years). I suppose that was the genius of the culture being player-driven: there was no one but themselves to blame.

Alex nods. She talks of the little things that seemingly went the team's way. Beating America 2–1 in the last five minutes of the last pool match to avoid Holland in the semi-final. Beating Argentina 3–2 when one of their opponents' players was denied a goal by the post. Momentum? Luck? Fate? I've heard it called many things – but neither of us are buying it.

'Those tiny margins in our sport are kind of the bits that you'd practise so hard for,' she says. 'Every team that goes to the Olympics has a shot at winning, but the ones that win, I think, have learned through practice to make the right decisions under the highest pressure load. I think we were able to replicate that really well as a squad back in our training environment, so we kind of knew what to do, when it was tight in matches, at the right time. Very few people go to the Olympics and win by goals and goals. It will always be the finest of margins.'

We're back to the sage advice that Malcolm, my old running coach and mentor, once gave me: 'You can win Olympic gold – but never believe you can win by more than a stride.'

Margins at the top of sport are tight. How those margins are swung in the right direction is the holy grail of sporting high performance. There are the almost robotic-looking clinical performances. Think Jonny Wilkinson kicking for goal. But there are also the chaotic make-it up-as-you-go-along calls, often taken at moments of incredible stress and tension. The most crucial decisions, by definition, have to be those taken under the greatest pressure. Think of decision making as a combination of how well you can fit past learning experiences to the current situation. Think of past experiences as a library of information. How encyclopaedic that information is not only depends on experience and practice, but also on how good we are at learning from those experiences and assimilating the information. Does a learning experience from a real-world hockey match have a greater informative impact than learning the same thing from a video? I think it does.

Alex's training had allowed her to build up a library of relevant information. Match experience and creating high-pressure environments in practice trained her mind to access the relevant information at the right time to aid her in the most important of moments.

Alex continues: 'Don't get me wrong, there were lots of things that were out of our control, but we couldn't really focus on those. You look at London 2012: Kate got hit in the jaw – had her jaw broken – in the opening game against Japan [one writer would later joke that she collected two pieces of metal at that tournament]. Disaster. But you had to stay focused on the bits that you could control, and if we could become masters at those parts, then the bits that involved a bit of luck would sort of work themselves out. Yes, you could argue in Rio that they hit the post in the final, they hit the crossbar. But I think we felt we had luck on our side because we did everything else well. The more you practise, the luckier you get, as they say.'

Curved sticks aside, hockey and golf have very little in common. One is highly dynamic, the other methodical. One, reliant on teamwork; the other, individual mastery. The ball barely stops in hockey. Move it in golf, and everyone gets a bit sweary. I've tried it. As you're perhaps sensing, I'm not really into golf. At least, I wasn't. Until I discovered the Ryder Cup.

For those of you who've never crowded around a tee while wrapped in the Stars & Stripes or (an awkward look, these days) the European flag, shouting 'in the hole', the Ryder Cup is a biennial tournament that dates back to 1927 and sees the best 12 golfers from Europe take on the best 12 golfers from America. It's everything day-to-day tournament golf isn't: tribal, patriotic, energetic, noisy. Three days, every two years, of high drama. And, in the premium it places on teamwork within the sport, it provides some helpful parallels with Alex Danson and those triumphant women hockey players.

After winning gold in the London Olympics in 2012, I decided to let my hair down a bit. We're not talking mid-1980s international cricketer levels, but I took some time out, attended a party or two, and caught up with everyone I'd not seen in the four years of preparation. Probably the best thing about time away from elite sport is freedom from routine. It's amazing how liberating it is to be able to say yes to meeting your mates at the pub because you don't have to be up early for training the next morning. Particularly when that's all you've been doing for the past four years: 35 hours a week over 45 weeks of the year, on average, plus countless hours of massage, physio and all the rest.

During that downtime I remember sitting down one weekend to watch the Ryder Cup, which was being staged at a country club just outside Chicago. This event has since come to be known as the 'Miracle of Medinah'.

Coming to the end of the Saturday (day two of three), the European team were dead and buried. They were 10–5 down, their biggest two-day deficit in more than 30 years. The American fans were getting raucous, the 'in the hole' shouts becoming more vociferous. Tiger Woods, Phil Mickelson, Bubba Watson and all the others on the American team were visibly swelling with belief. Home advantage was being rammed home. It was looking bleak for anyone this side of the pond.

But there was one match left to play out – a four-ball tie (two against two, with each of the four players playing every hole, and the lowest score from each side contributing to the running tally). Jason Dufner and Zach Johnson against Rory McIlroy – the Northern Irish wonderkid who'd won his first two majors, the US Open and the PGA Championship, in emphatic style over the previous 15 months – and Ian Poulter.

Poulter had never won a major. He still hasn't (though he's had multiple tour wins over his 20 years of playing). But put him in a Ryder Cup setting and he becomes one of the most lethally effective players ever to pick up a golf club. On that late afternoon, the Englishman, in his white visor and maroon team colours, played like a man possessed. He outshone his illustrious teammate by a distance, birdying the final five holes in succession to clinch the tightest of games and snatch a late point for Europe. His eye-bulging, chest-thumping celebrations had a galvanising effect on the team. Now trailing 10–6, rather than 11–5 or 10.5–5.5, overnight, they suddenly believed they had a chance.

The details of that final day make lousy reading if you're an American golf fan, and I have no wish to rub it in. Europe won 8.5 points out of a possible 12 (Poulter comfortably beating reigning US Open champion Webb Simpson to add another point) to win the clash 14.5 to 13.5. And I, for one, was hooked.

Most could retire on that performance. For Poulter, it's just another set of stats in a Ryder Cup career of almost unprecedented success. It began back in 2004 when, as a rookie, he won his singles match with ease, stretching all the way to 2018 and his wildcard selection to play at Le Golf National outside Paris, where he helped Europe to a convincing victory. Cue more eye-bulging self-CPR. Such is his record in the Ryder Cup, they call him 'the Postman' (you can work it out). And like my postman, he proved frustratingly elusive to track down.

When I finally did, we were both driving. Him off the practice tee, speaking on his hands-free. Me, on my way back from the European Triathlon Championships in Weert, in the Netherlands.

So just what is it that gets into him when he's playing in the Ryder Cup? And how on earth does he deal not just with the pressure of arguably the highest-profile event in golf, but with the expectation of being 'the player who always delivers'. His answer? Enjoyment.

'You have to embrace it, otherwise you're going to struggle. It's the biggest stage to play golf on – and it's the most enjoyable stage to play golf on. You've worked your entire career for the opportunity to play in those three days. So you shouldn't be nervous. You know you're one of only 12 players in Europe that's got that opportunity to represent your country, your continent. It's a pretty big position to take up, and you should enjoy every single moment of it. And I love it. I'm still just as excited by it as the first time I played.'

Golf's a strange sport in that it offers so little opportunity to taste victory. Most players are serial losers. I don't mean that disrespectfully; AP McCoy says the same of himself in Chapter 8. Tennis analytics experts point out that the No. 1 player in the world each year only wins around 55 per cent of the points they play. Since turning pro in 1996, Poulter has won a couple of World Golf Championships. He's won the Moroccan Open and the Italian Open. He's had some top 10 finishes in the Majors (sixth in the 2015 Masters; second in the Open in 2008, at Royal Birkdale). He's reached world No. 5. But arguably that's not a great return for a player who, on his day, is borderline unplayable.

'There's nothing I can put my finger on as to why you win tournaments,' he tells me. 'Obviously, if you're confident, you're comfortable, you feel like you're swinging well ... all your ducks are in a row for that given week, then you have the backbone of a successful week. But you need to capitalise. I mean I've played 500 or so events in my career and won 15 of them. Mine is a sport where you compete with 166 guys every week that have the opportunity to win, and can win. Wins don't come around that often. So you have to try and take those chances when they arrive.'

And the Ryder Cup, with its focus on match play rather than stroke play, offers a regular supply of such chances, not to mention the teamwork, the patriotism, the cut-and-thrust of high-intensity competition – all the things that a heart-on-his-sleeve player such as Poulter craves.

'The Ryder Cup is the Ryder Cup, and you're incredibly switched on from the first tee shot,' he tells me. 'The pressure is higher, your excitement level is a lot higher, the adrenaline is a lot higher, and in those Ryder Cups I've played some of my best golf. Because you're under the spotlight, you're under the heat. Match play is the purest form of golf because you're playing against one other person. I feel that when you've got the Ryder Cup shirt on, if you're placed in the team, you're gonna give everything you've got and try your best to deliver that point. I feel very comfortable with that on my mind, with that on my conscience.'

Listening to him talk, you can't help but feel that this is a competitor somehow stuck in the wrong sport. Yes, the Ryder Cup offers a biennial release. But just imagine Poulter in a high-intensity team environment week to week. He seems to have so much in common with Alex and her teammates.

Given the depressing win–lose ratio of even the very best golfers, a high premium must be placed on confidence and belief. I wonder about the psychology of this. How is it possible to convince yourself that you can win when faced with overwhelming evidence to the contrary?

Poulter, at least outwardly, has never shown signs of being short of self-belief. In 2008, he was mocked for an interview he gave to a golfing magazine in which he said that, when he started to play to his full potential, 'it will just be me and Tiger'. He claimed that what he said was taken out of context. But appearing nude on the cover, with just a pink-and-black golf bag covering his modesty, told its own tale. As did the flamboyant look he's always cultivated on the course: the crazily patterned trousers, the pink golf shoes, the bleached hair and Claret Jug-emblazoned outfits. This was a man who wasn't just happy with attention, he courted it. Bring on that 'heat'.

I ask him about this aura of confidence. Is it something he's worked on?

'I don't know anyone who can fake confidence,' he says. 'If they can, someone let me know how they do it because I'd love to know. If you believe in what it is you're doing, and you trust what it is you're doing, then you should have a level of confidence about your job.

'Some people are more outwardly confident than others: some people wear their heart on their sleeve more than others. And everybody has their own personality. You know, there are a number of players who don't show any confidence at all. They're super-quiet, they're super-reserved. You see no facial expressions and they give you no real feedback on how well they're doing or not doing. And you've got other guys that are completely the other end of the spectrum. It's a personality thing, I think, more than anything else.'

Poulter was wrong in his controversial 2008 assessment. Once he started playing to his full potential in the Ryder Cup, he didn't just match Woods, perhaps the greatest to ever play the game, he far outshone him. At the 2018 Ryder Cup, where Poulter ended up charging around the green in a postman outfit commandeered from a fan, Woods lost all four of his matches. At the time of writing, he's lost 21 games in the event over the years, one of the worst losing streaks in its long and esteemed history. Poulter has lost just six.

I love what he said about Tiger (if indeed he did) and that, clearly, he believed it. If there's one message to take from this book it's that, just possibly, the greats may not be as great as you think – and that taking them off their pedestal is the first step in the process of raising your own performance to those heights. Not them and me. Us. Poulter has always instinctively understood this.

'Look,' he says, as I listen to him crack another ball into the distance. 'I believe the most successful ones are more ruthless and more dedicated. And they have a heightened level to win. But I don't think anybody has a God-given right to be more successful. I know that when I play my best golf, it's good enough to beat the best players in the world.

'Over my 20-year career, things have changed an awful lot – technology's changed, my family situation has changed, my ranking has changed. But my drive for the game is still there, my passion for performing to the best of my abilities is still there. I love competing, I love what competing means to me, and I embrace that as much as I possibly can. I feel as motivated today as I did in year one.

'I never knew what it was gonna take to get to where I've got to. I never knew when I was a four handicapper that I would have a career like I've had. I understood that I was comfortable in myself, comfortable in my personality, comfortable in my mindset, comfortable with playing against other players that are super-successful, and because of that I feel comfortable in that environment. I think that is part and parcel of what's allowed me to play at the top level for so long.

'I feel I'm just as entitled – "entitled" is the wrong word – I feel there's no reason why someone else could be successful and not me. No one's born with the gift of being the perfect golfer, no one's born with the gift of having the perfect mindset. It doesn't give anyone else the right to be successful and you not to be. I understood that at an early age.'

Poulter's final comments take me back to a conversation with Alex. She also came to understand this point, though it took a little longer. She tells me about playing her first international in 2001 as a 16-year-old – 'just a kid, really' – and being in awe of those she was playing with. She'd be content to sit on the bench, perhaps come on for the last two minutes to sample the atmosphere and try to learn. One can't blame her.

The first elite race I participated in was the Salford Triathlon World Cup in 2007. There wasn't even a place for me on the start line at Salford Quays, so I had to start behind another athlete. I was delighted to be there and overawed at being surrounded by some of my heroes. So much so that I ended up diving straight on top of the bloke that was unlucky enough to be in front of me.

But for Alex, her outlook changed on the long and difficult road to Rio. 'As a youngster I'd look up to people who had achieved things and assume they had some different, magical upbringing or they were just extraordinary people doing unachievable things,' she says. 'One of the greatest lessons I think sport has taught me is that we are very ordinary people. I don't mean that disrespectfully – we're just ordinary people who have worked very hard at honing one, or in your case three, skills.

'I guess it's about taking people off a pedestal and just breaking down what makes a person successful. I've always believed that the most talented people aren't the most successful; it's the workers, the ones who want to achieve something a little bit more than the next. In our case, the last to leave the training session or the one that's willing to go and do the training when no one's looking.

'That's pretty much been the premise of my career. I definitely wasn't the most talented when I was younger but I was probably the most desperate to achieve or to play for my country or to make a team. Extraordinary people are not born – extraordinary people are made. And they're made by doing the simple things repeatedly.'

As I know only too well, the autumn of your career is when perspective, with all its pros and cons, tends to start rearing its head. What Alex has been through in the past 16 months has understandably accelerated that. In February 2020, after a brief comeback in a bid to make the squad for the Tokyo Olympics, she announced her retirement, saying her priorities had changed and if she couldn't be 100 per cent committed, she didn't feel she could continue. 'I'm all in or all out,' she told BBC Sport.

She retired with the satisfaction of knowing she'd helped leave the sport of women's hockey in a far better position than when she found it: professional contracts rather than the training-after-work gauntlet she had to endure on the way up; one of the best-funded Olympics sports; high expectation levels; that middle-class, genteel, strictly amateur ethos that once prevailed in women's hockey replaced by a ferociously competitive environment; and, most importantly, an Olympic title to inspire the next generation.

As a born scrapper who revelled in having to overcome the odds, Alex is a touch uneasy about one aspect of the new era, though. 'People are now coming in with an expectation of being a full-time athlete, and everything that comes with that. That has massive, massive positives, but sometimes when things are there and waiting for you, you don't develop the skills that you do if you have to fight for all of that.'

Overall, a fantastically successful and varied sporting career, then – and so lucidly described that it leaves me confident she can make a full recovery from her debilitating brain injury. 'My career was stopped, you know, by something out of my control, something reasonably innocuous – nothing on a hockey pitch,' she says. 'And it's funny, because as I come back into the programme now, I remember so clearly our assistant coach saying to me once, "Al, you need to have some perspective," because I was always very driven. She was like, "Al, please – it's just a game of hockey." I remember thinking, "I can't believe she doesn't think I have any perspective." But the irony is, you don't realise you don't have perspective until you have some.

'This year, with my health, with my sister, it's just made me realise how thankful I am that I lived my career as I did. I've had a very fortunate career where I actually didn't miss a tournament in 18 years. I've had injuries but I've always got back, I've been very, very lucky. Some athletes go through an absolute rollercoaster, selected one time but not the next. Very, very few athletes get to leave sport on their own terms, completely satisfied.'

It seems to me that three things – and three things that are perhaps relatable to all sports – have provided the foundations for Alex's stellar career: she loves what she does; she relishes the process of individual and collective improvement; and she genuinely believes that elite sport (and therefore elite sporting achievement) is a club that's open to all.

Alex agrees. 'We're so lucky to do what we do. That's been the biggest factor in what people perceive as a long career: I enjoy the game; I love, love being in a team environment, and I love competition. I love the thrill of *trying* to win. Actually, the winning is just not as great, is it? It's the pursuit of winning for me that's all-encompassing.

'I think it's fine to look up to others, to want to emulate them, but don't believe they came from somewhere else. Don't believe they were gifted, that they were naturally talented and didn't have to work for it. As I've said, I've found the most talented aren't the most successful. It's the grafters, and the ones who enjoy what they're doing a bit more than the next.

'That's how I always used to think throughout my career. I've done that extra hour because I bet no one else will have done that. And I think that was the collective approach in our gold medal-winning team that gave us the edge. You can always work harder than you think; always put yourself one step ahead of the next person. Set your heart on something, and make decisions that move you towards getting there. Break it down and, you know, anything is possible.'

5

DRIVEN

I'm standing in the field in front of my house watching Mark Webber hurtle towards me. He's well over a mile away, but closing fast – definitely in excess of 100mph. For a man who spent 12 years in Formula One, winning nine Grands Prix and standing on 42 podiums, it's exactly the arrival I expected.

I've known Mark since a chance encounter a couple of years before. I'd been training in the Yorkshire Dales – a long, torturous ride in the middle of winter. He'd pulled up in a big van with Dougie Lampkin, the seven-time motorcycle trials world champion. The pair had been trials riding – a radical departure for an F1 driver, you might say, but typical of Mark as I have come to know him: sports mad.

'G'day, Alistair,' he'd said, leaning out the window with a big smile.

We'd stayed in touch and, the following year, when I was in Australia for a month preparing for the Commonwealth Games, I'd accepted his invitation to a barbecue at his beach-view pad in Noosa Heads, north of Brisbane. He'd fully retired from racing the year before, and it seemed to suit him. Mark, as anyone who crossed racing lines with him in F1 will tell you, was never exactly the most highly strung on the grid, but now he seemed even more chilled out.

We'd hung out that day, relishing our shared love of sport, and swapping insight and gossip from our respective worlds. A keen cyclist and runner, he'd been full of questions about the intricacies and challenges of triathlon. Growing up, motorsport had never really grabbed me. It just seemed the antithesis of what I do. But my appreciation for the skills of those at the sharp end of the sport has grown exponentially the more I've learned about the demands, and meeting Mark accelerated that process.

One thing I particularly admired in him was his longevity. In a sport where the financial stakes are so colossal that a sequence of poor drives can see you kicked off a team, possibly never to be heard of again, his dozen years and 215 starts in the head-spinning circus of F1 seemed remarkable. The amiable Australian finally retired from racing in 2013 at the age of 37.

To put that in perspective, that's 20 years older than the age at which Belgian–Dutch prodigy Max Verstappen – another guest at Mark's barbecue that day, sipping a beer in the shade of the fierce Queensland sun – competed in the 2015 Australian Grand Prix. The following year, in Spain, Verstappen became F1's youngest-ever winner. Mark, who has organised epic, multi-day adventure bike races in his time, had been dragging Max round the trails of Noosa on foot and bike.

Sitting there, Jonny, our training partner Mark Buckingham and I were gripped by the conversation. I'd never quite appreciated just how monumental an F1 team is. How the driver interfaces with the rest of the set-up varies enormously, and it appeared Mark and Max were at opposite ends of the spectrum. Max, young and bursting with confidence, didn't seem to feel the need to get involved in every technical detail. Mark? Obsessive.

I didn't get the chance to quiz Mark about his longevity that day – the physical and mental strategies he used for prolonging his career so effectively. But I'm going to today. Just as soon as he arrives.

Mark slows as he approaches the house, and I squint up into the cloudless sky as, rotors thudding, he performs a little recce of the field, finds a level spot and expertly lands his helicopter. When we were setting up this get-together, he'd ended the conversation by asking for my postcode, then adding: 'Hey, mate – there aren't any cows in your field, are there?' It doesn't seem such an odd question now.

He performs his post-flight checks as the rotors slow, takes off his ear defenders and hops out of the white AS350 Single Squirrel. It's a freakishly hot April day – 22°C here in Yorkshire, which must be some sort of record – and he's made the hour-long flight from his Buckinghamshire house to see me. Dressed all in black – T-shirt, jeans and trainers – he looks lean and considerably younger than his 43 years. He's got a full head of black hair, and that ready smile that made him such a popular member of the paddock.

With him is his instructor and co-pilot, Al Gwilt, an ex-Army aviator who was F1 supremo Bernie Ecclestone's pilot for 16 years. We're going to talk about the ways one fills the void of no longer racing multi-million-pound machines at upwards of 230mph on a week-to-week basis. I think I can guess one.

'Yeah, it's amazing in sport how quick you get old,' Mark says, with a laugh. We're sitting round the table in my dining room a short while later, sipping glasses of water like the couple of health obsessives we are. He's run 13 miles earlier in the day; I've done 200 lengths of the pool at a mostly leisurely pace as it's Friday, my 'rest' day. Eight days later I'm racing a long-distance triathlon event in Spain, so recovery is at the forefront of my mind.

'One minute you're with all these guys that you've grown up reading about, and you're ahead of them on the times, and you're like, "How the fuck am I ahead of these guys?" They've done 150 races and I'm five, six races in. And then you look around a few years later, and you're like, "The guys I'm racing aren't even shaving yet." But you know what? You're wiser. You've got composure, right? "Composure" is a huge word in sport – having belief in yourself at key times, when it's hotting up.'

So true, I say. In triathlon, you're often racing the same guys day in, day out, week in, week out. Then you get to the Olympics – one race every four years – and, technically, everything is exactly the same. You're on a pontoon. You're diving in the water. The bike and run stages lie ahead. But you look around and you just know that a big proportion of your competitors are probably going to race worse than they would in the usual course.

In F1, that pressure is amplified by a factor of 100. 'We're a beacon for the team,' says Mark. 'At Red Bull we had 850 people at Milton Keynes, a €300 million budget. Thousands of hours have been spent on the car, and now it's over to you. You're going to back yourself to do what you can on that particular day, whether you're at the back of the grid, the front of the grid, whether it's raining, whether it's Singapore, brutal humidity, freezing, whatever. So that's a tremendous puzzle. I loved that.

'The best mechanics in the world and the best engineers in the world know that we're on a tightrope of performance. Emotionally, you go through a lot of micro tugs-of-war. The stress can be there, the responsibility can be there, the occasion is there. And there are all these moments you're constantly faced with where you have one chance: whether it's a qualifying lap, whether it's a particular corner, and you're like, "I have to nail this." All the time. So there's this respect for what you as a driver have to go and do.'

He explains that, as a driver, it's entirely possible to make an error, push too hard and destroy the car. That may result in 15 guys having to work 17 or 18 hours each to get it back to race level. 'You come back in and that discussion will be over inside 30 seconds – it's just that respect both ways,' he says.

The demands placed at the door of an F1 driver – the relentless schedule of testing, qualifying, racing, travelling, fine-tuning, media, sponsors, the lot – dwarf those of many sports, mine included. And we haven't even touched on the risk. We will, though.

How does he cope? 'The nerves are high. Like I used to get nervous, absolutely. I would go to sleep pretty well, but wake early. I'd struggle to put good food down. There's a tremendous amount of unknown in our sport. With tennis or golf, the equipment's gonna be pretty stable. In our sport, the equipment is not overly stable. We're dealing with a very, very dynamic piece of machinery.'

I think a mistake the public sometimes make is to view sport as a profession like any other. Lawyer. Teacher. Accountant. Sportsperson. The reality is that, if you've heard of a figure in sport, if there's any recognition factor at all, then you're most likely looking at someone in the top 0.1 per cent of their field. They've had to drag themselves upwards to the very top to be able to poke their head out of the hopelessly overcrowded ranks below and say, 'Look at me.' And then they've got to try to stick around.

Heard of Antônio Pizzonia? Me neither. Antônio was a Brazilian racing driver who was Mark's teammate at Jaguar in 2003. He'd performed well in the junior categories, and hopes for him were high. Alarming for Mark, too. 'We're two guys, same team, and you've gotta beat your teammate 'cos you've got the same equipment. All winter he was laying down these massive times. And I'm thinking, "This could be the end of my career; in six months, I could be replaced." In testing, Pizzonia – oh my God! And you could see the dynamics of the team, see people getting a bit sexy towards him, and I'm like, "Fuck, he's gonna be quick."' He pauses. 'When we got to the big events? Crumbled.'

Aussies have a way of emphasising certain words, really wrapping their mouths around them. Mark does this with 'crumbled'. He practically adds an extra syllable. Why did that happen with Pizzonia, I ask? Talented, but not cut out for the very highest level? Mentally overawed?

Mark looks thoughtful. 'In the junior ranks, you don't have the envelope of operation of the car; they're very standardised. You've only got your limits within that. They can be good guys that are really hard to beat in those environments, and then you put them in the bigger environments – bigger teams, more technology, more things to deal with, more things they've gotta focus on to get their performance to a higher level, more things they have to integrate with, whether it's the tech side, whether it's the media, whatever. Travel, dealing with money. And some guys …' He exhales.

Mark was a decent junior but really flourished on the biggest stage. 'I think I just managed to stay relatively normal with it, to be as calm as I could,' he tells me. We're back to composure again. Pizzonia, meanwhile, was dropped by Jaguar mid-season. He moved around teams, won a trickle of points and two years later was out of F1 for good. Shortly afterwards he was driving in the Champ Car World Series in Long Beach.

'He really underperformed. He just couldn't deal with it,' recalls Mark. 'And what it is, is that when we go through testing, you have a lot of time to get your eye in. But at a race weekend? Very limited time to hit that bullseye. So every time you go out, you have to deliver; put the car on its tippy-toes every single time. And when there are guys that need more practice to get up to speed … well, F1 isn't the time for that.'

He talks about the 'frame rate' and how this ramps up in F1, the information that needs to be consumed and filtered. He uses the analogy of the downhill skier. The snow conditions are always changing so they've got to try to imagine how a run is going to go. They go through the first two gates – 'Right, that's the snow conditions.' Once they're at the third gate, the skier will then naturally react as they need to. They're versatile. 'The guy that's fifth in the world, he might learn that at gate seven, and that's the fucking difference. Because your mate learned it five gates earlier, and now he's three-tenths up. Because he clicked. All the greats, they're clever – sharp. They know what to work on.'

He then says something that surprises me. 'The thing is, Pizzonia had more talent than me. All day long. But when it came to all the other columns, big Xs – because he couldn't handle it. Now what is that? Is that professionalism? What are those extra columns? Look at Nick Kyrgios in tennis. Insanely skilful. The most skilful player in the world, arguably. Unbelievable.'

I'd have to agree. At Wimbledon 2019, he even managed to ace Rafael Nadal – with an *underarm* serve. The great Spaniard, to his credit, seemed to enjoy it.

Mark continues: 'But is he a good tennis player? That's the question. He can win three-set tournaments, but slam tennis is best of five for two weeks, and his fucking mind can't do it. He can't do it. So where's the talent there? He's talentless, mate; he's talentless in some columns. Nick's trophy cabinet? It's like this table. Which is bullshit for the skill he's got.'

Kyrgios, for what it's worth, agrees. In an interview after that Wimbledon he said: 'I'm a great tennis player but I don't do the other stuff, you know. I'm not the most professional guy. I won't train day in, day out. I won't show up every day. So there's lots of things I need to improve on to get to that level that Rafa brings, Novak brings, Roger ... have been doing for so long. So it just depends how bad I want it.'

It was Mark's misfortune, it seems, to race at a time when F1 was packed with some of the biggest beasts ever to bestride the sport. Mark's nine F1 victories, and his near world title in 2010, need to be put in the context of this. It's something that we'll address – the difficulty of judging champions in isolation.

Of more interest to me is to what degree being surrounded by such spectacular strength, week in, week out, and having to measure yourself against a ludicrously high bar, elevates your performance. It's like an extension of the Köhler effect – the phenomenon identified by groundbreaking psychologist Otto Köhler – in which weaker competitors attain higher levels of performance when paired with stronger ones. Had he not been confronted with the triopoly of Federer, Nadal and Djokovic, Britain's Andy Murray would almost certainly be a more decorated player. But would he be as good?

I put this to Mark. He laughs. 'Yeah, mate, it was an absolute joke. Michael [Schumacher], [Kimi] Räikkönen, [Fernando] Alonso, Lewis [Hamilton], Seb [Vettel], myself, Jensen [Button], Rubens [Barrichello]. That patch ...' He puffs out his cheeks, shakes his head. 'The pace, and the risk, and the times that were going down. If you're there on your own testing, you're never going to go to that level.'

He gives me an example. 'You've done your lap time and you come in and you're just like, "Where am I gonna find that extra two-tenths? Where am I gonna find it on a one minute 30 lap?" And you gotta find it. And it's not about being scared. You're not scared – you want to find it. But it's like, technically, where am I *actually* going to find it. And then the guys are into you and you've gotta start soaking up the information and you've got three minutes to turn around and go again and try to find it. And you might actually find those two-tenths and then you're on pole. And you've not been pressurised into it, but you've sort of …'

Raised your game.

He takes a sip of water and continues. 'I would have won every race if I stayed in the category below, so what are you looking for? To be on the podium with those guys and every now and then be in the middle … those, mate – those are the special photos to have.'

Mark talks of how, to the untrained eye and even sometimes to the trained one, F1 races can sometimes look like an uneventful procession. Four or five cars, one after the other, with no change in placement or in the margin between them. 'You watch it on TV and it can be like watching paint dry,' he says. But what you can't see is that all four or five of those drivers are just going for it. They're on the absolute limit. 'And as drivers we'll laugh about that afterwards. Some guy's like, "Remember Suzuka 2010" or whatever.'

Who impresses who within the closed ranks of the world's best F1 drivers can vary from track to track, Mark explains. 'I think that naturally when you go to all of those circuits around the world, all those different combinations, you get guys that will pull away. I did some guys' heads in at certain tracks because they couldn't live with me.' He talks about his two wins at Monte Carlo, the showpiece F1 event, when he felt 'he had the car on a string'. 'There were tracks where I was given the acid and there were some tracks where I was like, "How is he doing that?"'

Inevitably, certain names caused more awestruck incredulity than others. I think we can guess a few of them. 'With Michael

[Schumacher], I saw him do things in the car and was like, "Fuck, mate." You can't even relate to the risk that was involved. Michael went off the road a lot, though. He did make a lot of mistakes. Yeah. But when it counted, he was exceptional.

'It comes back to versatility. Senna was amazing on one lap. Alain Prost? Bernie Ecclestone, who ran the sport forever, said Prost is probably the greatest ever. Now Prost was not dramatic, he wasn't flamboyant. He wasn't sexy. None of that. When it comes to one-lap qualifying, which is what all the people love to watch: the guy putting the car totally on the edge, brushing walls. That's not Prost. Prost is Sunday. Tactically just coming through there with his tyres. Like he just gets through in the most boring way possible. And gets the job done. He won four world titles, and had 51 victories.'

The criticism sometimes levelled at F1 is that it's all about the car. It's the F1 equivalent of Ronnie O'Sullivan and his 'genius'. Denying credit where credit is due. I read somewhere that British F1 driver and long-time commentator Martin Brundle once said that if you gave every driver the same car then there'd be no more than half a second between them. Apart from Senna.

Mark agrees, but points out that half a second is 'a truck-load' in F1. 'I tell you now, though – if it starts raining in the middle of a Grand Prix, if there's drama or you start getting involved in a scenario, that guy in that car is going to struggle. That's why the best guys are in the best cars. Lewis? He'll adapt very quick: composure, the rate of learning of new scenarios – these are very high. Whereas some guys need to see too many balls – they need to see it too many times and will get there eventually – we don't have that luxury. It's like a boxer, right? If you're missing moves, then your opponent is gonna win the fight. Lewis? He's gonna see the move coming.'

I think of Hamilton's thrilling final lap in Brazil in 2008 when he overtook Toyota's Timo Glock on the last corner to take fifth, and win the world championship by a single point. 'Lewis has gotta be up there in terms of all the strings to his bow. His stats now are massive. Massive [95 Grands Prix and seven world titles, by the end of 2020].'

Mark doesn't mention his former Red Bull teammate Sebastian Vettel, the youngest-ever triple world champion. For anyone who knows F1, that's not surprising. For a while, the two drivers' rivalry was so engrossing that even the Queen was intrigued. Christian Horner, the Red Bull team principal at the time, tells a story about being invited to Buckingham Palace for a lunch in 2013, shortly after the notorious 'Multi-21' incident at the Malaysia Grand Prix – and having the Queen quiz him about it.

To recap, with Webber leading the race from the German, the tyres getting fragile, and no threat from the other cars – team orders were given to hold position for the final few laps through the coded 'Multi-21' (2, Webber's racing number, coming before 1, Vettel's). Webber eased up, as instructed, 'turned the engine down', as he later put it, and awaited what would have been his final F1 win. Vettel was having none of it. He closed in on him, fighting to pass, racing wheel-to-wheel with his teammate and eventually inching past to claim victory.

Cue bedlam. 'Multi-21, Seb, Multi-21!' Webber remonstrated with his teammate in the pre-podium waiting room. There followed – and I've seen a fair few close up – one of the most awkward podium ceremonies I've witnessed in any sport. The interviews afterwards, with Lewis Hamilton in third looking on, were even more toe-curling.

It still grates with Mark to this day. 'Mate, it was toxic. I mean, we went to all levels of what shouldn't have been discussed publicly. I'm on the radio saying to Christian, "How big are your balls now?" The team are involved, there's a position being made clear, and then the individual overrides all that. That would have been a very, very hollow victory, and it still is to Sebastian to this day. He got the victory on paper, he's the winner, but the industry was like, "Mate, that was pretty average." It was pretty underhand, because it went against everything that the team had agreed.'

It seems an apt moment to talk about ruthlessness – that edge that seems to separate the top 1 per cent from the rest. Did he feel there were those he raced against, and not just Vettel, who crossed lines that he wouldn't have crossed himself? He talks about a 'natural ceiling' you're prepared to go to, particularly in a sport as manifestly dangerous as F1, and how this is informed by a driver's moral compass, how they were brought up. 'I did have issues with some guys on the track and sometimes I did have to dish out stuff that I wasn't overly proud of. There might have been some retaliation involved or I'd want to stamp my authority on someone,' he tells me.

'Early in my career you'd have guys like Michael coming up in your mirrors and it's like, "No, I'm going to be a bit of a prick here," because it's like a test. Because if you just roll over every time, team bosses see that, everyone sees that. So you need to be tough in that situation. I did have some very, very heavy fights on track, absolutely. But I would be shattered if the boys I raced with said I was doing cheap shots. There was nothing underhand – it was to what I felt was the limit.'

And, by extension, without that moral compass – would he have won more, been more successful? The question hangs in the air, the pause growing ever more articulate. 'Yeah, could have done,' he says, eventually. 'But I think culture comes into it, you know? We gotta look at how certain nationalities might look at how they are perceived. Different parts of the world have a different style, the way they can have things

DRIVEN

wash off their backs that little bit easier. I was hard, fair and honest.

'Both Michael and Sebastian, the Germans, sort of had that component of just going about it, right or wrong. Maybe I got hung up on it a bit too much, saying, "Well, actually, I'd prefer to win a different way." Don't get me wrong: Seb's got a better trophy cabinet than me for lots of different reasons. I'm not saying I feel hard done by. But that was an average day for him.'

For balance, it should be pointed out that Horner takes a different view of the Multi-21 incident – and didn't see Webber as entirely blameless. In a *Beyond the Grid* F1 podcast in 2018, he said that Vettel's actions in Malaysia were '100 per cent' payback for Mark squeezing the German up against the pit wall at the start of the championship decider in Interlagos, Brazil, the previous season – something that ultimately resulted in Vettel spinning after contact with the Williams of Bruno Senna.

When he got his damaged Red Bull facing the right way again and resumed, he was 22nd, and last, in the race. While Button and Hamilton engaged in a thrilling race for the lead, Vettel worked his way up through the field all the way to sixth, enough to narrowly beat Fernando Alonso to the world title.

Horner said that during his time racing for Red Bull, Mark struggled to accept that Vettel was the quicker driver and would 'use whatever tool he could to try to get under his skin'. In the podcast he says: 'Mark was a great competitor. A ruthless competitor. He'd read every mind-management book in the business. One of his heroes was Roy Keane. Mark would use whatever tool he could to ruffle Sebastian and if that meant using the team to do that, he would do that.'

Before Mark goes, we must talk about danger. Go on to YouTube and there's a 'Mark Webber crash compilation'. It lasts nearly five minutes and features, among others, the race in Valencia in 2010 when he gets almost as airborne as he'd been in his helicopter earlier today. And it doesn't even include his two worst ones, during the infamous 1999 Le Mans race weekend, when he flipped in qualifying and then, remarkably, with the car having been rebuilt, again in practice. Driving the same aerodynamically flawed Mercedes CLR a few hours into the actual race, teammate Peter Dumbreck endured one of the biggest horror crashes of all time, somersaulting four times and ending up over the barrier and in the trees. Remarkably, he was uninjured. Mercedes rapidly abandoned its entire sportscar-racing programme.

Yet Mark was among the lucky ones. You think of Niki Lauda being maimed in that inferno at the Nürburgring in the extraordinary season of 1976. The high-speed, fatal crashes of Roland Ratzenberger and Ayrton Senna on successive days at Imola in 1994. Sir Jackie Stewart has attended 32 funerals, Mark tells me. Risk, for all the safety modifications in the sport in recent years, is a constant presence in F1.

I'm interested in how Mark processed this. Was it something he simply embraced, enjoyed even? And how did his attitude towards the perils of F1 motor racing change over his dozen years at the top? He smiles. 'Yeah, I take the piss out of top-flight tennis players. I know a lot of them really well. They're super-overpaid, and they have a rough day and it's a double-fault. I'm being sarcastic, absolutely, but …'

He's too polite to include triathlon in that, but my sport is also (mercifully) low on the risk spectrum. I've seen some nasty bike crashes in my time. An incident that still makes me shudder happened in the Olympic race in Rio. I turned round on a fast section of the course (probably to yell at someone) and with one hand on the bars hit an enormous hole in the road. My hand slipped and for a millisecond I was braced for impact.

Fortunately, the hand reconnected with the bars. Any other day, I could have been sliding along the tarmac with my prospects of gold disappearing up the road.

Journalists seem only too willing to attribute 'courage' or 'heroism' to sport. After the incident with Jonny, in Cozumel, Mexico, in 2016 – when I helped my brother to the line in the World Triathlon Series decider after he became jelly-legged with heat exhaustion – I read a number of reports using such terms. Ridiculous, of course. I certainly wasn't endangering myself in any way by offering assistance (though he might have thrown up on me, I suppose).

In F1, these terms are completely warranted. I think of Niki Lauda getting back in his Ferrari at Monza just 42 days after being given the last rites in a hospital bed. His ear was missing, his face scarred by burns so recent that they became aggravated every time he put on his helmet. The track was wet. Yet the defending world champion was determined to make a statement at Ferrari's home course. Battling mental demons few of us can possibly fathom, he fought through to complete the race, finishing fifth.

James Hunt was once asked how he continued to be so quick on the track. 'Big balls,' he responded. Given the stories of his insatiable womanising, that would have made a fitting epitaph. But his off-the-cuff response was grounded in truth. To drive quickly, particularly in his era, you did need extraordinary courage. And it didn't pay to entertain either fear or doubt.

'You know, we've seen guys have massive shunts and maybe leave in a helicopter,' says Mark. 'And you've got to get back in the car half an hour later. That's just how it is. 'Cos you still believe in yourself, you believe in your car, your mechanics. But that changes. Eighty-five, 90 per cent of your career, it isn't like you're prepared to pay the ultimate price, but you just never see how close the walls are. And if you could see people thinking about that stuff in certain places, then that was where you were gonna push it to the limit. Or in tricky conditions, if visibility was really low, then you'd be like, "This is an opportunity to do something really ridiculous." You just think, "I'm ready for this. I'm gonna go out, make a statement, to myself, to everyone else." It's very cavalier. But when you get older, you start to see those closer walls, you start to see the tricky conditions. And the downsides are higher than the upsides.'

Just at that moment, my painters walk through the open doors (I'm in the process of renovating my house), jolting us out of the moment. I realise we've been talking for well over an hour. Mark nips off for a break, giving me a chance to have a chat with co-pilot Al, who has sat throughout, quietly listening. Mark started flying in his final year in F1 and now takes the helicopter out around half a dozen times a year. He loves the technical challenge of flying as much as the adrenaline kick; the layers of difficulty and the constant room for improvement. Given Mark's background, he must have a number of advantages in the cockpit, I suggest.

Al nods. 'His reactions and ability to take in technical details are a cut above,' he says. 'He wants to know everything technical, the aerodynamics, everything.' The pair have been flying together for five years, not always in the air. 'Mark scared the shit out of me on the track at Silverstone doing 180mph in a Porsche,' Al tells me. It's said with no hint of humour or fondness at the memory. 'He was in total control.' What makes him unique? 'He can walk away; he doesn't hold anger in the way some drivers do. It can be corrosive. Mark always had the respect of those in the pit crew. He was the technical driver; Seb less so.'

I'm intrigued by this technical side of Mark Webber. He's such a laidback character, the archetypal likeable Aussie, whose fondness for practical jokes in the pit lane was well known. Yet allied to that was a forensic knowledge of the workings of the car: the minute adjustments, the impossibly tight parameters of engineering performance. It's almost like he's an amalgam of those two protagonists in the 1976 season: James Hunt's easy charm, Niki Lauda's studious intensity.

When he returns to the dining room, I ask him whether the latter came naturally to him. Or was it just another example of a sportsperson smart enough to recognise that adding to their suite of skills was the best way to extend a top-flight career, in the same way that he kept himself physically primed throughout his time in F1 through cycling, running and paddling?

His answer is characteristically forthright – with obvious echoes of Ronnie O'Sullivan. 'As a Formula One top-flight racing driver, you have to continue to reinvent yourself all the time. If you're a one-trick pony, you're fucked. I was pretty skilful, but I wasn't, you know, Michael Jordan – someone who even at 85 per cent is going to have a good day. That wasn't me, you know.

'The tech and the data and all the engineering side of it: I was initially like, "I don't need it, I'm old school." But you gotta work hard at it. I had to get rid of the "She'll be right" mentality, and to say, "No, I need to start sleeping with these cats." I need to start hanging out with these guys, with the aerodynamic guys, where there's electronics, gearbox, all this stuff. And, mate, they don't get outside much, these guys. So it's a challenge for you to connect with them, socially. But you just know that they're so gifted at what they do. And you've got to be able to communicate, to translate what they say and what you want.

'In my career, the tech ramped up at a rapid speed. We had no simulators when I started, only at the end. Now, they've got

£20 million simulators. For me, I'd look at the calendar and see I had 20 simulator days, and I just dreaded them. My wife said that she knew when they were coming up. It did nothing for me. But I said, "Mark, you have to adapt," because this is going to come back to trophies, it's going to come back to prep, getting the guys more comfortable with how we're going to land on these tracks and get the job done. It's about body language and energy. If the team can see that you're not enthusiastic towards something, that's a negative.'

We're back to those 'non-sexy' factors, as Mark might put it, that keep coming up in relation to sporting achievement: structure, discipline, consistency, logistics. Mark tells me that a key innovation he made was to abandon his custom of leaving on a Sunday night after a race 'ballistically dehydrated', keen to get home but having no real need to do so. He tweaked his schedule. Stay another night, eat well, hydrate. Suddenly he was finding he wasn't getting so run down. Obvious, you might think – but in the breathless existence of a professional sportsperson, all too easy to overlook.

'It's about looking at your career holistically. How is Roger [Federer] still going in tennis? Well, guess what – he looked at the timeframe right back when, and said I've got this many bullets in my career, and I'm gonna be efficient with every single one of those bullets. I'm not gonna fire them in practice. I'm gonna fire them when it fucking counts.'

Mark and Al gather their things and we stroll out into the sunshine to where the chopper is waiting. We chat about retirement as we go and have a good laugh at the James Hunt cruise-ship tale. He was found by a friend in his cabin disconsolate after having bedded a beautiful woman, the story goes. 'What's wrong?' his friend was said to have asked, incredulous. 'This is all there is now,' came the answer. It's up there with the George Best squandering story.

'Walking away from Formula One, I'm never gonna replace that,' says Mark. 'Like you, mate – those last moments of a race you've got won, when it's just all so beautiful, and it's just coming together and all the prep, the thousands of hours, and you're … executing, executing on what you've planned. Mate, it's out there. What humans can do when pushed to the limit is fascinating.'

I find myself envying Mark. His legacy safe, his reputation intact, a wide range of friends, admirers and interests – from flying helicopters and riding motorcycles to cycling, running, punditry. And still only mid-40s.

Nine times he stood on top of the F1 podium, far more than any Australian before him. But if he's brutally honest, and even with the ridiculous strength of his opponents, I think he'd say he underachieved. And possibly the reason for that is the same reason I, and many others, have such a fondness for him. It's also why he won't spend his remaining years allowing that thought to overly bother him.

Perspective.

'We're not trying to invent penicillin, mate – we're driving cars,' he says as he slaps me on the back, hops back into the cockpit and once again hurtles off into the distance.

6

THE MAVERICK, THE CHOIRBOY AND RIDING THE TORPEDO

The Sheikh Zayed Stadium in Abu Dhabi is hardly the most storied of cricketing venues. But in October 2015 it was the setting for an innings that perhaps best encapsulates England's most prolific Test batsman. In the first Test against Pakistan, England's opener Alastair Cook top scored with 263 runs, a colossal haul for any international batsman. But the total wasn't the most striking thing about it. It was the time he spent accruing it: 836 minutes. There were no reverse sweeps or outrageous hooks off his nose for six and few eye-catching boundaries. Nothing, indeed, that the press box might term 'swashbuckling'. He just got into a rhythm and then proceeded to produce a nerveless, sweatless (we'll come to that) master-class of patience, precision and focus. Batting is a profession of near-constant jeopardy. Like sudden death in football, only every single ball. For the near-14 hours that Cook was at the crease – a period during which, according to BBC Sport, 215,688 babies were born worldwide (one assumes the two were unrelated) – he made run accumulation look easy. Inevitable even.

When he was finally out – caught at short fine leg sweeping a ball from off-spinner Shoaib Malik – his was comfortably the longest ever innings by an Englishman, and the third long-est in the history of Test cricket. Former England captain Michael Vaughan praised his concentration and mastery of 'low-risk cricket'. Cook himself spoke of 'mind over matter' and the joy of getting into a 'blissful routine'. Not the sexiest words you'll ever hear in sport, admittedly. And critics of Test cricket would no doubt argue that this is exactly why we should favour the shortened forms of the game. But no one questioned the immensity of the achievement – just another record to fall to arguably England's greatest ever batsman.

I've been fascinated by Cook for many years. The moment I began this project I knew I needed to include him. So numerous are the feats, and the plaudits, so neat the symmetry, so consistent the achievements, his looks like a sporting career conceived in its entirety, in advance. By a hopeless optimist. Cook made a century on début against India in March 2006. His (self-declared) final Test, in September 2018? Also against India, and another century. He's England's highest Test scorer with 12,472 runs, and the fifth highest of all time. He's England's most-capped player (161 Tests) and longest-serving captain (59 matches). He's the youngest player ever to reach 10,000 and 12,000 runs, and the first England player to take part in 50 Test victories. His haul of 33 Test centuries is an England record.

Cook's *annus mirabilis* came in 2010/11, when he won the International Cricket Council's Test Cricketer of the Year, still the only English player to have done so. It followed a period in which he scored – again, with limited fuss or fanfare – 1,504 runs in 12 Tests, including 766 runs in Australia to help England retain the Ashes. Only Wally Hammond had scored more in this most historic Test match series, way back in 1928/29. In all, he won the Ashes four times, as well as series in South Africa and India. And, playing slip, he took the most catches of any English player (175). Ordinary bowler, mind you, with just the one Test wicket, against India in 2014 (Ishant Sharma, for the trivia buffs).

I first met Alastair a few years back, when we had dinner one evening at a quiet pub in the North York Moors. We were both competing the next day, so we took it steady. I loved his company. My overriding impression was one of politeness and humility. A real gentleman. We talked about his club career at Essex, about farming (his other great love – he lives on the family farm in Bedfordshire with his wife Alice) and swapped stories about our respective sports.

I found him to be a sportsman in the same mould as me (albeit some way ahead in accomplishment): always keen to improve, taking nothing for granted, and enthralled by the mental battles all sportspeople have to fight. Old school, too. No pedalos, no fights, no tattoos (I'm guessing there). Not the sort to 'clear the bars', either – as they say of some crick-eters (Jofra Archer and Ben Stokes of the current generation) – though you wonder if that's merely because drinkers at Lord's or Headingley or wherever knew there was no hurry; Cook would still be batting when they made it back to their seats.

When we catch up again late in 2019 – him now retired (from Test cricket – he still plays for Essex) and a knight of the realm; me just back from an Ironman in Western Australia – I'm keen to press him on a quote I'd read in the intervening years. Essentially, that he believed the talents he was blessed with weren't so much cricketing, but mental: focus, concentra-tion, application. His long-term mentor Graham Gooch was another to speak of his phenomenal concentration – decent praise from a former England captain and the second-highest Test run scorer for his country (behind his protégé). When Cook finally retired, Kevin Pietersen – the very antithesis of

Cook as a batsman – said his former teammate's biggest attribute was 'his mental strength when batting'.

Was this what separated him from the rest?

Alastair pauses to consider my question. 'I suppose one of my skills was that I managed to, in a sense, treat every ball the same. It didn't matter what level I was playing at – Essex Under-17s or England – or the situation or circumstances of the game. It didn't matter to me. It was all about that one ball. I suppose that's what made me sort of stand out from other people – that what was going on outside of the game, external pressures, had less impact. I mean, of course it impacts you, no one's immune to it. But I reckon it impacted me less. The result was that I probably got the most out of my talent, and more than other people who might struggle with it managed to.'

Put like that, it all sounds so obvious. Concentrate only on the mechanics of your job and everything gets significantly easier. Achieving it – as I know only too well – is something entirely different. We're into the realm of the metronomic. Through mental strength and resilience, Cook effectively turned himself into a machine. Of course, this would have got easier for him. After all, he spent 37,308 minutes at the crease in his Test career – almost 26 24-hour days. He faced 26,562 balls – the sixth highest ever. Do anything for that length of time and you're going to develop coping strategies.

The difference is, as a batsman in cricket, none of that time is guaranteed. It all has to be earned. To an extent almost unmatched by other sports, you have to arrive at the crease for your first Test as close to the finished product as possible. Give away your wicket cheaply a handful of times and you're under pressure. Five and you're in a rut. Any more and the press criticism builds, the on-field sledging, the stick from the crowd – and suddenly you've entered a whole new realm of mental torment. Cook would have been painfully aware of that from the start; he made his Test début, aged 21, in 2006 as a late replacement for Marcus Trescothick, who flew home from India with a stress-related illness (a key theme in his excellent 2008 autobiography *Coming Back to Me*).

'As a batsman there always seems to be a disaster pending,' Cook agrees. 'You've been batting lovely up to 20, 30, 40, you make one mistake and you're out. So even during those big innings when you don't get out, you're living on a bit of an edge. I found that the aim of my batting was to get into a rhythm. All I tried to say to myself was "commit and watch the ball". Park everything else when the player is running in to bowl. Because ultimately cricket is a bit of a strange game: if a bloke bowls at 90mph, you don't actually have time to think and react.'

And what about when he got out: that flow cruelly interrupted in a millisecond – and no chance to make immediate amends? Plenty of cricketers have laid waste to the dressing room, though I'm pretty sure that wasn't Cook's style. How did he rationalise it and move on?

'It doesn't matter whether you're playing in the Ashes or wherever: when you get out, you get out. That's what cricket is. You know as a batter, particularly an opening batter, that the other bloke's getting paid to get you out. He must be pretty good, the best in his country, or else he wouldn't be there. So some days he's gonna win that battle, and other days I'll win that battle because I've been selected for my country to do the opposite job. I see it like that.

'[Former England captain] Mike Atherton was very good at that. When I was young I read something he'd said: the aim is to win more days than you lose. If you do that you'll be half-decent. And accepting that there are days you are going to lose. Being able to take your pads and helmet off, all that kind of stuff, and not have too much baggage. Of course there's some baggage; there always is. That's what sport is. But not have too much baggage once you've had your five minutes, or 10 minutes, of being frustrated. Try and move on to the next innings as quick as you can.'

We talk about the contrasting pressures on a batsman and a bowler. I get the sense that he felt he got away lightly. 'A batter gets out and you stew, but you sit away from the pressure. Whereas a bowler can be bowling terribly, and there's no hiding place. He can't sit in the corner of the changing room – he has to carry on bowling because there are only so many bowlers on the team. So his agony goes on. How do you then cope with that? That's interesting to me, those mental challenges. Jimmy Anderson [Cook's England teammate and the world's most successful fast bowler] and I played probably 130 Test matches together, both done OK, but both had very different mental things to deal with – even though we were playing in exactly the same team.'

Cook believes that self-belief lies at the heart of this. 'You've got to stay true to yourself. You nick off for nought and are like, "OK, the next time I bat, I still could get out for nought, but am I still doing the right things in my training? Am I still hitting the ball where I want to hit the ball? Am I hitting the ball straight? Are my feet moving?" But there's no doubt you can get affected by low scores, of course you do.'

It's a brilliant mentality. The ultimate in Waitzkin-like resetting; a stripping away of emotion to ensure effective execution of skills. In the middle, Cook tended to leave the sledging and confrontations to others, while away from the pitch he treated unnecessary attention like a dangerous-looking inswinger, deftly deflecting it away. 'His conduct on-field and off it has been impeccable,' tweeted Indian great Sachin Tendulkar – whom he supplanted as the youngest batsman to reach 10,000 runs in 2016 – upon Cook's retirement.

And what about luck, that recurring theme? Given all those records and plaudits, and the seemingly perfect career, I was surprised to find that there were a couple of key junctures where the bounce of a ball, a cheap run-out, or a momentary lapse of concentration (as if) could have killed off this most glittering of careers before it had begun. In the summer of 2010, Cook's form was poor. Captain Andrew Strauss, his fellow opener, and coach Andy Flower stuck with their young left-hander after a difficult summer. He responded with a century in the third Test against Pakistan on 20 August 2010 at the Oval to silence critics, and that winter he made 766 in the Ashes as England won their first series in Australia for a quarter of a century – the start of a record-breaking, and defining, year. Cook subsequently said he felt he was one innings from getting sacked.

The echoes of Manchester United manager Alex Ferguson in 1990 are considerable. The Scotsman was widely acknowledged to have been just a defeat or two away from getting the boot after four years without any silverware. Winning the 1990 FA Cup saved him, and 37 other trophies were to follow. Of course, you like to think that two such dominant sporting characters would have got further opportunities to shine. But in sport there are no guarantees; as Mark Cavendish puts it in a later chapter, in sport things move on so fast and you're easily forgotten.

We talk about Cook's time as a chorister ('This is gonna sound really sad,' he says – 'Don't worry,' I reassure him, 'I was also one'), and how this attuned him from an early age to performing under pressure and in front of large crowds. He quickly realised that it was irrelevant how many people were there because the music didn't change. It stayed exactly the same. He also learned about the importance of hard work. Seeing Cook at the crease, in full flow, it's easy to fall into the 'genius' label trap, as New Zealand captain Brendon McCullum did in 2013 after he'd scored yet another century against the Kiwis – much to Cook's embarrassment.

He's certainly blessed physiologically: 6ft 2in, rangy, athletic, and with great endurance. He apparently has a helpful trait of not really sweating, even in the hottest Test arenas in Australia or the Indian subcontinent (Cook would be thrown the ball to shine it as there was no danger of the rough side getting damp in his dry hands). But – yet again – it was all underpinned by a ferocious work ethic, which Gooch, a notoriously hard worker himself, helped develop but certainly didn't instil. A man not given to empty bragging, Cook says he never lost a beep test as a professional cricketer. 'The one thing I do know is that I did work as hard as anyone, if not harder, from an early age,' he says. 'At 14 I was running twice a week before school and swimming twice a week before school because I wanted to get fitter, because when you're fitter you end up hitting more balls.'

Plain old repetition, he believes, was a key factor. 'How you train your brain is by hitting lots of balls. You can't polish a turd but you can certainly make a difference, can't you? [Australian spin bowler] Shane Warne might not be the fittest bloke in the world and he quite likes a beer and a fag, but I bet he bowled a hell of a lot for a long time to be that good. He was naturally talented but he still worked bloody hard at it.'

Being a captain in Test cricket is a massive job, both on and off the field, requiring superb man-management skills, tactical acumen, leadership – and luck (Richie Benaud, the Australian cricketer turned 'voice of cricket', once said this was 90 per cent of the job). Assuming the captaincy places significant extra pressure on your individual role in the team, whether that be as fast bowler, 'keeper or batsman. Cook was named Test captain in August 2012 after Andrew Strauss's retirement.

On his first tour as full-time skipper, to India, he scored 562 runs, was Man of the Series, and led England to their first Test series win in the country in almost three decades. He was the first captain to score a century in each of his first five Tests in charge. Those extraordinary powers of concentration and mental discipline were simply transferred to the new task.

His success in the role reminds me of a passage in Mike Brearley's definitive book on the subject, *The Art of Captaincy*, published in 1985, the year after Cook was born. 'Charisma seems to me a most limited asset to a captain. It helps in the early stages but honeymoons come to an end and charisma does not imply steadiness, patience, concentration or considerateness, all invaluable in a captain.' The sport has obviously changed enormously in the intervening years. And yet that still seems to ring true to me.

Cook explains the competing demands to me. 'The trick is when you're batting, you're not a captain. That's laid into you very early. Can you cut it up and put it in little compartments in your brain? Obviously the hard bit is when you've spent all day in the field and it hasn't gone well, and you've got the last tricky half an hour to bat and you're mentally tired because it's been a stressful day and the team are losing.'

And the luck? 'As a captain you need to not take too much to heart because you can have things that you do that don't go well. You think you've got the right plan and then the bowler doesn't bowl at the right place, or there's a dropped catch that costs a lot of runs, and you get criticised for the end result. Well, it could have been a lot different.

'As a captain you don't actually know what to do, so you have to say, "This is what I want to do, this is what I believe in," and whether you're right or wrong, you make a decision on it. You've got to be stubborn, you've got to be tough, you've got to be ruthless in one sense – but also you've gotta be quite empathetic because it's a game in which a bowler could bowl brilliantly and not get any wickets. Perhaps beat the bat 15 times in a spell. That's the test of the player, when it doesn't quite go your way. Can he respond? Can you respond?'

His old mate Jimmy saw it differently, joking during a tearful interview on Cook's retirement: 'Who knows how many wickets I would have if he [Cook] could actually catch.'

But Cook's mental strength was not inexhaustible. He fought retirement for 18 months before he made his decision (he was still only 33, remember), but the relentless demands were beginning to take a toll, even on his Rolls-Royce mentality. 'It's sad, but that's kind of what can happen. You play 160 Test matches, grinding away against the new ball, against the best players, and they're always fresh. It isn't easy. And this isn't a sob story – that's just the nature of it. You throw a bit of captaincy in there for 59 games. You can see why it kind of chips away at you. I was ready to go. I'd had enough of putting myself under pressure. Also what made me different, which we've spoken about, was that I did train harder than other people, I did have that mental thing, and then towards the end of my England career I started losing a little bit of that. Whatever I searched for, I didn't quite find.' So he departed the main stage, and with a century. Timing. Essential in a good opener.

Tiger Woods has spoken about relishing 'the stress' of competing in a major, what's called 'counterphobia'. Wales and Lions captain Sam Warburton wrote in his autobiography, *Open Side*, about the 'horrific' nerves on display in team hotels or on tours, saying he'd often consider retirement such was the all-consuming anxiety. But I wonder, does Cook miss the pre-match nerves? The moments before he stepped out at Lord's, or the MCG, or even the Sheikh Zayed Stadium in Abu Dhabi to face the opening balls of the clash, when the bowlers are at their freshest, the ball at its hardest and the crowd at its most expectant?

He smiles. 'No, I don't. It is a drug, and it's a drug that – when you look at it when you haven't been playing – you think is nice. But when you are playing, it isn't particularly pleasant. That hour, that morning of a Test match or any game, is not pleasant: the anxiety, the nervousness about what's going to happen. I don't like that feeling.

'I can't say anyone enjoys that.'

I can think of one person who did – and he's sitting opposite me here in the courtyard of his home in rural North Yorkshire on a beautiful summer's evening.

His dog is sniffing its way round the beds and manicured lawns of the garden, and the shadows are lengthening as they did when he was lighting up Test matches in summers long since past. So ingrained is the 64-year-old on the British public's consciousness that it feels almost strange to see him in this setting, so far removed from the arena he once dominated. Reassuring, too; the public often forget that sport is just one element of a sportsperson's identity.

Sir Ian Terence Botham – England's greatest all-rounder. A combative right-handed batsman, a brutally effective fast-medium swing bowler, and a very useful slip fielder, 'Beefy' accumulated 5,200 Test runs and 383 wickets in 102 matches. He also took 145 wickets and made 2,113 runs in one-day internationals. Fantastic figures, but they take no account of context. And the context was that, throughout a large proportion of his 16 years playing international cricket, England were far from a world force. Often they were a laughing stock. His feats – not least in the 1981 Ashes ('Botham's Ashes', as they became known) when he turned a series pretty much single-handedly with bat and ball – made him a national hero.

British sports fans today take success for granted. My gold in Rio was just one of 27 won by the Great Britain squad, and we ended up second in the overall medal table; in the Atlanta Games in 1996, Great Britain got one gold and came 36th, the low point after a number of lean years. But over the following couple of decades, in women's and men's sport, in rugby, football, tennis, cycling, motorsport, netball, golf, hockey and a host of other disciplines, UK teams have been dominant. In one-day cricket, England are world champions in both the women's and the men's game as I write this.

In Beefy's day, however, the story was largely one of underinvestment, underachievement and confidence at rock bottom, and into this domain came a figure so dominant and apparently carefree as to be almost – and this was the greatest sporting compliment of the era – Australian. Going toe to toe, sledge for sledge, beer for beer with anyone and everyone. Flicking 90mph bouncers off his (unprotected) nose for six. Tearing in from the Pavilion End, chest puffed out and curly mullet trailing. Impulsive, unorthodox, confrontational, tetchy, charismatic, impatient. And superhumanly confident.

Similarities with Cook? Well, they both played cricket.

So what was it like to carry the hopes of a nation on his shoulders, to head out into the middle chasing a lost cause? He responds with a shrug. 'I just don't do stressed. I don't understand stress. I really don't. It's just the way I am, and it's the way I've always been, and I think that's part of my make-up. Pressure? You create pressure by failing, and if you take it on board and worry about it, then that pressure increases.

'I think it's about confidence in your own ability. And I think once as a professional sportsman you start to doubt the confidence that's got you to where you are then I think you're in real trouble. And I've never had that problem, even in the lowest points of my career, and thankfully there weren't too many. I backed myself, and I knew that I felt that I could always come through.'

Over the next couple of hours we're to discuss a wide range of topics, from his grandson's rugby to Beefy's obsession with fishing ('I just love it. I actually fished for about four hours a day last week on a river that didn't have any bloody fish in it.') But he's perhaps most interesting on the question of pressure, and his internal monologue during his playing days.

'Do you have a phrase that you quote to yourself? I had a saying, and quite often I'd use it, it could be anywhere, and I would just simply say, "You ride the torpedo to the end of the tube."' He pauses. 'People used to look at me and go, "What the fuck are you on about?"'

I try not to let my look say that. Beefy continues. 'And I'd say, "I'll tell you what I'm on about. You get on, you're in for the trip, you'll have lots of things going on around you, but you ride it to the end of the tube. And if you haven't won, and you haven't done your best, then that's your problem. But you ride it to the end of the tube." And I always did that. That's always been my saying since I was a kid. I don't even know how I came across it; whether I made it up, or whether I heard it from someone. But that's how long I've had it – since I was an 18-year-old.'

It's clearly bonkers (I'm no expert in nautical warfare but, well, I have a few questions …). But I love it – absolutely love it – and I know exactly what he means, too. It's about commitment, backing yourself, conviction (yes, that word again), following a chosen course of action because you know that self-doubt is your biggest enemy. It's what AP McCoy terms going 'all in', and what Alastair Cook was aiming for with his own, more prosaic mantra of 'commit and watch the ball'.

I'm curious to hear what Beefy makes of sports psychologists. He looks at me suspiciously. 'Has someone primed you on this one?'

I shake my head. 'I've never met a psychologist who has lasted more than two and a half minutes with me,' he says. 'And I mean that. I remember I was doing some commentary at Eden Park, in Auckland, and there was a tap at the door and someone popped their head round to say there's this guy who wants to see you. He said he was writing a book about sports psychology and that he'd been told to speak to me. I know immediately someone's been winding him up. So I thought, "OK, I'll go along with it." He said, you're walking out at the MCG on Boxing Day with 100,000 Australians there, what's going through your mind? Not very much. I'm not really thinking about anything, because it's a 100-yard walk, so I'm just enjoying the atmosphere, soaking it in, and I get to the middle, then I take guard, then I look to see around the field. I don't even hear them. "What do you mean you don't hear them?"

'And this conversation went on and on, and in the end, I just said to him, "I'm going to ask you one question before you go any further, because I'm getting bored of this: What sport did you play?" Oh, you didn't. "OK, so you didn't play international sport in big arenas?" No. Well, that's the end of the conversation, isn't it? And that was my attitude; it's always been my attitude. And sometimes I've embarrassed my family, and sometimes I'm a lot stronger than that. Sports psychology I think is the biggest con.'

It's interesting to set this against Beefy's record when captain. Given his totemic role in the England side, it was no surprise that the captaincy came to him in 1980. But, in contrast to Cook, his form dipped when he took on the mantle, as did England's fortunes. They won none of the 12 games in which he was captain and he resigned the role after the first two Tests of the 1981 Ashes. And we all know what happened then.

In *The Art of Captaincy*, Brearley also wrote: 'Certainly the best player is not necessarily an adequate captain, any more than the best salesman makes a sales manager. Indeed, the outstandingly gifted may well find it difficult to understand the problems of the average performer in their field.' Brearley concluded that in Botham's case, sensitivity to criticism compounded the problem. 'He allowed people to niggle and upset him.'

I have no intention of letting either of these things happen, but I have sympathy. To me, for all the benefits I accrue from my training group and companions, sport is an individual pursuit. Given how selfish I am around my own performance, and around optimising the environment in which I feel I can be at my best, I have no doubt I would be a terrible captain. But I find the flick-switch model he speaks of very relatable – the idea that, in sport, you must be capable of mentally adjusting your entire focus as the occasion demands it. I ask whether for him, as an all-rounder, this process posed a constant challenge.

He takes a sip of his G&T. 'I think the all-rounder status was actually very important for me because, first and foremost, I have a very low boredom threshold, so I need to be involved in all parts and acts of the game. So if I fail with the bat, I can make it up in the field, at slip, or I can make it up in the bowling department. So I actually have three strings to my bow. Someone's who's a specialist batsman has one string – there's a lot of pressure on that. But, like I said, pressure … Kath will tell you. When was the last time I got stressed?'

His wife Kath walks past and smiles. 'You don't get stressed,' she says.

Chatting to Beefy about these things, I'm reminded that pressure is entirely a self-imposed thing. Broken down into its constituent parts, everything is exactly the same whether you're turning out for the village cricket team or taking on Australia in the Boxing Day Test at the MCG in Australia (the litmus test for any cricketer). It reminds me of that saying, coined, I think, by Eleanor Roosevelt: 'No one can make you feel inferior without your consent.'

The pressure of competition – diluted for me by both the profile of my sport and the protracted nature of it – is something I've grown to welcome. I've certainly got better at harnessing rather than fighting it. The heart beating explosively in the chest and up the neck. The adrenaline surging through the bloodstream. The knowledge that the next moments of your life could define it. Some people live for this. Cook battled but could not ultimately overcome it. Beefy somehow seemed to swerve it altogether.

'Look, I think that everyone who played with me would say … the phrase that was used in the dressing room was "the most confident bastard I've ever played with". I think that actually I took a lot of players with me on that boat. I think there were a lot of guys who maybe were tottering and maybe got in the slipstream and off we went. Certainly on that tour in 86/87.'

Ah, the fabled Ashes tour of 1986–87 to Australia. England were given no chance, written off not just by the notoriously partisan Aussie press but at home too (their 5–0 thrashing in the West Indies, followed by home series defeats to India and New Zealand prompted Martin Johnson's famous quip in the *Independent* that there were only three things wrong with the England side – 'They can't bat, can't bowl and can't field').

Back then, England's chances of winning on the road were hampered by archaic rules that kept players' partners and families at arm's length – 'the stiff, egg-and-bacon, MCC way', as Beefy puts it. He – and Kath – were having none of it. She flew out, stayed for the duration and the Bothams took a suite wherever they went – 'at the end of the tour we were in negative equity' – which became the team/family room.

Here they'd refuel on pizza and the like ('at the end of a long day's cricket, all you want is stodge'), have some drinks ('in those days there was a bit of a culture, you know – you celebrated') and bond, with each other, with the families – even with Elton John. 'He used to come along. We used to call him "EJ the DJ". He'd come and play the music, take the guys out. He rescheduled his tour so that he was playing concerts in the same cities where we were playing Tests. That room changed the whole atmosphere. You knew that if you had a bad day, by the time you left the team room it was a good day.'

The power of affiliation in sport, of comradeship, is something we'll look at in due course. It can be a potent weapon. Success duly followed, with England winning the series. 'We were invincible on that tour. By the end of the third Test, the Australian press were talking about the rugby league. That's how you win in Australia. And without doubt, every single player that played will tell you it's because we had the team room.'

It's good to hear of a time when alcohol was more a part of sport. For Beefy's 'bit of a culture' read 'regular and spectacular piss-ups'. In his book *Pushing the Boundaries: Cricket in the Eighties*, Botham's teammate Derek Pringle recounts drinking 17 pints during the rest day of a Test match against India the same year as that team-room Ashes tour. Three years later, Australian batsman David Boon reputedly managed to squeeze the contents of 52 cans of Victoria Bitter past his handlebar moustache on the flight to England for that summer's Ashes (which the Aussies won 4–0). The same was true of top-flight football at the time, although its deeply ingrained drinking culture was on its last legs. I'm not advocating that, but nor would I call for the teetotal approach. For me, a drink or two has always provided a mental line in the sand at the end of a day, the point at which the 'work day' finishes and you can switch off. An athlete's job can easily become 24 hours a day, seven days a week; there is always more stretching to be done, or exercises from the physio, or course maps to be studied, or kit to be readied. For all this to be sustainable, you need to step outside the bubble of intensity.

The team-room idea shows not just Beefy the non-conformist, but Beefy the innovator. In a similar vein, he later became the first England cricketer to wear sunglasses during a Test to reduce the glare and improve his fielding. It's a common thing in cricket nowadays, but at the time it made the front pages. In endurance sport, people talk about the advent of sunglasses being a massive thing because you can hide your eyes – the clearest sign of whether someone is struggling. We've all seen images of Tour de France riders battling to stay in touch with the peloton on a climb; mask your eyes and it's possible to look almost comfortable. Well, until you blow up completely.

Beefy wasn't going to be coerced into wearing a helmet, though. 'I think that helmets have made a lot of very ordinary players a lot braver and lot more successful,' he says. 'I've played against the West Indies – four bowlers itching to get at you, bowling at the speed and height that they did. It never even crossed my mind to wear a helmet.' He stops and smiles. 'I took some quite fierce blows but, at the end of the day, prob-ably the most solid part of my anatomy is my head.'

Kath pops over again and we finish up our drinks. As we're walking out to my car I ask him whether he feels that confi-dence – his or others' – is innate. 'It's a very hard question, if you've never not had it,' he says. 'Self-belief and confidence have given me a hell of a lot. I think they're my biggest asset.'

For all Beefy's confidence, he strikes me as endearingly lack-ing in arrogance. He seems humble, appreciative almost, of what he has achieved. And, like Alastair Cook, the only other

England cricketer of the modern era to receive a knighthood, accepting of the role played by fortune.

'Do you know, the biggest thing is the rapport between myself and the public. I've always been the man on the street. I've always been that guy, Beefy. I think that's really quite important, and I like that. Just because you've had an ability and a lot of luck, and you were at the right place at the right time, that doesn't give you any right to be an obnoxious prick.'

7

THE PRESSURE AND THE PAIN

Can there be a hotter event in the world of athletics right now than the marathon (and I don't mean 2019's comically sweltering Doha World Championships débâcle)? Growing up, it was a fringe race at best, at least in my eyes. One for the eccentrics, the hollow-eyed loners, the moustachioed masochists. I loved long-distance running. But even I looked at those runners, that never-ending tarmac, and thought, 'Nah.'

But in recent years it has undergone a transformation. At the elite end of running, the world's best are now moving up from track events such as the 10,000m much earlier in their careers, lured by the marathon's prestige – and the money that has poured into the event. At the same time, the mass-participation charity thing, driven by the runaway success of city marathons, particularly London's, has been a driving force.

The first London event was held in 1981 and – like seemingly much of that decade – it was completed in drizzle, with just over 6,000 runners braving the course from Blackheath in south-east London to Constitution Hill, next to Buckingham Palace. In 2019 (the last mass-participation event pre-pandemic), on a now-amended course finishing in the Mall, there were 42,549 finishers. That's more than the capacity of Elland Road.

It's a monster of a race, with huge crowds, multi-million-pound sponsorship and broadcasting deals, a total of more than £1 billion raised for good causes since its inception, and a regular flow of world records. And beyond London, with the fabled sub-two-hour mark within tantalising reach, the marathon has transcended athletics to become almost a benchmark for human performance; how fast can we go not just in a race, but as a race.

In 2017, Nike's Breaking2 project came within seconds of success in Monza near Milan; the Ineos 1:59 Challenge, in Vienna, two years later, achieved it, with the Kenyan world record holder Eliud Kipchoge, assisted by 41 pacemakers, becoming the first person to run under two hours. Given the contrived nature of the event, the International Association of Athletics Federations (IAAF) didn't ratify the time, but that wasn't the point. The bar had been raised; others will now surely follow, and the ranks of those from all walks of life wishing to tackle the 26.2-mile distance will swell still further.

Just look at the proportion of the applicants for the 2020 London Marathon who'd never run a marathon before – 56 per cent. But the most striking stat, for me, is that nearly half the record 457,861 people who registered for a ballot place were women. And to understand the catalyst for this, we need to go back to the extraordinary events of a beautiful spring day in London in 2003.

At that year's marathon, running with her distinctive nodding gait and dressed in a red two-piece running suit and (what looked a lot like) magician's gloves, Paula Radcliffe pulled off the greatest trick ever seen in women's distance running: she ran 2:15:25, in just her third competitive marathon. She beat her own world record by nearly two minutes and ran more than three minutes faster than any other woman had run before (and nearly 45 minutes quicker than the British women's record set in that very first London Marathon in 1981). She won by a mile. Literally. The second-placed athlete finished four and a half minutes behind. London's race director and former 10,000m world record holder Dave Bedford called it the greatest distance-running performance of his lifetime and compared it to Bob Beamon's era-defining long jump record at the 1968 Olympics.

Having just competed in the mini-marathon for West Yorkshire I was standing on the Embankment listening in to the excited commentary on someone else's radio. The excitement in the air was palpable and built to a climax as Paula flew past, her focus absolute and inspiring to a 14-year-old me.

What was notable was the number of men Radcliffe beat that day. Remember that the respected Boston Marathon only began allowing women to officially compete in 1974 – the distance was felt to be too gruelling prior to that – and the women's marathon only became an Olympic sport in 1984. With Radcliffe as the poster girl, a boom in women's running in the UK and beyond followed.

Radcliffe's time sent shockwaves around the athletics world. Critics made much of the two male pacemakers who started the race with her – never mind that most of the women's marathons at that time were mixed races, and that Radcliffe conspicuously failed to draft them (i.e. run in their slipstream, to benefit from lower wind resistance). The rationale for using men was simple: at the time there simply weren't any female pacemakers who could deliver the sustained speeds that Radcliffe was capable of running. The record stood, though it was subsequently decided that two benchmarks would be recorded: mixed competition (women running with men) and women only.

I've met Paula a number of times at sponsorship events and dinners, and always enjoyed her company. She's reserved, but also great fun, and has an obvious intelligence (she got a first at Loughborough) and an eye for detail – she can happily trot out exact times and placings from races throughout her career.

Masochism was top of my list of topics to discuss. You don't become (in Radcliffe's case, moving up from the 10,000m and 5,000m) an elite marathon runner unless you're prepared to spend the majority of your working life in discomfort, if not outright pain. Following her 2003 record, the details of her training regimen were pored over and analysis always seemed to come back to the same thing: her unbelievably high pain threshold.

I have a little bit of experience of marathon running myself. In 2019, I ran three of them. Unfortunately, on each occasion, after a very long swim and bike ride. The one at the World Ironman Championships in Hawaii was a particularly bad experience. By the end it took every ounce of willpower I had just to put one foot in front of another. It's a brutal event, Ironman, and when it goes wrong, it's hell. If it was around in the 14th century I think Dante would have probably pencilled it in as one of his infernal circles.

I recall Radcliffe, in the aftermath of that landmark run in London, challenging those who said she'd set 'the unbeatable record'. 'I don't think I'm someone who has way more talent than everyone else [yet another for our collection],' she said. 'Somebody is going to come along and beat it. But I do think they've got to be prepared to hurt in order to push themselves that hard.'

We talk a bit about her early years, competing from the age of nine in a mix of cross-country and 800m races and as part of successful girls' teams. Also the superstitions that stayed with her throughout her career – lucky breakfast (porridge with a bit of honey and dark chocolate in); lucky safety pins; lucky race-day jewellery; the same kit all season if she won in it.

Don't worry – we're all like that in sport. Shane Williams told me he always had to put his socks and rugby boots on left-side first and be the last out of the changing room. For many years I used the same Adipro racing flats in my races. Every time I wore them, I finished on the podium; when I didn't wear them, I'd have a shocker. Until, that is, the Beijing Olympic Games, where a 20-year-old me stood on the start line without a hope of success but with my 'lucky' shoes waiting for me in transition. They carried me to a respectable but disappointing 12th.

Rafael Nadal, the Spanish tennis great, is particularly neurotic in this regard, arranging and rearranging the bottles by the side of his on-court chair in strict sequence. And I once heard of an athlete who had to separate their trainers the night before competition. The evening before the big day, they would knock on the door of the neighbouring hotel room to ask if they could leave their left trainer with the confused guest. The reason behind this? When the trainers were reunited the following day they would be happy to see each other and perform well.

Bonkers? Obviously. But also not. To me, sporting superstition has always seemed like a natural extension of the obsessive attention to detail all top sportspeople must deploy. It's a question of correlation or causation. Take my shoe anecdote as an example. The logical explanation for my success in the shoes is not that they made me run faster, it's that they were quick, lightweight ones that I only wore when I had the confidence to wear them – due to fresh and healthy legs, and being in an optimal mental state.

As Radcliffe's career developed, she showed a willingness to innovate. She never did 'shake-out' jogs, as they're called, ahead of events, just completely rested (48 hours before a big race, 24 hours before a normal race). She lived and trained at altitude, took ice baths, endured punishingly deep deep-tissue massages and tried out altitude tents before they were really a thing.

'Alec [Stanton], my coach, from the beginning, was always reading books and talking to people. He spent a lot of time chatting to Harry Wilson [coach of Britain's Steve Ovett through countless world records and 1980 Olympic 800m gold, who believed in training tailored towards athletes rather than set methods] and Peter Coe [father–coach of Seb, who won gold in the 1,500m in 1980 and 1984]. Just trying to learn things from them.'

One of the key training sessions she used, she tells me, was something called Bondarenko repeats. Created by Olga Bondarenko, the Soviet athlete who won the first ever Olympic 10,000m for women, in Seoul in 1988, it's essentially a rolling fartlek (a training method of moderate to hard efforts, with easier efforts between; the term, which is Swedish, translates as 'speed play'). Each rep is 2km, divided into 400m, 300m, 200m and 100m, each run at middle-distance or sprint pace and followed by the same distance at the slower marathon pace. 'It became a key session in the end,' she says. 'So things like that – learning and innovating.'

And what about the altitude? Back when Paula was breaking through, it was far less common than it is today – and not everyone had the luxury of being brought up in a mountain refuge like Kílian Jornet. 'Altitude training was something I loved,' Radcliffe tells me. 'I came to Font-Romeu [in the Pyrenees in the south of France near the Spanish border] for the first time in 1995 on my year abroad, and I knew straight away that I'd found another level of training here. It worked really well for me. Because the training was harder, I could work much harder; I could push myself to a different level, and also do greater volumes, for more effect, if you like. So I could do 110 miles a week and it was worth 140 at home, but without the extra pounding on your body.'

Training at altitude affects different people in different ways. For me, there is undoubtedly the physiological benefit: increased haemoglobin, the oxygen-transporting protein in red blood cells believed to give those who train at altitude a competitive advantage once back at sea level; more capillaries and mitochondria in the muscles. But let's not forget those intangible benefits around environment, too. The quiet, the detachment, often the beauty. By their very definition, altitude camps have to be in the mountains and probably fairly remote. I've been lucky enough to try all kinds of locations in my quest to find the perfect spot. The most memorable is a mountain hut on the top of the volcano in Tenerife. Only a wood fire for heating, only a generator for electricity and zero phone signal after 8pm. Bliss.

Radcliffe's physiologists would analyse her and say she was a non-responder at altitude, that she didn't get much of an increase in haemoglobin. 'But I did race way better, so how could I be a non-responder? It worked really well for me, and I think that was because the training was harder – I could work much harder and push myself to a different level.

'You learn to push yourself through that fatigue, which I think is particularly important for endurance training. I mean, I've always done the head-bobbing thing, but it was only after I came to altitude for the first time that my mum noticed something else. She was like, "Oh my god, your eyes are rolling right back! During the race they're rolling right back in your head." And they think it was a response that I developed, after I came up here for the first time, to turning off pain.'

*   *   *

Top athletes' relationship with pain is something that Dr Michael Joyner knows all about. Dr Joyner is a fabled figure in endurance sport. A more than decent marathoner in his own right (his PB is 2:25), the 6ft 4in US anaesthesiologist and physiologist at the Mayo Clinic, an academic medical centre in Minnesota, is one of the world's leading experts on human performance and wrote an influential paper in 1991 suggesting that a sub-two-hour run was physiologically possible. At the time, the record was nearly seven minutes off that.

I speak to him just days after arguably the biggest weekend in marathon-running history: Kipchoge's landmark achievement in Vienna on the Saturday, then Kenyan Brigid Kosgei breaking Radcliffe's 16-year record by 81 seconds at the Chicago Marathon the following morning (Paula, magnanimously, was there to congratulate her).

We talk about the legendary Lloyd 'Bud' Winter, an athletics coach and conditioning expert who helped prepare more than two dozen Olympians, including Tommy Smith and John Carlos – the black athletes who raised their fists in a Black Power salute during the playing of 'The Star-Spangled Banner' at the 1968 Olympics in Mexico City.

Winter also coached Joyner's coach, so the professor is better acquainted than most with the former PE teacher's methodology, refined while helping to prepare fighter pilots physically for battle in the Second World War. Winter noticed that those who performed best in aerial dogfights were those who, against all odds, were able to relax. He developed this philosophy, which is loosely translated as 'relax and win'.

'Kipchoge's face when he's running,' says Joyner. 'That's what you're seeing. We're not supposed to talk about Lance [Armstrong] any more, but Lance had a great phrase, and I don't know whether he came up with it or it was just something in cycling: "How do you manage your suffering?" There's the suffering day to day, week to week, month to month, and riding out the training, and then there's the specifics of how you manage your suffering in a race. And the question then becomes, "How is your training preparing you to manage your suffering?"'

Joyner has written about the 20 × 400m, a brutal workout that's designed to acquaint you intimately with suffering. It draws on the interval-running approach honed by the great innovator Emil Zátopek, the Czech athlete considered by many to be the greatest Olympian of all time. Zátopek won a gold in the 10,000m at the London Olympics (1948 rather than 2012) and missed out on another in the 5,000m by a whisker. Then, four years later, at the 1952 Olympics Games, he did the distance-running hat-trick: the 5,000m, the 10,000m and – on his first attempt at the distance – the marathon. Over the course of a little over a week. Just incredible.

The aim with the workout is to increase the pace of the laps while not going into the red (adhering to the 'no bend-over rule' at the end of each rep – if an athlete has to do this to catch their breath, then, as a crude measurement, they're overexerting and are not under control). Between each rep is a jog. Who needs heart rate and lactate measurements?

I've never actually tried the 20 x 400m, but I've done countless similar sessions over the years. The physical and anaerobic benefits of such a workout are clear but Joyner sees this as something more psychological. Like Froome altering his perception of effort, this is about meditative rhythm trumping all those pain receptors trying to make it through to your conscious thought. It's about embracing, then transcending pain, to reach a state Joyner explains to me as 'hyperfocus' – what some might call being 'in the zone', with heightened performance but also heightened awareness. Relax and win.

This goes back to the Marcora discussion about the differences between dissociative and associative strategies. It's also about efficiency. If you can focus on the physical movement to make it as optimised as possible, while distracting yourself from the noise in your head that starts out as a quiet 'stop' then grows into a screaming 'STOP!', you're on your way.

Joyner likens it to sticking your hand in hot water ('short-course triathlon is hot water,' he tells me, 'and Ironman is warm water') and learning how to relax as you do. 'Kipchoge's obviously the recent master of this. Frank Shorter was very, very good at it.'

Shorter, known as 'the father of running' in America, was credited with launching the running boom in the US in the 1970s and making it cool, as Radcliffe did for British women 30 years later. Shorter won marathon gold in the 1972 Olympics in Munich in a race broadcast live in America, and silver four years later in Montreal (beaten by East German Waldemar Cierpinski, later implicated in state-sponsored doping). I love watching videos of Shorter: that ridiculously efficient style; the low gait; the smooth cadence; the bushy moustache. He liked a drink, too, by all accounts – rumours persist that he was out on the town the night before the final in 1972, enjoying a German beer or two.

'The people that are exceptional at it are doing it under control,' says Joyner. 'The 400 [-metre] hurdlers – they have to really push themselves to keep their stride. They have to almost learn it better than anybody else because any kind of breakdown in their tempo or rhythm and they're screwed. You see it in all sports, though. You have to not be afraid of it. To learn where your edge is and just how to get on the edge and stay there.

'You watch Secretariat [the American thoroughbred and Triple Crown winner] winning the Belmont Stakes in 1973. He wins by 31 lengths – the largest margin of victory in the race's history. The sense of rhythm and tempo. And I think that's why this sort of interval training, where people descend workouts, is really important.'

He says this translates to day-to-day work. Joyner uses interval principles with his medical students – telling them to use the principles when they're studying: do an hour hard, go for a walk, get a coffee, switch venues, do it again. To maximise their time but break things into bites, recover, do it again, recover, do it again, recover, do it again.

'And it's a learned skill,' he says. 'I think all of this is highly learnable. You even read it in Roger Bannister's description of his four-minute mile. And once you learn to do it, you have this sense, this altered state and tremendous sense of command you can feel. That's what I describe it as: you're in command, and while it hurts like hell on one level, it doesn't hurt, because you're driving it. You know what I mean?'

I do. I've done my share of intervals over the years. In three different sports. The intervals Joyner is talking about are the lung-bustingly tough ones. You might be doing 3, 10 or 30 of something. Maybe 100m in the pool, three minutes on the bike or 400m on the track. But each interval is a race and a challenge. It should be irrelevant that you still have 29 to go. You have to try and pour everything you have into each one, physically, technically and mentally.

I want to know what he thinks of Kipchoge's 'record', particularly given he called it so many years ago. Was he surprised? Impressed? Joyner says he felt the Kenyan had various things going in his favour: he's a 'generational' athlete (Olympic champion, world record holder for the distance in an officially sanctioned race – 2:01:39), who runs a high volume of miles (130–140 a week) at high altitude and doing interval work. The course in Vienna was perfectly optimised for the attempt and for him – it was flat, low altitude, low humidity and low temperatures, and it was close to the same time zone as Kipchoge's Kenyan base, meaning little disruption to the athlete's schedule.

The custom-made Nike alphaFLY shoes created for the challenge, with multiple air pods and carbon-fibre plates, surely also helped. Versions of the shoe have been used in all but one of the fastest marathon times run in the past two years, and variations are flooding the amateur running ranks, too. 'I think the shoes are worth 1 per cent, or a little over a minute – about 80 seconds,' he says.

'And then I think that the pacing really, really helped him, because he was able to get behind those guys, and some of it's drafting, but some of it's sort of psychological sucking – and if you look at Paula Radcliffe's 2:15, that was in a mixed race, where she had guys around her.'

He's surprisingly relaxed about the contrived nature of the attempt and the footwear innovation, pointing out that the advent of so-called 'brush spikes' on the track in the 1960s – velcro, with multiple spikelettes like tiny teeth under the ball of the feet replacing the individual metal spikes – had an equally devastating impact. 'Bannister had special shoes, and the track at Oxford had just been fixed, and Brasher and Chataway, who were world-class runners, paced him through the first 1,200m or 1,300m. So I think Kipchoge's getting a bit of a bad deal.'

While the world of athletics gasped at her achievement in 2003, Radcliffe and her team were already looking ahead. On the horizon, the following year, was an even bigger prize: the Athens Olympics, and the marathon in Marathon. Her greatest chance. The greatest expectation. Relax and win? Easier said than done.

* * *

With apologies to Paula, to Britain's Jess Ennis at London 2012, to Carl Lewis in Los Angeles in 1984 and his compatriot Michael Johnson a dozen years later, and to countless other home-grown stars, any discussion of Olympic pressure and expectation begins and ends with Cathy Freeman.

The 400m runner went into the Sydney Olympics in 2000 as an overwhelming favourite for gold. She was the world champion, the world No. 1, and in her previous Games – in Atlanta, in 1996 – she had taken nearly a second off her personal best to claim silver and show her extraordinary promise. Now, with the 27-year-old at her peak, the Games was coming to her backyard, she was lighting the Olympic torch – and only gold would do.

My obsession with the greatest sporting event on earth started in 1996. My first memory? Reigning 100m champion Linford Christie throwing his spikes away after being disqualified in the final for a second false start. To say it was a marginal decision is an understatement – he was adjudged to have reacted 0.014 seconds too early to the starter's gun. By 2000, the Olympic flame in me was well and truly stoked. I was obsessed, staying up at night to watch the first-ever triathlon events. The men's race was won by my now friend Simon Whitfield, the two-time Canadian Olympic flagbearer. But the Cathy Freeman dynamic was something else.

It was not just the hopes of the sports-obsessed Australian nation that she carried on her shoulders – she was the only prospect of athletics gold on the track – but also those of the Aboriginal race. Memories of the so-called 'stolen generation', Aboriginal children who were removed from their families under Australian government policy in the first half of the 20th century to aid 'assimilation', were still raw. Freeman's own grandmother was taken away from her mother as a child. Her gold, it was hoped, would be like a beacon for reconciliation.

But first, she had to win it – and in one of the most tricky events in all of track and field athletics.

'You've definitely got to have a screw loose to run the 400m.' This is Donna Fraser, the long-striding Croydon Harrier and Great Britain athlete, who won a string of medals at world, European and Commonwealth championships until her retirement in 2009. Why? Because the 400m sits somewhere between an all-out sprint and a feat of endurance. Its demands are both aerobic and anaerobic. You need the explosive start of a sprinter, and the willpower to push on in the final 100m despite your lactic system being agonisingly overwhelmed. There's your lane position and two bends to consider. And your strategy, and pacing, have to be inch perfect. No wonder some call it the 'death race'.

'Do something just a little bit wrong and it can throw the whole race out,' says Donna, adding with a chuckle: 'I always think 400m runners are quite eccentric to do what we do – like triathletes, probably.' Ouch.

Once the 2000 Olympics began, the eyes of the world were firmly fixed on Freeman. But in the months leading up to the Games, pretty much the only person who saw her was Fraser. The two spent the summer leading into the autumn spectacle training together in Windsor in an initiative organised by their respective coaches. It made perfect sense for Freeman. If she'd stayed in Australia, she'd never have escaped the public and media scrutiny, and that buckling pressure would have begun months out, instead of days.

In Windsor, she was largely unrecognised and could go about her preparation in peace. For Fraser, too, who was training with the world's best and pitting herself against her most fierce rival day after day. It's something that I know; years of training alongside my brother Jonny offers huge benefits.

'We were based in Windsor that whole summer,' recalls Fraser. 'We were usually the only ones on the athletics track at that time.' Her memories of it are rose-tinted. 'It worked so perfectly. We just gelled. Our coaches' mindsets were the same, mine and Cathy's too – easy-going but giving 110 per cent in training, that deep competitiveness. It was an amazing experience and we're still in touch. Looking back, the Windsor track felt a lot shorter for some reason.'

It was probably just that they were covering it at such a rapid rate, one matched by few female 400m runners before or since. Fraser paints a picture of training nirvana: low pressure, high performance, that wonderfully satisfying trajectory of measurable improvement. Pushing each other on, they achieved something close to peak physical and mental fitness – and she learned so much about the champion mentality.

The training sessions weren't that much different from what she was used to in terms of structure. Just a darn sight harder in terms of pace. 'My first session compared to how I finished going into those Games, I was a completely different person. That first session I was miles behind, struggling. Oh my god – it was so hard: the pace, the tempo, everything was raised. I realised, "This is how champions train. I need to raise my game."'

I'd make two points here: the first, which we've already encountered, is the way in which a trailblazer can make others believe they can achieve amazing things. The second benefit is more subtle. It's about learning how well the process can be carried out – maximising the science or nutrition or psychology of what you do, or simply training more or harder.

'It was Cathy's whole approach. Every session, no matter how tired she was, she'd put everything in,' recalls Donna. 'It's a valuable lesson. If you feel a bit off, you still give it everything because you don't know how the session is going to end up. That gap got progressively smaller and smaller. By the end I probably didn't realise how fit I was. I didn't see it as, "Oh, I can win the Olympic Games." I just saw it as training. Probably that was my downfall.'

And those looming Games? 'It never came up. We'd talk about everything except Sydney. Looking back now, I can't even imagine the pressure she was under, and lighting the Olympic flame as well. She was carrying all of Australia on her shoulders. But we didn't talk about it.'

The date of 25 September would have been firmly ringed in both their diaries, though. Once the Games began, Freeman and Fraser progressed smoothly, reaching the final as the first and fourth fastest qualifiers, respectively. And then came the climax. Despite having watched it back on numerous occasions, it still retains a dream-like quality for Fraser, she tells me. The deafening noise generated by that remarkable crowd of 112,524 people. Freeman's green and gold jumpsuit, and her yellow and black spikes honouring her Aboriginal heritage. That expansive stride, the wrists cocked, the clinging on.

Fraser, finishing strongly in lane two having been miles adrift, claimed fourth. She was the first to congratulate Freeman, whose face was blank, impassive. Never had a gold medal-winning athlete looked less elated. 'What a legend, what a champion ... what a relief,' says the commentator, judging the mood perfectly.

'I had to go and hug her because I knew that it meant so much,' Donna remembers. 'It was strange – I was feeling the pressure for her, being her training partner. Immediately I crossed the line I went straight to her because I knew that was a huge weight off her shoulders. How she did it ... I've got to take my hat off to her. No one knew what would happen – you never know in a 400m.

'I said, "You did it, you did it." She was absolutely over-whelmed; just a huge burden off her shoulders. When you win any race you're just kind of thinking, "Thank god." I've had that before. So if I times that by a million, I can understand what she was feeling.'

Just 0.68 seconds separated their times. For Freeman, once the relief had passed, a lifetime of joy and achievement. For Fraser, a lifetime of 'what if?'. Such are the margins between success and failure. Fraser ran a PB, she came fourth in one of the most iconic Olympic races of all time, but it's clear from chatting to her that this is absolutely no consolation, even nearly 20 years later.

'I'm so proud, looking back, to have been part of it. I watch it now and I get goosebumps and think, "How on earth did I cope with that atmosphere?" But I was devastated – I still am to a degree, even though I believe things happen for a reason and I have no one else to blame but myself for the way I ran that race. I was so in the zone, I wasn't aware what everyone was doing or how far behind I was until the last 150m, and that's when I started to run the race. My one regret is I wish I'd followed Cathy because that would have been the norm in training just to tuck in and stick with her because I could hold that pace. Things could have been different.'

How different, I ask? If that race was re-run 10 times, what would happen? I've been asked that very question before and it's annoyed me – but Fraser indulges me. 'From what I know now, and given the shape I was in, I would say nine times out of ten I would have come second.' And the other time? 'You never know, I might have beaten her.'

You sense Fraser, on some level, would have been devastated to have denied her great rival and friend her date with destiny. 'Cathy was just such a role model to be around. She's a cham-pion, a born champion. I learned so much from her, particularly this: that the only pressure you have is the pressure you put on yourself.'

Fast forward four years and it's Paula Radcliffe's turn to wrestle with that mind-blowing pressure. The Athens Olympics isn't at home, but given her feat the previous year at the London Marathon, she's as red hot as a favourite can get, and the British fans are busy rearranging their Aegean holidays in their thousands to ensure they can witness Paula storm to victory in the Marathon marathon (it begins in the suburb, north-east of the Greek capital, from which the event takes its name). Hundreds line the hilly course on the day of the event, a mass of red and white flags and pink flesh (it's one of the hottest days of the summer – 35°C – and humid, too). Thousands more gather in the Panathenaic Stadium, where the race is due to culminate with a final lap, watching on giant screens. The mood is jubilant. It doesn't last.

There's an Olympics saying – one Radcliffe herself trotted out four years before after finishing in this position in the 10,000m in Freeman's Sydney Games, to add to her fifth in the 5,000m in Atlanta in 1996: 'No one remembers who came fourth.' But such was the drama and emotion of this race, few, bizarrely, remember the winner. It was Japan's Mizuki Noguchi, and her passing the habitual frontrunning Radcliffe around 15 miles into the race, and pulling away, was the first indication that all was not well.

Radcliffe's head roll became more pronounced, her stride less fluent. She appeared to be struggling for breath. Brendan Foster, commentating, said: 'The heat is taking its toll, the hills are taking their toll.' This was the biggest day of her running career, her life, and it was unravelling fast. At the red 36km marker, she pulled up, looked round disorientated, almost panic-stricken, gasping, bewildered, unsure what to do.

She tried to continue, running a few strides, then stopped. It was clear she had nothing left, and she knew it. The tears came. She collapsed on to a grass verge, folded up like a thrown jockey and racked with pain, and wept. The Panathenaic Stadium went silent. When Noguchi crossed the line several kilometres later, it was in a time 11 minutes slower than Radcliffe's London world record.

Radcliffe's plight was agonising for any athletics fan, British or not – like Usain Bolt ripping a hamstring coming out of the blocks in the 100m and having to limp over the finish line. I remember it affecting me deeply as a sports-mad youngster. Unfulfilled talent on the grandest stage; someone who wants something so badly having it cruelly denied – that's sport, I suppose.

'I'm hurting so much inside for myself, but I also feel I've let everyone else down,' Radcliffe sobbed in a television interview later, having been put on a saline drip and had some time to recuperate. The inquest began. Was it the heat and humidity? She denied it was either. The anti-inflammatory drugs for a leg injury sustained a couple of weeks before the Games? Possibly. Was she simply a quitter? The British press thought so. Radcliffe herself was baffled. She said she 'just felt totally empty out there'.

There's a fine line between top-level fitness and injury. I've heard it described as 'teetering out on a knife edge'; the further you move along it, the more chance you have of falling off. But it's easy to reflect with the benefit of hindsight. What if Paula had taken her foot off the metaphorical gas in the weeks before that race and focused on being healthy? Conversely, what if Paula always took the 'safe' option and didn't look for that extra one per cent? My gut feeling is that she would have never got there in the first place.

We've discussed in these pages already how the imperfect

nature of sport is one of the things that makes it so appealing. The elite may strive to turn themselves into metronomes; Froome and Cook have perhaps come closest. But this can never be an exact process.

Professor Samuele Marcora, whom we met in an earlier chapter, is fascinated by this. When you're talking about the elite of the elite, where there are very small differences, it's not about fitness. So I think from a scientific perspective there are things that you cannot control. He's done studies to try to find out why athletes have good and bad days. 'If I can crack that, I'm sure I can become a bit rich,' he says to me, chuckling. We discussed races where it has gone well, and not so well for me, and the preparation for those. There's very little to put my finger on that's different. 'Exactly,' he says.

The issue is that athletes, in all their imperfect, rationalising, sometimes superstitious ways, aren't great at offering objective analysis. Marcora conducted a study to show as much, fabricating a 'bad day'. Participants were asked to run on a treadmill at the same speed on two consecutive days. Unknown to them, the inclination of the treadmill was increased by 1 per cent on one of the days – 'which makes quite a big difference in terms of energy expended, and on perception of effort, right?' says Marcora.

'Obviously they felt shittier in the conditions where we'd had the inclination. And then we asked them to compare the two days, the zero per cent and the one per cent, and give explanations for why they felt that way. And people, as you said, come up with all sorts of "attribution", we call it, because they didn't know the real explanation. They came up with all sorts of things that clearly were not the reason why it felt harder that day.

'So I don't think you can rely on the athletes too much to explain this. Of course, there could be something that had clearly gone wrong, like you couldn't sleep at all that night or you had a bit of a sickness a few days earlier. But sometimes it's just a bad day that's out of your control, right?'

I ask Radcliffe about this. She says: 'When you know that the training's gone really well, and you know you're in shape, and you know this is what you're gonna do ... when you really believe that, that's when you're at your most dangerous. The risk is when you've got a doubt there; so if you've missed some time. That's what I've always found if I've missed time with injury or I know that I'm not quite as strong as I could be, but I'm still gonna try and bluff it.'

I tell her that I think that one of the areas where an endurance athlete is different is that confidence can't be faked. When you're on the start line you know you've done the work and can see the correlation. Or you haven't. Bluffing the triathlon is a lot harder than say a snooker or tennis match.

She agrees. 'You've gotta be a lot better than the others to do that, when you know you haven't done the training. Especially when you go longer. So when you go 10k, half-marathon, up to marathon, if you haven't done the work, you just can't. The best way to get back from it is to get out and be able to give it your best, and to kind of reassure yourself that it's still there, that you can still do that.'

That's what she did in Athens, starting the 10,000m five days later. She had a great support network with her coach, and her husband and long-time manager Gary Lough. But this was one of the few times she worked with a sports psychologist – Steve Peters, who'd helped Ronnie O'Sullivan. She recalls: 'After what had happened in the marathon, I wanted to run the 10k, and Team GB didn't want to let me. So we agreed that I had to talk to the psychologist first and if he said that it was OK, then I could do that. So we kind of went in, and he talked about all the things that would happen if I dropped out again and if I wasn't able to finish. And I talked about how much worse it was to sit in the stands and to be thinking, well, what if I could've made it, what if I could have salvaged something from that Olympics?

'The worst had already happened in the marathon, so if I couldn't finish the 10k, I couldn't finish the 10k. It wasn't that big a deal compared with what had happened. So in the end, he just said, "Yeah, she's OK to start it." They never said this to me – but I think they just checked that I wasn't going to become a basket case if I tried to run the 10k and had to drop out. So I think it was more he was assessing me on that.'

Again, Paula dropped out – with eight laps to go. Her Olympic record read: fifth, fourth, DNF, DNF. In Beijing four years later, she wasn't fit, still recovering from a stress fracture to her leg, and came 23rd. And then, in what would have been her fifth Olympics, in London 2012, as a 38-year-old mother of two, she had to pull out of the marathon a week before the race due to medical problems. For another 'generational' athlete, it's a woeful record.

How did she stay motivated through all the ups and downs? She says she believes it was different things at different times. A perverse pleasure in subjecting herself to punishment. Seeing how hard she could push herself and what performances she could wring out. 'So there's kind of that personal challenge,' she says. 'But then there are still times in training when you're just knackered and you don't want to get out of the door. And then it's about the end target, the goal you're working towards: Olympics, World Championships.

'It was always a big goal of mine to see how fast I could go. So that was a big motivator in races. And I think in training, I just enjoyed pushing myself. So the hard sessions that really hurt the most, and you kind of had to work the hardest, are actually the ones that you walk away from the most satisfied.

Deep down you're still just that nine-year-old cross-country runner. You just wanna get out and race.'

I love this. Similarly, my goal as an 18-year-old was to see how good I could get, not how many medals I could win. 'You train too hard,' and 'You won't have a long career,' I kept getting told. My reply? I'd prefer to have two cracking years than 10 average ones. Of course, as an 18-year-old you tend to think you're indestructible.

Did Paula enjoy it, looking back?

'Yeah, I think I would still be doing it now if I could.' But, as she once said in an interview, running has broken her heart and spirit many times over.

8

RIDING WITH THE PUNCHES, IDOL TALK AND GOING ALL IN

Self-control can be defined as the ability to regulate behaviour, emotions and thoughts in the face of temptations and impulses. We mostly think of this in relation to, say, not having that second or third pint. But in elite sporting terms, the temptations and impulses are to slow, to ease up, to stop, to get complacent. In this respect, all those we've met so far have astonishing self-control.

I do wonder, though, as with many of the subjects in this book, whether the ability to do what they do – the preparation, the drive, the resilience and all the other elements that go into success – is actually some sort of gift, or even a form of genius (to use that much-hated term), albeit a less exciting, more multifaceted sort than sporting talent in itself. The levels of self-control, the way they can harness themselves, the manner in which they adapt and innovate – is that in fact the gift, rather than the manifestation of it seen on, say, the Formula One track in Monte Carlo or a football pitch in Saint-Étienne or in the Alps at the head of a peloton?

Professor Samuele Marcora touched on this in memorable terms, saying: 'There are some things you can't do anything about. It's like, for example, I sweat a lot. And sometimes, maybe I'm in the disco and I'm disco-dancing with a lady, and it would be lovely to tell my armpits to stop sweating, but I can't. So that's something that's out of your control. But you can control, to a certain extent, your behaviour – and that's especially true among elite people who have the same physiological capacity as each other. That's where you can gain the edge, and I guess you have done that.'

For the record, when he says 'you' and 'edge', he's not talking about my disco dancing.

But there's control of self, and then – in certain sports – there's control of other elements. Sometimes machinery. Sometimes conditions. Sometimes, even, animals. On my way to chat to legendary jockey AP McCoy, I find myself turning over a phrase from Mark Webber again and again in my head: 'In our sport, the equipment is not overly stable.'

Well, one sport that makes the equipment in F1 look as reliable as a cherished family Volvo is horse racing. Obstinate, highly strung creatures given to unexplained shifts in form, bursts of overexcitement, neurotic meltdowns. And that's just the jockeys.

I'm joking, of course. Mostly. And in a race like the Grand National (when it's not run virtually, as it was in 2020), you've got no fewer than 40 of these creatures riding in close configuration and hurdling 30 fences over a 4.5-mile course. For a jockey, it must feel like competing in F1 – sitting on top of the car.

The National is the showpiece of the jump season. But from the top down, racing is a sport that places unimaginable demands on those competing – and not just on race day. Falls aren't just a possibility; they're a racing certainty for all riders, of whatever standard. Being 'unseated' is the euphemism. It makes it sound like someone has pinched your seat at the pub rather than what it is: being thrown from a half-ton animal thundering along at up to 40mph into the path of multiple other half-ton animals with neither the time nor the inclination to avoid you.

The injury rate, as we'll see in a moment, is off the scale, and with depressing regularity these injuries can be career- (if not life-) ending. During the Cheltenham Festival in 2018, *The Times* ran a piece on jump jockey Ruby Walsh and his 21 major injuries. There was a helpful graphic: ruptured spleen, fractured hip, cracked jaw, crushed vertebra …

George Chaloner, a Royal Ascot-winning jockey, retired in 2017 aged 25 with 27 screws inside him. The final straw came when he raced (inadvertently) with a fractured back, fell again and broke it. Told by doctors that he'd been a centimetre away from being paralysed, he reluctantly threw in the towel. 'I'd be worth a fortune in scrap metal,' he said later, his jokey manner masking immense disappointment.

Take a look at the website for the Permanently Disabled Jockeys Fund, an organisation in America that looks after 60 paralysed or brain-damaged former jockeys. The shots of riders lying prone, broken or balled up in agony in the gutters of the dusty courses, their fellow competitors having long since charged off and their careers now hanging in the balance, are heart-rending. It feels more like the aftermath of warfare than sport.

Then there's the 'wasting' (a more apt euphemism). This is the ongoing struggle jockeys face to get down to the weights needed to ride racehorses. Saunas and hot baths, perpetual hunger, sweat sessions in the gym, and barely a cucumber-topped rice cake to look forward to at the end of the day.

Two-time Grand National winner Richard Dunwoody tells a story about trying to get as light as he could to qualify to ride a prospect trained by Martin Pipe. He lost 10lb in 24 hours, cramped up so badly before the race that he couldn't get his feet into the stirrups and – having sweated out the diuretic hormones – didn't go to the toilet for two days afterwards. Not much fun, and that's before you get to the complications around concussion and dehydration.

Many riders are self-employed, so there's also the politics of keeping owners and trainers happy. Who's in favour, who's out. But it's the logistical overload of being a jockey that really gets me. And particularly if you're trying to become Champion Jockey.

Most sports – football, rugby, cricket – exist on weekly cycles of training, playing and recovery. Cycling has its grand tours, golf its majors. Events are structured, with time between for preparation and travel and to give competitors the best chance of arriving at the start line or the first tee or kick-off in optimal shape.

Jockeys often compete in multiple races a day, several days in a row; brutal, daily examinations of their skill and stomach for the fight (though after certain painful defeats, I'd have welcomed the chance to make immediate amends). And if you're competing to be Champion Jockey – the title given to the rider with the highest number of winners at the end of the season – that schedule shifts from relentless to ridiculous. It's like Serena Williams entering not just the grand slams and Masters events but also every Challenger Tour match and qualifier that will have her. Anything that might net her another win to throw into the pot.

And every victory counts. Richard Dunwoody's battle with Adrian Maguire to be Champion Jockey in 1993–94 transcended racing, such were the neck-and-neck tallies of the two riders, Northern Irish and Irish respectively, and their fixation with the prize. It came down to the last day of the season, with Dunwoody a short nose in front. He rode three winners that day, to Maguire's one, and won the accolade 197 to 194.

Maguire retired a few years later with the tagline 'the best rider never to be Champion Jockey'. It followed a fall at Warwick in which he broke his neck and was lucky to avoid paralysis.

Which brings us back to risk. Every time a jockey mounts a racehorse, they're moving a step closer to another fall. And yet to become Champion Jockey you have to be riding as often as you physically can. Bangor, Carlisle, Chepstow, Newcastle, Exeter on a rainy Tuesday evening. It's a marathon of sprints, with no allowance made for peaking, for tapering, for recovering – either physically or mentally.

'You have to compete every day. You have to win every day. There is no time to be getting injured or sore or feeling sorry for yourself. You have to be prepared to go deeper, and further, than everyone else.'

This is Tony McCoy. For 20 years, from 1995 to 2014, his entire professional career, McCoy was Champion Jockey every season. In 2001–02, he rode 289 winners, beating a record that had stood since 1947. Over his time as a jockey, he amassed 4,357 winners; at the point he retired in 2015, no one else had passed 3,000. This amiable but intense Northern Irishman was also the first jockey to really break into the mainstream. In 2010, he won BBC Sports Personality of the Year, the first in his profession to do so. This followed his win in the Grand National, at the 15th time of asking, riding Don't Push It. Given McCoy's ferociously competitive spirit, it was one of the most ironic pairings in sporting history.

I've been trying to chat to McCoy for weeks. When I do track him down, our chat is one of the most enthralling hours of my year. 'Like everything, you get better,' says the Co. Antrim man when I ask him how he reconciled himself to the constant punishment dealt out by his sport. 'You get better at winning, you get better at falling, you get better at coping with pain and injury. You have to. Pretty much the only bone

I didn't break in my career was my femur. I broke my ankle, I broke my leg, I broke my arm, my wrist. I've had two metal discs in my back, four screws between my T9 and T12 vertebrae. I broke all my ribs, I broke my shoulder blade, my sternum, my collarbones, cheekbones, pretty much all my teeth …'

He pauses. 'It's one of the very few sports – and walks of life – where there are two ambulances going around behind you. And no matter how good you are, you're going in one of them.' In fact, the better you are, the better the chance you're going in one of them. 'I rode in over 18,000 horse races,' he tells me. 'If they say that one in 15 horses fall, or one in 20 or whatever it is … I spent a lot of time in hospital and I've seen a lot of ambulances.'

The racing driver James Hunt once said that the closer you are to death, the more alive you feel (it didn't sound so clichéd at the time). AP agrees. He says that there was nothing he enjoyed, or wanted, more than to compete and to win. Now that he's retired, the one thing he misses more than anything is winning on a big stage, in front of people. 'But – and this is a very difficult thing to say because I saw colleagues fatally injured and I have images in my head of suits hanging up and lads never coming back – I genuinely miss the risk. I miss living on the edge. Going in a 24-runner race at Cheltenham or Newbury or wherever, and falling in front of all those horses and thinking as you're on your way to the ground, "Oh my god, this is going to hurt." And you get kicked all over the place, and then you kind of get up and you think, "I got away with that, that wasn't too bad."

'With the amount of races that I rode, there'd be times when I would end up breaking my arm or my leg or my back, and I'd say to myself, "Do you know what, I haven't broken it for a year and a half, what do you expect?"'

There's a parallel with boxing here. It may not be your opponents looking to pummel you (though that can happen inadvertently), but that pummelling awaits nonetheless, and a key part of your job is to convince yourself that you can withstand it. That you're unbreakable. This is another thread of metacognition – controlling how you think to ensure an optimal outcome.

AP, growing more animated, gives me a vivid example. 'You're lying on the ground after breaking eight ribs and puncturing your lung and fracturing your sternum, and you can't get a breath and you think you want to die. But you have this sixth sense thinking, "I'm invincible." You know what I mean?' he says. No. Not in the slightest. Thankfully.

Then: 'You end up in hospital and you can't remember where you are and you're having your dinner through a tube and they're pumping morphine intravenously into you every half an hour to try to kill the pain ... and there's still something in you that makes you wanna get back out there.'

What I've always loved about horse racing is the big characters. There's something about the danger, those challenges we've discussed, that is self-selecting. In racing, there are no passengers. You need extraordinary drive to get anywhere near the sport, and an iron will to stay there.

Richard Johnson is the man of the moment, one of the most likeable characters in any sport. He's certainly the most persistent. Sixteen times he was runner-up to McCoy to be Champion Jockey. Twenty-one times he's ridden in the National (a record). Twenty-one times he's failed to win it. With McCoy gone he enjoyed a swansong, claiming four titles before announcing his retirement in April 2021, aged 43.

He's fascinating on the subject of how racing has become more sophisticated – better-trained horses, better conditioning, and medical and mental-health support (jockeys are disproportionately prone to mental-health issues). But every victory he notched up – by the end of 2020 he had claimed his 3,749th win – made you ponder: would he still be going had McCoy not raised the bar to such stratospheric levels? So often in sport, champions beget champions. Someone an aspiring player relates to in some way – be that their character, where they're from, their style – blazes a trail that they're able to follow. It's not really a mentor–mentee thing; indeed, it's often unspoken. Think of Ronnie O'Sullivan practising Steve Davis's walk round the table, mirroring his clothes.

'I think in sport, as in any walk of life, you have to have someone who you look up to, who sets the benchmark,' AP tells me. 'In my case, it was Woody. When I started riding he was Champion Jockey and as far as I was concerned he was the best, and I wanted to beat him. I'd find myself watching him and analysing things: the ways he was better than everyone else; why he won; more importantly, why he won more than anyone else.'

Dunwoody had the aura at that time. He won the Grand National on West Tip in 1986 in just his second year as a professional. He won it again eight years later on Miinnehoma. He triumphed in the King George VI Chase four times, twice on the legendary grey, Desert Orchid. And he was Champion Jockey three years in a row between 1992 and 1995.

AP was entranced. 'I saw someone who was meticulous, almost unbelievably driven. He was probably the most mentally and physically strong person I'd ever seen. Not probably – he was. I watched him and thought, "That's what you have to go through to be Champion Jockey." I saw him when I was a young jockey coming in after a really, really bad fall, and going back out [to race] again. If that's what you need to be a champion, I thought, then I'd better get used to it.'

So, what Dunwoody offered was a template for success. A walking, talking, often limping blueprint. A few months earlier,

I'd met up with Richard. He'd recently returned from North Korea, where he'd run the Pyongyang Marathon. Since retiring, he has become a globe-trotting photographer and adventurer still subjecting himself, perhaps for old times' sake, to punishing extremes. In 2008, he completed a 48-day charity trek to the South Pole. The next year he walked the same mile loop in Newmarket 1,000 times in 1,000 hours for various charities including the Jockey Club. In 2017, he was at it again, completing a 2,000-mile walk over the length of Japan to raise money for Sarcoma UK.

Richard and I meet near my West Yorkshire house at a hotel where he has checked in with his girlfriend Olivia and daughter Milly. He's been at an event in Northumberland and is en route to his home in Madrid. Now 55, he looks fit and lean, though his face bears the lines and scars of a life led at the coalface of sport. Six hundred and eighty-two falls he had in his career, before a debilitating neck injury dragged him kicking and screaming into retirement. Six hundred and eighty-two! And that doesn't include falls in practice or in races where he remounted. And Woody was very much of the old-school jockey ranks, what you might call the 'drive-yourself-to-A&E' era.

We share tales and insight, and Richard is as interested in my experiences as I am in his. There is no hint of frustration at my relatively limited knowledge of the sport that consumed him. We laugh about the crap mechanical horses available to train on in his day, light years from the slick simulators favoured by the new breed of jockey today. We talk focus and risk – 'Four or five friends got killed – you just accepted it. It doesn't make you think differently about what you're doing. You have tunnel vision.'

Talking in a calm, measured voice that has me occasionally leaning in to hear him, he tells of the time that he broke his sternum two weeks and three days before Cheltenham, where he had loads of favourites lined up to ride. You can guess where this goes. He had a few days in Sunbury intensive care, leaving him 13 days to get himself fit.

'First I couldn't even walk. I was in bits. You can't really do anything for a sternum except you definitely don't want to cough,' he says with a smile. Gradually, painfully, it healed, or at least it healed enough for him to be able to convince a doctor to let him ride. He made it to Cheltenham – and had three winners. Then he adds quietly, 'I did have about three or four falls during the festival, but I was able to take them and get up.'

I'm beginning to get a sense of why Woody made such an impression on AP.

We discuss wasting and some of the sacrifices he had to make – while gorging on pie and chips, ironically. Richard is 77kg now, close to his natural weight. When he was racing, he was 63kg. 'It was a pretty hideous existence,' he says flatly.

In my career, I've always been quite relaxed about diet. It helps, when you're training long and hard days, to have something to look forward to. Often that's a pie or fish and chips. In my home village of Bramhope there's a bakery, a chippy, an Indian takeaway. I'd be lying if I said I haven't given them more than my fair share of business over the years. Balance and common sense have been among the cornerstones of my career. But if eating freely helps you to get through a torturously long day, then get up and do it again, so be it. That's always been my view.

There are so many uncontrollables in horse racing, with metaphorical loose horses coming at you from all angles. But arguably what proved most significant in laying the foundation for AP's period of dominance was his innovative approach to the things that could be controlled: namely, logistics. Horse racing in the late 1980s and early 90s, the era of Peter Scudamore and then Richard Dunwoody, was still in the dark ages. Richard rode seven days a week, he told me, with days off only for injury or bad weather. One year he rode in 900 races, the majority of which he drove himself to.

Sometimes the schedule became comical, at least in hindsight. He tells me a tale of him and two other jockeys driving at 120mph down the M4 to get to Sandown Park, in Surrey, from Chepstow, in Monmouthshire, after the helicopter that had been lined up to take them couldn't fly because of fog. Another, of him racing in England on a Saturday, North Carolina on the Sunday, and back in England again on Monday. After that red-eye nightmare you'd be forgiven for getting the two ends of the horse mixed up.

'I felt I didn't manage my life very well – there was a stage between agents where I was doing everything myself,' says Richard. 'I drove myself everywhere because that's what people did when I started. I'd drive up to Sedgefield, in County Durham, for one ride, and then drive all the way home. It was madness. And I'd also be trying to sort out rides, speak to trainers, speak to owners. Yeah, it was nuts, and I didn't get a secretary until I was halfway through my career. You need to have someone to manage all that.'

Which was what McCoy recognised. 'AP, whether he learned from my mistakes or not, saw that. He got a manager who knew the game inside out. Then he'd have a secretary as well, a driver, and a really good agent, the best in the country. AP had a driver right from the start. He slept. He'd sleep until 10am if he needed to, and was able to get to races rested and ready to perform. I'd get there late, I'd be stuck in traffic ...'

AP would always have done well, you suspect, but the foresight to grip this as things started to fall in his favour surely meant a lot to the longevity of his career. 'If he had a bad fall, again he was prepared to do whatever he needed to do to get back quickly,' says Richard. 'I remember he broke his back once and he was straight in the ice chamber to help the healing.'

When I put it to AP that he may have capitalised on his old mate's mistakes, he agrees. 'I learned a lot from Richard, both good and bad. Things that I thought I could make easier for myself or that would make my career last longer. You spend a lot of your life in a car as a jockey. I could concentrate more on being a jockey rather than worrying about whether I wanted to drive three hours to bloody Sedgefield. I didn't want to wake up one morning and think, "I've been travelling for the last five days, I've been in Edinburgh today, I'm in Exeter tomorrow and I'm too tired to go to Bangor or Haydock on Friday." When my agent, who booked my rides, rang me up and said, "You know what? You're in Scotland today, you're in Wales tomorrow, you're in Devon …", I'd be like, "No problem."'

'I dunno if I was an innovator, but I guess time moves on and you have to make sure you move before it. You have to be the first one to move. It can be the smallest detail. But some-times that's enough. And you have to be prepared to make a little change – it might not work, but you have to be prepared to make the change. I think in sport you have to find an edge all the time – to try and find something that gives you an opportunity of being better.'

McCoy's meticulousness was another edge. It's amazing in top-flight sport how often you meet characters who appear to be leaving their career progression to chance. Or, worse, to others. I've always felt it important that I have total autonomy over my career – my tactics, my preparation, my diet, my race schedule. There's no one to blame when things go wrong. But the flipside is that you're perfectly placed to make the fine-tuning that might be needed. I find the responsibility empowering.

AP, like Mark Webber in Chapter 5, was the same. He tells me he had to have the whole picture in his mind when he went out on a horse: their speed, the going, the point the horse can't run any faster. 'Probably like you, with the running side of triathlon,' AP says. 'You're always looking up thinking, "Can I beat whoever's in front? Am I in a position, am I too far off, is he going too fast, am I out of range?" You're always trying to give yourself the opportunity or put yourself in the position where you can win. I never wanted to be dependent on others; I wanted for me to make the decisions.'

Something AP and Richard shared was an unwavering, often alarming focus. *Obsessed*, Dunwoody's excellent autobiography, contains disturbing admissions. About his (now ex-) wife Carole's suicide attempt, in the wake of which he went to race rather than visit her in hospital. His rage at losing and the torment of defeat, which at times he seemed only too happy to share with those around him. He was a self-styled 'horrible bastard', something that is almost impossible to reconcile with the character I meet. His psychologist, Australian Peter Terry, labelled Richard Dunwoody 'a perfectionist with intrapunitive tendencies' – that is, someone who grows self-destructive if they can't reach the (impossibly high) standards they set themselves.

These are not traits that play out well in the real world. But all us sportspeople are guilty of them to a greater or lesser extent. I recall hearing the 'separate checks' story about Tiger Woods, first reported in an ESPN article in 2016. After training with the Navy SEALs, with whom the golfer felt an affinity (even if it wasn't always mutual), a group of five or six of them ended up having a meal in a restaurant. When the waitress brought the bill, the table went silent. Surely the man worth

$1 billion would cover it. Nope. Everyone looked at one another awkwardly. Finally one of the SEALs said, 'Separate checks, please.' One of the guys later said: 'That's weird shit.'

I wouldn't defend Tiger – and I'm a Yorkshireman! – but I know that Richard and AP, like myself, would recognise something in this tale. The neglect of social conventions. The extreme self-absorption. The tunnel vision, to use Richard's phrase. Some of the stories that competitors could tell about me from my racing career don't make pretty reading. The number of times I've left my mates waiting in the rain at the side of the road for me to turn up after I've prioritised something else is, frankly, embarrassing. But when you're an athlete, there can be no half-measures.

I ask AP whether he changed in any way when he became a father – his daughter Eve was born in 2007, after IVF, since exposure to daily hot baths and saunas had obliterated his sperm count. After all, he knew the odds of being paralysed, brain damaged, even killed doing his work. There's a pause. 'I always knew this job was dangerous, and I got to know it at a very early stage. I wanted to beat everyone else, so I was going to have to get used to dealing with the dangers of the sport. It's just the way it is.

'But I never thought for one moment, "God, what happens if I'm killed and my kids grow up without a father?" or whatever. Because I never genuinely thought it was going to happen, even though I saw it happen to other people. It's not an attractive trait at all, that selfishness, but you need to have it. It needs to be all about you.'

To say we do what we do for the love of the sport or for the buzz of winning is a massive oversimplification. You get locked into a spiral, as I've found in the latter stages of my career. AP is so articulate about the tail-chasing that characterises sporting dominance. 'I always thought that when I was lucky enough to beat the records that Richard set, that I wanted to beat my own records,' he tells me. 'I wanted to beat me. But I had this fearful thing that if I could beat me then someone else younger was gonna beat me. And that would really annoy me.' He once said that he'd often forgotten about the victory, or at least put it from his mind, 'by the time I'd taken the saddle off'. That isn't obsession. It's addiction.

We're back to that idea of shifting normality. Fans assume that sports stars exist on a plane of constant euphoria – 'If I'd scored the winner in the FA Cup Final, I'd retire on the spot and dine out on it for the rest of my life.' You would, but only with your current outlook. If you have the experience, the opportunity, the ability to be tucking away that goal on such an elevated stage, then what you've created is simply a new normal. 'Most human beings have an almost infinite capacity for taking things for granted,' wrote Aldous Huxley. It's why we can endure such hardship, and it's why arguably the greatest jockey to have ever mounted a horse can make the following, startling admission to me.

'I was never content in 20 years. Never satisfied. I never felt I was different from anyone else,' he says. 'Definitely through the first half of my career, the first 10 to 11 years of being Champion Jockey, I wasn't confident in myself. It was only probably when I rode my 4,000th winner that I felt a sense of achievement, you know what I mean? When I rode my 4,000th winner, I was thinking, "Do you know what, this is actually going OK."'

He adds: 'The one thing I got better at was being level: not getting too up or too down. Sure, if I won a Grand National or the Cheltenham Gold Cup I'd be excited for a little longer than in a normal day. But I was good at not getting carried away with myself. I was good at not letting the whole thing get to me.'

Not getting too up or too down. That's called being phleg-matic. People see it as a positive, something pulling you up from the down times. But not being able to properly appreciate the successes, to allow them to wash over and energise you, is a dangerous game.

Professor David Lavallee, of Abertay University in Dundee, is the world's first Professor of Duty of Care in Sport. An expert in the trajectory of sporting careers, he speaks of the 'Faustian bargain' that athletes make: the more someone focuses and develops a strong identity around what they do, the more likely they are to perform. In short, you can't just *pretend* it's the most important thing in the world to you. But the problem comes when that thing – whether it's competing or winning – is taken away.

There's far better support for mental-health issues in sport today, both for competitors and retirees. And, interestingly, sports psychology was one area in which it was Dunwoody, not AP, who was the innovator. Today, a sportsperson using a psychologist is positively de rigueur. But when Richard started working with Peter Terry, he had to hide it.

'The *Sun* newspaper got hold of it and they had all the head-lines: "Dunwoody – off to the psychologist". You wouldn't believe it,' he tells me. 'Five years later, they were all using psychologists, and now it's just par for the course. I would get so wound up early in my career. Just couldn't let it go. I only used Peter for 18 months, but his lessons stayed with me for the rest of my career. "Control the controllable" was the mantra.'

He goes on: 'I had a massive fear of failure. Massive. Not making myself look an idiot – that's what drove me. The fear of making a mistake kept me as focused as anything else.' He asks whether it's the same with me. It's not. At least not very often. There have definitely been times where I've been more driven by fear of being beaten by, say, my brother, but that was more when I was younger. I remember I'd race one week and say I'd be worried about being beaten by Jonny, and then be racing exactly the same people the next week and I just wanted to win. I realised that these shifting outlooks could potentially change the decisions I was making and how I went about the race; if I raced defensively, for example. So I purposefully didn't make that my focus.

It hit me once big time – the first time I won the World Triathlon title in 2009, in fact, when Jonny wasn't in the race. The World Series is a number of races, and it worked out that I needed to come fifth or better in the last one to win. I started thinking there are these three guys who might beat me, and what if I get a puncture, and this and that. Then I thought, I've won every other race this year apart from one – this is completely the wrong attitude. Control the controllables. I won the race and the world title.

It's a little-realised fact that AP was a serial loser. If you play Premiership football, then even an average team is going to win a fair number of games. The best will only lose a handful. A jockey can ride 38 races in a week and there's a good chance that they'll lose at least 30. 'What you do in racing, more than any other sport, is you lose,' says AP. It's yet another facet of the sport that places enormous emphasis on mental durability.

I'd read somewhere that AP once said he had 'more will than skill'. I ask him about this. He says that he didn't think he was the most naturally talented person but was able to 'mechanically' get himself where he wanted to be. It was his refusal to back down that is striking.

'Up until the day I retired, I genuinely, every time I went out, thought, no matter how hard I get kicked, I will get up,' he says. 'You have to have that mindset, you have to. I broke my back, I fractured my T9 and T12 in 2008, and I lay on the ground for three, four, five minutes until the ambulance and the doctor came, and I didn't know whether the sweat was running down my forehead from the pain or from the fear that I couldn't move, you know what I mean? I can still picture it in my head.

'Then, half an hour later, the doctor and the ambulance drivers and the medical staff put you on a spinal board, you can see them lifting your feet, you can see your legs and you think, "Ah, I'm alright." You go to the hospital and you convince the doctor who wants to put you in a body cast for three months that that ain't gonna work because you need to be riding at Cheltenham soon. And then the doctor puts two metal discs, four screws in your back, and you ride a few weeks later.

'I wanted other jockeys to see that, even if I'd got kicked all over the place or badly hurt, I'm going back into that changing room. I want them to see that if you're gonna beat me, this is what you're gonna have to do.'

There's loads more I want to ask AP about, not least the exciting emergence of female jockeys. Bryony Frost, at the 2019 Cheltenham Festival, became the first woman to win a Grade 1 race, making the front page of *The Times* in the process. After Katie Walsh came close on Seabass in 2012, Irish rider Rachael Blackmore became the first female jockey to triumph in the Grand National in April 2021, riding Minella Times. This could prove to be the most welcome of tipping points, but, we've seen, in racing there are no guarantees. Four days after her Cheltenham win, Bryony fell at Southwell and fractured her collarbone.

I'd like to ask all this, but we're out of time. AP has a racing event to get to (suited, rather than in silks), and I've got to go and delete all the social media posts I've ever made moaning about ankle strains and other minor injuries. Not for the first time in the process of writing this book, I feel humbled. They say jockeys have a screw loose; well, if that's true, it's usually only because it has been dislodged by the most recent fall.

We leave this chapter with probably my favourite quote from McCoy, whose extraordinary willpower drove him to unimaginable heights in this merciless sport, setting records that may never be broken. It's one I intend to reflect on until I'm also dragged kicking and screaming into retirement.

'You get a lot of sportspeople who retire and think, "Do you know what? I'm not sure I went to the absolute red zone, to empty. I'm not sure I made all the sacrifices that I could have to make myself better." I think I had a lot of will, and I do think I was prepared to go to the end. As far as I was concerned, I was all in.'

9

THE MAN-BEATER, THE MISSILE AND THE POWER OF OBSESSION

This is a tale of two cyclists. One male, one female. One a revered pro, the other a rhubarb-pulling amateur. One, a fêted and well-rewarded star of cycling's biggest spectacles (the Tour de France on the road, and the Olympics on the track); the other, denied a shot on either stage. One – a giant of the carbon-fibre age – (very much) alive; the other – a throwback to the steel frame and toe clips days – greatly missed.

Dig deeper, though, and the picture that emerges is not one of difference but of similarity. Both, as we'll see, are outsiders, blinkered and uncompromising, prickly and confrontational, unorthodox and unapologetic, gripped by an all-consuming rage to win.

I'm enthralled by both. Obviously, I only had the opportunity to meet one of them, though I had to fly 4,000 miles to do so. With the other, I settled for the next best thing: a leisurely day out in the saddle chatting to her daughter, also a cyclist, about the mother in whose shadow she still, to an extent, lives.

Compelling characters, the pair of them. My only sadness? That we never got to see them on a tandem.

* * *

'She was incredibly focused on what she needed to do, to the extent that nothing else – no one else – mattered. In this respect she was very selfish.'

Denise Burton-Cole is discussing her late mother, as we negotiate the Beryl Burton Cycleway between Knaresborough and Bilton, in West Yorkshire, named in her mum's honour. If there's any residual hurt in what she's saying – Denise, as Beryl's only child, would have borne the brunt of such blind dedication – then she's hiding it well. Either that, or the nuance of her words is getting lost in the humid summer air as we zip along the banks of the River Nidd.

A petite lady of 64, Denise is in impressive nick. She wears Lycra, rides a road bike with an 'under saddle' and a handle-bar bag that hints at a passion for long-distance touring, and has the sort of easy confidence and presence in the saddle that you can't fake. The pace, if I'm honest, is keeping me on my toes.

It's a beautiful day. The morning rain has long since dried up in the sunshine and the daytrippers are out in force, ambling along the path or inexpertly rowing up and down the river in hire boats. This is a route I've pedalled half a dozen times and driven past countless more. And the story of the lady behind this cycleway has long intrigued me.

Listing the full roster of Beryl's achievements requires the sort of stamina that she became known for. In a career spanning five decades, the Yorkshirewoman won seven world titles (two road race championships and five world pursuit victories on the track) and 96 national titles: 12 road race champion-ships, 13 national pursuit championships and 71 time trial titles.

Starting in 1959, the Morley CC rider also claimed 25 consecutive Best British All-Rounder (BBAR) titles, awarded by the Road Time Trials Council (now Cycling Time Trials) to the rider with the highest average speed in time trial races over the course of the season. In 1959, Beryl's winning average was 23.724mph, and she only improved with age. Her peak was 26.665mph, set 18 years later in 1976. But the most remarkable stat contained within these figures is that, during her quarter-century of BBAR dominance, her winning average speed was – for 13 years, all told – faster than the men's.

There were other gender-breakout feats that had the cycling world, home and abroad, shaking their heads in astonishment. The greatest, arguably, came in 1967. That year, Beryl set a women's 12-hour time trial record that was to stand for 50 years. Picture that: a benchmark established in the same year as Tom Simpson's notorious death on the slopes of Mont Ventoux during the ill-fated 13th stage of the Tour de France, one that lasted until a year after the Rio Olympics.

The distance she covered, 277.25 miles, was nearly a mile more than that of Mike McNamara, who set a new men's record the same day. As she overtook him, in a moment that has passed into Yorkshire cycling folklore, she offered him a liquorice allsort – a gesture of both solidarity and nose-thumbing dominance. 'Ta, love,' was apparently all he could muster.

Beryl's 50-year record was finally beaten two years ago by Alice Lethbridge of the Drag2Zero team, at the Eastern Counties Cycling Association 12 Hours Championship. Chapeau to Alice. She was understandably ecstatic. But to see the pictures of her on her carbon fibre time trial bike, her skin-suit coated in sponsors' logos, with her aerodynamic helmet and visor, merely amplified just how ludicrously ahead of her time Beryl Burton was.

As one comment on the Road.cc website discussion board following the breaking of her record put it: 'Burton was a once-in-a-lifetime freak of nature. Add in a massive dose of

Yorkshire grit and determination to push where others would fold and you have a superlative athlete that none has matched. Only technology has bested her.'

Denise looks proud. 'In this country, she was the biggest thing in cycling. I can remember going down south weekend after weekend. The people down there thought the world of her; they thought she was amazing. I meet up with people and they still talk about her. She loved it, and that's part of what made her want to do well. You can tell in people's faces – she loved it: the winning, the attention.'

I feel a close affinity with Beryl. She was twice the athlete I'll ever be but her success, like mine, was forged on the same Yorkshire roads and in the same famously variable conditions. Riding out to the coast for the day – to Scarborough or Bridlington. Up the Wharfe valley, out towards Otley, Ilkley and Bolton Abbey, then looping back around. Into the heart of the Dales, perhaps as far as Buckden to tackle climbs such as Kidstones or Fleet Moss up to the highest road in Yorkshire. Beryl would have had the same internal battles, the same mechanicals, the same agonies, the same euphoria.

I doubt there's more than a handful of rural roads in our great county that we haven't both shed sweat along. On a good day, when you're in form, and the weather is on your side, there can be few better places in the world to cycle. But when both desert you, not so much. In a sporting sense, however, our experiences are a world apart. Beryl had no access to the coaches or training facilities, the nutritionists and gels, the aerodynamics and the microscopically tuned bikes, as well as all the other marginal gains that I take for granted. When I get on my bike before an event, I know instantly if any of the adjustments are a millimetre out. By comparison, Beryl, and many of her generation, pretty much just winged it.

'Her trademark was that she always rode with one hand higher than the other,' says Denise. So consistent was she in this quirk that it has even been immortalised in one of Knaresborough's 'Town Windows', which I passed earlier in the day on the way to meet Denise. The town has turned some of the many blocked windows on its Georgian frontages – a legacy of when families, who were charged tax based on the number of windows on their property, bricked them up – into trompe l'oeil paintings portraying well-known figures linked to the area.

Mother Shipton is there – the 16th-century witch was said to have been born in Knaresborough, and her cave, at the start of the Beryl Burton Cycleway, is regarded as England's oldest tourist attraction. Not much of a cyclist, mind. Some of the figures perch on the painted window sills or lean out surveying the town. Not Beryl. The rider, who once raced for Knaresborough, explodes out of her window on her red bike, with short curly hair, back low and ruler-straight and, yes, one hand higher than the other on the drop handlebars.

I say to Denise that these days you'd have a fleet of specialist coaches trying to correct such imperfection. At the very least, a specially adjusted bike made for you. 'We didn't then. You just went with the fashion of the time,' says Denise. 'You put your heel on the pedals, said, "That feels about right," and then you'd race. Nothing fancy. Training was "Yorkshire", too: high mileage, simplistic. Beryl was a "peddler" who had the strength to push high gears in racing.'

Beryl resisted the siren call of professionalism throughout her decades of success. Raleigh offered her a contract to ride purely for times (there were no professional races at the time), which she turned down as it would have meant her being banned from the rider-against-rider competition she craved. The result was that she had to go on working – mostly at that rhubarb farm in south Leeds.

I've not done a lot of rhubarb pulling in my time. But I can see it's backbreaking work. Denise nods. 'It was a hard manual job; she didn't have to do weights,' she says, with a chuckle. But in her own way, and in the spirit of the age, Beryl made it work for her. Rhubarb is a winter crop, so the job left her summers free to race. The repetitive, demanding nature of her work would have helped her build the rock-like core needed to remain locked in an ultra-low cycle position for up to 12 hours at a time. The bending helped the flexibility. And what better to toughen you up mentally for an unrelenting time trial than exposure to a Yorkshire winter?

Denise and I have covered just over five miles now, and at a decent lick. We pull up in Ripley outside a teashop, park our bikes and go in to order tea and scones. Solid cycling fare. It's busy. We pull up a seat in a quiet corner and keep talking. I want to know what she thought gave her mother that all-important edge. Was there one thing she felt had more bearing on Beryl's success than any other? Her drive? That unbreakable will? Her focus?

'She had Dad there,' she says, matter of factly. 'She had a shoulder to cry on, a mechanic. He used to take her everywhere, and he didn't do it grudgingly.' She looks rueful. 'To have that level of support must have been fantastic. When Mum died, Dad didn't know what to do with himself. All his adult life was planned around her.'

This was Charlie Burton, who met young Beryl Charnock in the mid-1950s when she was 16 and they both worked in a tailoring firm in Leeds. He got her into cycling, bought his then girlfriend her first bike, and introduced her to the club culture. Denise's eyes shine as she talks about the social side of cycling. 'It was a good scene,' she says. 'Friends for life. Club dinners and dances that you'd ride to with your dress in the saddlebag. A wonderful life. Fabulous memories.

'But then the cycling bit starts to grab you. It's wonderful – and a curse at the same time. You can't get rid of it.'

It certainly grabbed Beryl, who eclipsed Charlie so completely that – inverting the social conventions of the day – he dropped pretty much everything to support her. This was how he described her early development: 'First of all, she was handy but wasn't that competent: we used to have to push her round a bit. Slowly she got better. By the second year, she was "one of the lads" and could ride with us. By the third year, she was going out in front and leading them all.'

Charlie was a superb mechanic and would drive his wife all across the country to enable her to race or ride. He worked hard to help fund her cycling, even taking an evening job. And of course there was Denise to think of. 'He was driver, mechanic and childminder,' Denise once put it.

It's a fascinating image, isn't it? Charlie, the uncomplaining, unfailingly loyal consort. And Beryl, with her short hair, ferocious single-mindedness and invincible aura, obliterating social stereotypes. In this latter task, there was no one to draft, of course; she was out front, alone, taking the brunt of the (social) resistance. To be treated as the equal of male riders, it was painfully clear to her, she had to not just match but consistently best them.

We finish our tea and scones. On winter days, these same cafés are empty, save for cyclists looking to refuel, to warm cold hands on mugs. Yorkshire is steeped in cycling history – bolstered by recent initiatives such as the Tour de France staging its *Grand Départ* in the county in 2014 and the now-annual Tour de Yorkshire, which began the following year. And it's a fraternity that both Beryl and later Denise belonged to – though rarely together.

The Beryl Burton story would be remarkable enough on its own. But the relationship with her daughter adds an extra layer and may help us to understand something of the nature of this true sporting 'gripper', to borrow Seb's phrase. It's why I'm so keen to meet Denise.

She was born in 1956, the year after Charlie and Beryl married, and was two when her mother won her first national title. She got her first bike when she was nine. Google their names together and it's possible to find black-and-white shots of Beryl teaching her schoolgirl daughter the basics.

But when Denise also excelled as a cyclist, it seemed to be despite – rather than because of – Beryl's best efforts. Nature, without the nurture. 'It was secret and competitive,' recalls Denise. 'She didn't share training tips. Sometimes I'd say, "Where are you going, Mum?" She'd say, "York." I'd let her go off and then follow on. I knew which route. When I saw her, it would be, "Hi, Mum."'

Home life was dominated by her mother's dedication, and selfishness. Beryl refused to have a TV or a phone in the house, lest they prove a distraction, and Charlie was forbidden from also providing his daughter with mechanical support when she emerged on the international scene in the early 1970s.

'Mum was incredibly competitive in everything she did. Everything. She liked gardening, knitting, baking – but she had to be the best and the fastest. She wanted to win.'

Which meant that there were always likely to be fireworks when Denise's emerging talent pitted them together as rivals. Denise wasn't allowed a place in the car on the way to the national championships in 1975. 'When I was about to put my bag and self in the car to go, Mum refused to let me in and told me I had to ride out (about 25 miles). I persuaded her to at least take my kit bag in the car. My dad got my bike off the car roof and my racing wheels as they weren't allowed in either, fixed them on my bike with sprint carriers and I set off on my own. It did not particularly bother me. I just shrugged my shoulders and thought, "Oh well, it's a good warm up."' In the race, Denise outsprinted Beryl to win the title, and Beryl refused to shake her hand on the podium. 'I don't know what came over me,' Beryl would later say. 'I just felt Denise hadn't done her whack' (lingo for taking your turn at the front).

I'm no stranger to familial rivalry. Jonny and I have shared many a frosty podium after a row about some sort of real, or imagined, slight or tactical foul play (I'm yet to make him walk home, though). But siblings is one thing. We're almost expected to compete. Parent and child? Very different.

Denise seems reflective, but also detached, as we talk about this and other stories. At times it's like she's recollecting a story in which she played no part. There is no suggestion that her mother was not happy and proud of her daughter's success. Just that these emotions were overshadowed by the insatiable competitiveness that had served her so well for so long. As Beryl said in her 1986 autobiography, *Personal Best*: 'Our bitter conflict played out in an almost gladiatorial fashion.'

Beryl passed away – out on her bike, of course – just short of her 59th birthday in 1996. She was entered to ride the national 10-mile championship the following weekend. Ironically, for someone blessed with more heart than almost anyone I can think of, she died of heart failure.

Hers was a glittering career. As well as the records and the medals, she received an MBE in 1964 and OBE in 1968, the year after she came second in the BBC Sports Personality of the Year (something else we have in common). She's had a radio show and play made about her life, and, in 2009, she was included in the new British Cycling Hall of Fame in the Manchester Velodrome, one of only 50 inductees.

Yet there's a sense that, remarkably, she could have done even more, have been even bigger. Her obituary in the

Independent in 1996 said: 'Beryl's achievements were impossible to ignore ... but she never felt that either the local or national press properly appreciated her efforts.' Being denied those two key stages, the Tour and the Olympics, lay at the heart of this.

Through barriers that she'd helped to bring down, a women's Tour de France (Tour Cycliste Féminin) was finally launched in 1984; prior to this, women riders were not felt to have the stamina to ride stages of more than 80 miles over the course of three weeks (note, this was nearly 20 years after her 277.25-mile humbling of Mike McNamara). Aged 47, Beryl wanted to compete in the inaugural race but was prevented from doing so for not having the right road-racing credentials.

'She wanted to ride the very first Tour towards the end of her career and the British Cycling Federation didn't pick her,' recalls Denise, who finished the first women's full Tour de France in 1986 and was prevented from entering the 1987 edition by a freak training accident involving a snapped spindle and a broken back. 'She should have gone. Imagine the attention in the media it would have got. She was best British all-rounder, and one of [the races] is 100 miles, so I think she'd have had the stamina, don't you?' She adds: 'She still rode her bike and did her time trials. She was still winning. But that [rejection] really finished Mum.'

As for the Olympics, women's cycling didn't become an event until Beryl was 47. Too late, even for her. Just think of the medals and records she could have accumulated. Then the press would surely have appreciated her.

'It's impossible to imagine what she would have achieved,' says Denise, as she unlocks her bike and we part with a firm handshake (seems strange to recollect in these socially distanced days). There's pride there, but also that ... detachment. Sporting families. Always complicated.

So that's Beryl Burton: ruthless, relentless, brilliant, belligerent – and quite possibly the greatest Olympian Britain never had.

It's more than a year later and I'm out in Bahrain watching Mo Farah compete in an Ironman. A bit back to front, right? Let me explain.

Sir Mo has been selected as part of a Legends relay team taking part in the 70.3 Middle East Championships. 70.3 is one of the fastest-growing sectors in triathlon. It's another name for a half Ironman (70.3 is the number of miles you cover in total – 1.2-mile swim, 56-mile cycle, half-marathon run). There are thousands of amateur athletes competing in the event and some professionals, too – there's a whole race series, which had culminated in the World Championships in Nice, France, a couple of months before, in which I'd come second.

Midway between short-course Olympic triathlon and the full mental and physical torment of Ironman, 70.3 is one of my new fixations, and something I'll be focusing on more intently in the coming years. It's still got the tactical element of the shorter-course formats, only with the added challenge of racing for nearly four hours. But today, having just returned from another race in Western Australia, I'm here as a spectator. And also because I want to catch up with another member of this expensively assembled dream team: Mark Cavendish.

'Cav' has already done his bit, effortlessly nailing the 56-mile ride. Handing on to him was the third member of their team, Australian swimmer Chloe McCardel, who wouldn't have found the distance much trouble – Chloe is the veteran of 29 cross-Channel swims and world-record holder for the longest unassisted ocean swim, 77.3 miles. Now Cav and I are watching Mo passing every 20 minutes or so as he laps his way to 13.1 miles in the bright sunshine. It's quite therapeutic.

Cav is a real Northern boy's sporting hero. Widely regarded as the greatest sprinter in the history of cycling, he's claimed 48 Grand Tour stage wins during his career (the third highest in history), and 30 at the Tour de France. Only the great Eddy Merckx, with 34, is above him in cycling's greatest stage race. He's notched up 150 UCI victories in his career and, in 2011, he became Britain's first world road race champion since Tom Simpson won the event in San Sebastián 46 years earlier.

Back in 2012, while riding the Tour as part of Team Sky with eventual winner and runner-up, Bradley Wiggins and Chris Froome, he became the first person to win the final Champs-Élysées stage in four consecutive years. And four years later he claimed a quartet of stages in the 2016 Tour de France, including the opener, Mont-Saint-Michel to Utah Beach, putting him in the yellow jersey for the first time. You could see how much it meant to him.

Perhaps my favourite Cav Tour de France stage win came in Paris, in 2009, the year he took six stages. As is customary in the Tour, the winner of the general classification was already settled and uncontested – Alberto Contador, of Astana, with Lance Armstrong, also riding for Astana, in third (his placing was subsequently voided due to the doping revelations, with Bradley Wiggins, then of Garmin–Slipstream, promoted to third). But the most prestigious stage was still very much up for grabs.

The aerial footage showed the high-speed snake of riders sliding through the cordoned-off streets of Paris, building to the sprint finale. 'Everyone wants the wheel of the fastest man in the world, Mark Cavendish, and they're bumping shoulders to get it,' said the commentator. A sprint in cycling is highly tactical. You need to be positioned near the front to be able to challenge when the final sprint begins, but go too early and you give someone a free ride drafting you ('sitting on your wheel', in cycling terminology), possibly resulting in them using the saved energy to storm past you in the final metres. To add further complication, it's a team event, with lead-out riders doing their best to chaperone their top sprinter into a position from which they can be catapulted into the final frenetic, vein-popping acceleration to the line.

Stick on Cav's wheel, his competitors would have reasoned, and you at least stood a chance. But they had to be able to keep up. None could. The Manx missile, behind Mark Renshaw, 'the fastest lead-out man in the business', won by a huge margin, seemingly half the length of the Champs-Élysées, underlining his dominance.

I want to ask Cav about the Tour, about those explosive finishes, about the strain of riding a 200km stage that comes down to the final few inches. So, too, about trying to stay in a three-week race up and over those brutal Alpine or Pyrenean cols when you're built for sprinting. Cav has been called the Usain Bolt of cycling. But I don't recall Bolt ever having to run the 10,000m before lining up for the 100m.

But first I want to hear more about where he's from. Draw a line between my house and Belfast and it cuts straight through the Isle of Man. Given its topography and the conditions, it may as well be a small part of Yorkshire in the Irish Sea; if you're going to ride a bike there, you have to really want to. Cav – still – really, really does.

'Home environment is so important,' he says. 'I think it boils down to it taking you back to why you started, you know? I started racing when I was 11 maybe, and getting out wearing a jumper and some leggings from Next or something. And just riding out, being freezing, but just loving it. I think ultimately I'm still doing that. It's why I'm here. It's still the same roads.'

He tells me about the strong cycling heritage on the island, the group of riders that meets at the National Sports Centre in the capital, Douglas, every morning at 9.15am no matter what, to head out for a ride. Man or woman, weekend warrior or pro, five-hour loop or 90-minute blowout – everyone welcome to join. It sounds like the groups I've been part of all my life.

'We've all got the same mentality: that we go out and enjoy riding, race for signs, stuff like that. And there's always gonna be someone there you know. And whether they just do half the ride with you, or the whole thing, it doesn't matter. That's how it's been since I was young, and it's still like that.' I smile at the thought of, say, a junior lady or a grizzled veteran suddenly finding themselves locked in a sprint to a road sign with a 30-time stage winner of the Tour de France.

He explains that he's only really started doing 'efforts' in his training – targeted distances or set paces – in recent years. Prior to that it was mostly improvised, and seemingly all the better for it. 'I just love it. I never did specific efforts until just a couple of years ago. In fact, when I started doing them is when I didn't really win as much, you know? Like we always joke about that: our efforts came from racing. There's lanes here – it's like Yorkshire, you know – little lanes you can go down and so you'll race to get the best position, you're trying to brave it up in the crosswinds, and you regroup at the end. Every ride, someone just presses on, swinging their dick a bit. But it'll drive you on to stay with them.'

We stop talking and enjoy the race playing out in front of us. There are hundreds of runners, endorphins flowing. It's a great sight, and Cav – new to the world of triathlon – is impressed. He shakes his head. 'I've been to some sporting events in my time but I've never seen so much enthusiasm,' he says. 'That's Ironman,' I reply. Few other sports or events inspire such dedication.

I've known about Ironman since I was about nine. I was just discovering triathlon and my uncle was competing in them. The 2.4-mile swim, 112-mile bike ride and a marathon to finish seemed like a ridiculously long way then. It still does. The Ironman World Championships in Kona, Hawaii, have been on my radar ever since. It's been a matter of when and not if I would have a crack at the event. When, in 2019, I stood on the start line in Hawaii, it was only my second race over that distance ever. The first had been in Cork, western Ireland, when the swim was cancelled and it rained for every single one of the eight hours I was on the course. It didn't stop thousands of spectators from lining the streets and rural lanes. After the race, which I won, a local restaurant was kept open for me late into Sunday night, and I spent the whole evening being referred to as 'The Ironman' and not being allowed to pay for anything. An experience that definitely lived up to its reputation and the two-decade wait.

The race in Kona didn't go as I'd hoped and I immediately understood why so many had told me that it's such a hard race to get right. I was reduced to walking down the highway between the aid station oases, where I'd try to immerse as much of my pale Yorkshire skin in the ice buckets as I could. It's a brutally hard event. And it's one I want to conquer. It will be my primary focus in sport after this year.

We spot Mo, who's nearing the end of his second lap. He takes a wrong turn towards the finish. Spectators shout but he doesn't hear. Cav sprints off down the finishing straight – you can take the Manx Missile off the bike … – to put him right. A minute later, Mo is on the course again and Cav saunters back.

His relaxed demeanour belies a tough couple of years. Dimension Data, the South Africa-based team he was racing for, wasn't a great fit for him. He wasn't included in the team's roster for the 2019 Tour de France, the first time he'd missed the race since his début in 2007. This came after the team's performance manager, Rolf Aldag, who has worked with Cav for years, named him in the team's final eight, only to be over-ruled by the general manager, Doug Ryder. 'We've selected a team based on the route and how hard it is this year,' Ryder said at the time. 'Mark is a legend of this race and it's sad for this race that he's not here.'

This followed two nightmare seasons of illness and injury. In 2017, he had glandular fever for the first half of the season – a constant worry for athletes because it can lead to chronic fatigue and have you out for months, even years – before breaking his collarbone in a crash at the Tour de France and having to withdraw. Then, he was eliminated from the 2018 Tour mid-race after failing to make the cut on the short, very sharp mountain stage between Albertville and La Rosière, finishing just over an hour behind stage winner Geraint Thomas. The aim had been to get him through the mountain stages so he could challenge for more sprint stage wins later in the race. As Ryder commented: 'Cav has worked hard but the sport is brutal.' Mark later announced that he'd been struggling with Epstein–Barr virus, which causes glandular fever.

Now, having rejoined Deceuninck–Quick-Step after a diffi-cult year with Bahrain–McLaren, things are looking up. He narrowly missed out on his first win in three years at the one-day Grote Prijs Jean-Pierre Monseré in Belgium in March 2021 and picked up four wins in the Tour of Turkey a month later, and talk has turned to the possibility of his involvement in the delayed Tokyo Games, although he has conceded that it's highly unlikely to be on the track.

For someone so decorated, Cav's Olympics medal haul is modest. While there was a British cycling 'gold rush' in Beijing in 2008, he underachieved. This seemed to spur him on to his unprecedented period of success in road cycling. It was not until Rio, his third Games, that he had a medal of his own – silver in the men's omnium.

But where his dominance has never been questioned is at the sharp end of a road race. Let's for one moment put aside the considerable challenges – physiological, mental and technical – of getting yourself into contention for those final couple of kilometres. What about the decision-making under pressure, the pace judgement, the fearlessness in this game of high-speed chess? If you want to see just how incomprehensibly hard it is to win a sprint stage of a big race I urge you to watch the final stretch of his World Championships win in Copenhagen in 2011: a 260km race, 5 hours 40 minutes and 27 seconds of riding, and he wins by half a wheel. His breakthrough win in Milan–San Remo in 2009 was even tighter.

He smiles. 'I think there are two types of people, and this doesn't necessarily just apply to sport: racers and non-racers. You, you're a racer. Even if it looks impossible for you to do something physically, you're like a pitbull – you just grab on. I'm like that.

'But part of my nature as well is to obsess over stuff. Even as a kid. Things had to be in their place and things had to be right. The bike had to be right. Even my fucking knife and fork drawer had to be the way that I wanted it. And if it wasn't, that wasn't good enough. In sprinting, romanticists like to hear about the adrenaline and the elbow-to-elbow action. But I was never really like that; I kind of just see the gaps more than I see the other riders. It's a calculated thing, more a kind of process, you know?'

He explains what he means. 'It's standard practice now to do stuff like go through course maps, but it's actually not too long ago that nobody did it and I was like the only person that did. I'd go through Google Street View and look at Tour de France finishes. It's an everyday thing now.' Cav's photographic memory is well documented. *Telegraph* journalist Jonathan Liew wrote a piece in 2013 in which he challenged the Manxman to describe in detail the last kilometre of that 2009 race into San Remo. He described the last 10km instead.

When it all goes well, a cycling sprint can look like a thing of precision engineering, of technical and tactical perfection. But it only needs a crash to remind you of just what vanishingly small margins these sprinters are operating within. Harrogate in 2014 should have been one of Mark Cavendish's finest moments. *Le Grand Départ* had brought the Tour de France to Yorkshire for its opening three stages. The opener, from Leeds to Harrogate, was a loop of nearly 200km through Otley, Skipton, Hawes, Ripon, along roads I know intimately.

It will be one of my lasting regrets that I wasn't in the country to experience it first-hand. Instead, I was on a training camp in St Moritz, Switzerland. We were following the race as we ploughed up Swiss mountains, and we stopped in a mountainside restaurant to watch the last 20km of the race, sipping on hot chocolate and eating Engadine torte as we saw the riders fly past the Yorkshire crowds.

Those crowds were enormous, as was the expectation: 29-year-old Cavendish was at his peak, the fastest cyclist in the world, and the stage win, and the fabled yellow jersey, lay within reach. Then, with Prince Harry, the Duke and Duchess of Cambridge and thousands of others looking on, and millions watching at home, Cav collided with another rider and was catapulted over the handlebars. He remained lying on the road for several minutes. Later it was found that he had suffered ligament damage and dislocated his shoulder. His Tour was over. He later admitted that the pressure he'd been under in the build-up to that race had been on another level to anything he'd previously known.

I ask him about his time with Team Sky, racing the 2012 Tour de France with Chris Froome, as well as Bradley Wiggins and Richie Porte. Cav has always been outspoken, always seen himself as an outsider (he once described himself as the 'runt of the British cycling litter'). He's super-self-assured and doesn't mind showing it. He thrives on confrontation and seems to get most from himself when he has a point to prove. None of these seemed like perfect attributes for joining the uncomplaining ranks of the machine-like Team Sky.

He's since been critical of the team's tunnel vision and the joylessness – but never their work ethic. 'Having worked with all them at Sky, Froome and everyone, I can say there's a reason they won that much, and that's because they worked harder than anybody else I've ever seen in cycling. And not just the riders. All the backroom staff, the mechanics, everyone,' he tells me. 'But it was like a regime, you know?'

'If you join that team [now Team Ineos], you will become, physically, the best rider you can possibly be, without a doubt. Froome will have a lot of time to enjoy the fruits of his labour, but I don't necessarily – and I might be completely wrong – I don't necessarily think he enjoys his life right now. He doesn't have a life, he exists for it, which is why he's so much better than everyone else. Brad was the same; absolutely blinkered when he was on. Just existed for cycling.'

But I wonder if there's really that much daylight between Britain's three most famous cyclists of the past 25 years. All share a desire for constant improvement. It's clear that Cav, like many we've so far met, sees his career as a giant learning curve, rather than a fixed course to a pre-determined goal. Complacency is the enemy. And that obsessiveness – as with Beryl Burton – can't be turned off, even if they (we?) might occasionally wonder what life would be like without it. That's what continues to push him, at 35, to sign new contracts, to tear round the world, and to spend long periods away from his wife Peta and their four children (he once estimated that he sees his kids as little as 60 days a year).

'Once you start looking back at what you've done without picking the faults in it, you're gonna stop moving forward. Even if you win, you still have to find out how you could better it for next time,' he says.

'How many people, not just sportspeople, do something in life and then just spend the rest of their lives looking back over their shoulders at it, with a smug smile on their faces. But as you know, you're only as good as your last result, aren't you? The last few years have taught me that. Everything I've done in my career, like, and then you get fucking Continental [the third tier of professional road cycling] riders laughing at you now. And you're like, "Are you kidding me?" But that's what it's like in professional sport. Things move on so quick and nobody misses you.'

But they do, and they will. Just look at Beryl.

Flicking through my notes from my meetings with Cav, and with Beryl's daughter Denise, I'm struck by the similarity of the following quotes:

Denise: 'Mum was incredibly competitive in everything she did. Everything. She liked gardening, knitting, baking – but she had to be the best and the fastest. She had to win.'

Cavendish: 'Ever since I was a kid, I had to win at whatever I did. I didn't always win, but I'd be pissed off if I didn't. Just striving to be the best you can be wasn't good enough for me – I had to be the best of everyone: spelling tests at school, athletics, everything. If I was playing Monopoly at Christmas, I had to win. It's not necessarily healthy but it's just how I was.'

Following up, Cav does say with a laugh: 'I'm better [at that sort of thing] now. I always said before I had kids that I'm never letting them win. And that just went out of the window!'

One up on Beryl there, then.

10

STRESS-BUFFERING, AFFILIATION AND FEELING THE LOVE

The Bob Graham Round is one of the most testing endurance events in the world – a 66-mile run around the English Lake District incorporating 42 mountains and 26,900ft of ascent. It's not a conventional race, as there are no course markers or marshals. It's a self-timed, self-navigated challenge. Most attempts come in summer, your best chance of avoiding the notorious Lakes weather, and all must begin and end at the Moot Hall, in the Cumbrian town of Keswick, and be completed in under 24 hours. It's a beast of an undertaking – completed by fewer than 2,500 fell-running enthusiasts since its inception in 1932. It's on my post-retirement list, for sure, though I'm not convinced that even a career of Olympic-standard endurance sport will be adequate preparation.

The slender, swarthy figure who set off on the loop just after dawn on Sunday 8 July 2018 wasn't aiming to complete it in 24 hours. He was looking for a time of roughly half that; he was attempting to break the seemingly unbreakable Bob Graham record, set by Lakeland stonemason and godfather of fell-running Billy Bland 36 years earlier. As word of the attempt got out, locals began to line the course and gather at transition points, spots where roads intersect the planned route, allowing for refuelling or a switch of support runners. The fell-running community isn't easily impressed, and would certainly never have their heads turned by hype, but they recognised that the humble, ferociously determined, boundlessly talented athlete in their midst was the real deal.

Rumours that Catalan endurance runner Kílian Jornet might have been lining up a Bob Graham record attempt had long persisted in the Lakes. And now here he was, out on the fells in his sleeveless blue vest, turned-around white cap and shades, with his more than one million Instagram and Twitter followers poised for updates – and presumably desperately trying to find Keswick on the map. The timing was a surprise: Kílian had broken his fibula in a skiing accident just four months before. He'd entered, and won, the Mont Blanc Marathon, with its nearly 9,000ft of ascent, a week earlier (recording a time of 3:54:54 despite the sapping heat). Clearly his leg was in decent shape – but would he be sufficiently rested for such a mammoth task?

This was a man, however, who has made a career out of achieving the impossible: winning numerous ski mountaineering world cups; obliterating the field in countless ultramarathons (technically, any race longer than a marathon), from the Ultra-Trail du Mont-Blanc to the Hardrock Hundred and the Western States Endurance Run; a multiple winner of the Skyrunner World Series; and (his most recent obsession) the holder of a string of FKTs, or Fastest Known Times, for there-and-back ascents of some of the world's most iconic mountains: the Matterhorn, Denali and Mont Blanc. And in the previous year, he'd blasted up Everest twice in a *single week* in an attempt to record the FKT, to the mountaineering world's astonishment. As the star of lavish, drone-shot films with emotive scores and stunning mountain backdrops, he's the closest thing the endurance-running world has to a rock star – and here he was, closing in on Billy Bland's record.

Keswick's market square was rammed with people long before Kílian ran back into town. A cowbell-jangling runner warned of his imminent arrival. The crowd parted to create a path up to the steps of the hall, which he climbed before collapsing onto the top step – 12 hours and 52 minutes after leaving that very spot. He'd broken the record by a full hour (and one minute). A beaming Billy Bland presented him with a glass of champagne (the last thing he'd have wanted) and sat down next to him. And there they stayed, the septuagenarian and the 30-something, the Cumbrian and the Catalan, as lines of people queued to climb up the steps and shake the hand of this slight, diminutive running giant.

It's not so much *what* Kílian has achieved, but *how*, that I'm keen to explore. His outlook appears different to other athletes. The records, the wins, the plaudits; they all seem almost a by-product of the life he has chosen, rather than the main drivers. When we speak, he doesn't talk of a training regime, he talks of life. 'Love' and 'fun' pepper his speech, expressed in his charmingly thick Spanish accent. He smiles often. And why wouldn't he?

He spends his days among some of the world's most ravishing peaks in the Romsdalen valley in Norway, around 60 miles from Ålesund, where he lives with his Swedish mountain-runner girlfriend Emelie Forsberg and their baby. It's a simple yet utopian existence, in which they have a house by the water and grow their own food. The surrounding mountains are where he trains, or rather experiments – sometimes with skis, at other times with trail shoes, occasionally with crampons and an ice axe. You and I would visit just to gawp at such natural beauty; he's out there for days at a time (do watch the

YouTube video of his attempt to tackle the seven summits of Romsdalen in one day – it's breathtakingly photogenic). It's one hell of a workplace – not that he would see it that way. And that arguably lies at the heart of his immense success.

Jon Albon, a world OCR (obstacle course racing) champion, and also a leading athlete in skyrunning – a series of steep-incline mountain races staged above 2,000m – has competed against Kílian. He thinks he's one of the most extraordinary athletes in history.

'There's something a bit special about him. From both an athletic point of view and also from an approach to the lifestyle and the racing – how he goes about doing what he does. He seems like a really nice, chilled-out sort of guy who would love to be in the mountains running around. Obviously he enjoys racing and is very competitive but it's more about the lifestyle, the ride.' The late Ueli Steck, the Swiss mountaineer and great friend of Kílian's who died in a fall on Nuptse in the Himalayas in 2017, said: 'Of course he does these amazing performances, but I think really in his deep heart, Kílian likes to play out there and to test his limits.'

The mountain environment has always been a part of his life. Kílian was raised in a refuge, Cap de Rec, in the Pyrenees, and by the age of five he had summited the highest peak in the Pyrenees, 11,167ft Aneto, with his mountain-guide father. He began his competitive career as a 13-year-old ski mountaineer. 'My parents loved mountaineering,' he tells me. 'I started walking at 10 months and we started doing long hikes: five, six hours in the mountains, climbing a summit. It's a game – you're outdoors, you are playing: who will be the first to find this flower, who will be the first to the summit. You keep doing that and finally it makes the processes of training invisible.'

I explain that it was the same for me, especially in the early days of my career. I did a huge amount of training from school, escaping in my lunch hour, and a lot of it would be just about 'I fancy running here today – I want to see what's there.' It was the same with cycling. I wanted to go out with my friends and track down a particularly big hill in the Yorkshire Dales. So it was kind of exploratory and I think a lot of that came from my parents, who would take us out on a lot of walks, hill climbing. Just that basic love of the outdoors.

We talk about how he trains for so many diverse disciplines, and the benefits of this for mental freshness and sharing the physical load on muscle groups. He has developed a system of pacing himself in the mountains – partly out of appreciation for the vistas, partly practicality. 'It's important to understand the terrain, where the snow or outcrops are. It's always easier if you are in a beautiful landscape. I get overexcited and say, "I should probably turn around, but it looks so beautiful." Then you train longer, and because you train longer, you do more hours and you run faster.'

Such a simple ethos.

I explain that I often have to restrict myself, through fear that a spontaneously extended session might impinge on the schedule for the next day. 'I'm more relaxed than that,' he says. 'Mostly that's why I hate racing – because before a race I must rest, which is not fun. It's strange, though: sometimes I rest before a race and the race goes well. But other days I have been training a lot, 80 to 100 hours a week in the mountains, finishing on a Friday and racing on the Sunday, and I'm expecting to be destroyed but I feel really, really good. It's like, "What's going on?" I think it's interesting to try things and see how it was, and to try to understand.'

I feel envious chatting to Kílian. Sometimes I have to explain to people that being a professional athlete means you don't get to do a lot of the things you'd like to do; I'd love to drop everything, meet Kílian in the Alps and run one of the iconic peaks together. But I'm already thinking about my training sessions tomorrow, my race next week, my commitments. It's a fantastic life, of course it is, but there are actually a lot of things out there that you can't do. So I guess that leads us on to the sacrifices that we have to make.

Kílian understands. 'I know that if you want to do something great, you can't do a lot of other things. If you want to open a door, you need to close another. It needs to be a conscious choice. I think the problem is when you just follow the mood, and then you just hit the wall because you haven't been thinking about it. But since I started to say, "OK, I want to be professional – I want to be doing this," then it feels less like sacrifice, more like prioritising.'

This ownership of the process is so important. I touched on this when I spoke about dropping out of Cambridge. I decided it was too hard for me to be able to do the training I wanted while studying. It was a really, really difficult decision and my parents weren't happy. Looking back now, with two Olympic golds in the sock drawer and a career I love, it seems like the right thing to have done. Hindsight. What a wonderful thing.

Kílian, it transpires, is the same. He wanted to go to Barcelona to study design, but didn't want to go to a city because it was not in the mountains and he could not continue training. So he moved to Font-Romeu to start studying sports science at the University of Perpignan. Font-Romeu was perfect – it's at altitude (1,800m), with snow on the doorstep and several alpine and cross-country ski resorts nearby. He'd go straight from university to training and not have a social life ('I'm not a very sociable person, so it was easier').

We've already looked at the science of suffering with Chris Froome and endurance-performance professor Samuel Marcora. People think that racing must be so painful, but it's often not, because all the time you're thinking about how to beat the person next to you, the tactics and the strategy of it. For much of Kílian's racing life, the competitors are more dispersed, and it's more of a solitary race (particularly for him, way out in front). How does he manage the discomfort, particularly over periods of 20 hours or more? What are the mental strategies he deploys?

'In longer races, you need to accept the pain for many hours, and then it can be many things. Things like counting the time to the next refuelling station, giving yourself small goals. You cannot think "It's 50 miles to the end"; that will destroy you. It's easier to say, "In two miles it's a refuelling station," so my goal is to arrive there, and then it's the next and then the next. So small goals.' This is like Alastair Cook and his ball-by-ball philosophy, which we heard about in Chapter 6.

He talks about the associative and dissociative thoughts we covered in previous chapters, and his experience of both. 'If it's very far and you are alone, you can let the mind wander, to imagine the area's history, but you need to mix this with concentration, to keep coming back every now and then and keep pushing hard. I think if you arrive at a race and you have been racing a lot before, and doing a lot of press conferences, or meeting with fans, you will not push as much as if you have been just training hard and visualising the race or visualising winning or doing something great.

'Then, for example, in high altitude your brain is kind of in disconnect, and the only thing you want to do, every second, is turn back and go down. It's too hard, and that's when your preparation and what you've done before is very important: the weeks before, the motivation, the visualisation.'

The high altitude, and all the associated risks, set Kílian apart. He's had both training and race buddies die. What's his decision-making like when breathing the rarefied air of Mount Everest or Denali, and how does he make sure that he's giving that part of his mind the right amount of energy it needs to make those really important decisions? The smaller mountains are fine – nutrition plan set up, a get-out plan if conditions deteriorate. But above 8,000m, in the so-called death zone, it's completely different, because your brain no longer functions as it should.

The effective concentration of oxygen at 8,000m is around 7.7 per cent, about one-third of that at sea level. The hypoxia induced by being at that altitude impairs brain as well as physical function. Early climbers called the condition 'mental laziness', believing that it was the mind's choice that it couldn't work effectively. More recently, it's become accepted that impaired vision and judgement, along with hallucinations, are all symptoms of breathing the thin air.

Kílian's response to this? Make the decision stark and binary. Yes or no. If I go on, will it kill me? At the same time as trying to haul himself up the highest mountain in the world, his impaired brain is making life-and-death decisions. He's not consciously weighing up the exact snow and weather conditions, his fatigue levels and the amount of food he's eating. He can't. He doesn't have the capacity to do so with his conscious mind.

Decision-making in sport is an enthralling topic in itself, irrespective of whether it's a matter of life or death. The leaders in the field of behavioural economics and decision theory are Amos Tversky and Daniel Kahneman. They argued that the subconscious part of our brain (System 1) makes the lion's share of our decisions because it has the processing power to do so. The conscious part of our brain (System 2) is slower and requires more energy, so the brain avoids using this where it can. In sport, psychologists talk about mental processes becoming automatic – unconscious, efficient and System 1. But this efficiency, according to Tversky and Kahneman, can come at a cost: heuristics. Mental shortcuts to save the brain time and energy.

The availability heuristic is probably my favourite. It means we make judgement on the likelihood of an outcome based on how easily a relevant example comes to mind. I had wondered for years why athletes seem to get exactly the same injury as each other within weeks of the first athlete suffering from it. Then I read about research that showed doctors with recent experience of a condition are more likely to subsequently diagnose that condition.

Kílian has a wealth of relevant experience and knowledge to rely on. By making his decision binary, he allows his subconscious mind to access this incredible resource and use its processing power to come to an optimal decision, hopefully without the conscious mind or an unwanted heuristic getting in the way and hijacking the process.

'You need to make things really, really simple,' he says. 'Not, "Should I hold off drinking now because it will be bad for my stomach?" or "This guy is attacking now." Over 8,000m, it's only two choices: if I continue, will I die or not? That is the only decision that matters. You know that you will be hurting, you know that it will be hard. I think you need to be able to strip away everything that is emotional, so take away happiness, take away fear, take away all the emotions, and to think only of the dangers.

'For example, if I get cold and I have hypothermia I die; or if I have a brain oedema [a build-up of fluid around the brain due to the extreme altitude], I will die in five hours, or if I fall … so all the time you are thinking, "Do I feel like I'm getting an oedema?" No, so I continue. "Do I feel cold?" No, so I continue. "Is this stretch too technical?" No, so I continue.

'So it's about only these decisions and about making the correct ones, because it's easy to get too excited. If you climb to the summit and are too excited' – so called summit fever – 'then you will make mistakes in the way down and you will probably die. So you must be super-cold-blooded. Not having any kind of emotion.'

The longer I speak to Kílian, the more I realise that he's a total one-off. He never stops innovating, even after reaching training and performance levels many of us would see as optimal. He shifts his focus constantly, keeping his body and his motivation sharp. He talks of using competition to benefit training, rather than the other way round, of finding stimulus in different methods – for example, training for 100 hours, super-hard, and then going to a race ('maybe it's worse and maybe it's not,' he says). This is incredible. Brutal trial and error. He's trying different training plans like others might try on outfits. And that, in turn, provides him with added impetus.

'To try these experiments, that's motivating. For example, high altitude and high intensity. I was at 6,000m in an artificial altitude [in a chamber] and I was training for one hour at 15km/h. And then I was doing flat, then incline, then on the VO_2 max for like five minutes, and then five minutes at normal pace. That was super-interesting' (most would call it barbaric).

'After that I was, maybe for three hours, numb. But afterwards it was a really big boost for the body, and it was super-interesting going to the high mountains afterwards. So I am excited about these kinds of things, and seeing how I can apply them to mountain projects.'

Innovation comes in several forms: the obvious technical or equipment improvements, and the more subtle mindset that enables someone to decide they can do something that no one has ever done before. Beryl Burton innovated to believe she could beat the men at a time when such things were unthinkable. Kílian decided he could run faster for longer than anyone else. He decided he could scale peaks more quickly and lighter than anyone who'd gone before: summiting Mount Everest in a matter of hours, rather than days, carrying light equipment rather than packs with sleeping bags and stoves. The FKTs trend is not his alone; it has been gathering momentum and popularity. But it takes a particular type of person to take this to the extreme of the world's highest mountain.

He's already thinking about what's next. 'Everest was very interesting for me first because I was able to get to this altitude, and second because it was possible to do really fast ascents and recover very fast. So I think that now we can possibly link different summits in the Himalayas. At home you can do like 10 summits and you can start running home. That's normal to do in the UK or here in Norway. But in the Himalayas, it's like you do an expedition, so you stay two months in a base camp and climb one summit. I think in the future it will be possible to be in a village in the mountains and stay there and maybe run to Everest and then follow the ridge to Lhotse and then go down to another village and then climb another summit. In a way I think it's what Everest was kind of letting me know – that this will be possible in the future.'

Of all the people I've spoken to, indeed that I've met, in top-flight sport, no one comes close to having Kílian's perspective. He has found a different way of doing things, turning everything on its head. Journey rather than destination, training rather than success, lifestyle first, achievements second. I wonder how much we could all learn from him. Never mind work–life balance. How about merging the two.

He's humble – but not in a calculating or contrived way; when he spends his days dwarfed by his working environment, it's not surprising. Above all, he recognises the fundamental silliness of what we do in equating sport with life in terms of importance. No great surprise given the brushes with mortality he's endured, the colleagues and friends he's lost.

'I don't think what I do, what we do, is anything important,' he tells me quietly. 'It's sport, so in a way it's a game and we are doing something that is very selfish. It's for the emotion at the end, it's nothing productive – we are not like teachers that are forming a new generation of people, or doctors helping people live.

'I think what separates those who are really at the top is knowledge of yourself and having the vision of where you want to go.'

I'm minded of these words when I meet Anna Hemmings. Anna had been recommended to me by a mutual friend as one of the world's leading thinkers on the transferable benefits of high-performance sporting mentalities and methodologies in business. Her theories are far from just theoretical; they're based on her own experience as Britain's greatest female kayaker. In her career, she won six World Championship gold medals in the K1 and K2 events (the numbers relating to the number of athletes in the kayaks), and competed at the Sydney and Beijing Olympics. Since retiring in 2009 she has set up a high-performance-training consultancy for business, Beyond the Barriers, and is a sought-after motivational speaker.

She's the ultimate high achiever. She's confident, broad shouldered, with a smile to match. But her career wasn't an endless procession of victory. She's known some incredibly low moments – and her insight is all the more valuable for it.

When we chat about how she got into kayaking as a nine-year-old, like Kílian she uses the word 'love' a lot. 'Excitement' too. It was about splashing around the river. At first. As a young member of the prestigious Elmbridge Canoe Club, on the Thames in Surrey ('our goal is to be the best canoe club in the country and then the world', its website proudly states), she remembers being inspired by older athletes returning from competition. One gave her a T-shirt from the Olympics. When British kayak legend Ivan Lawler won his first World Championship gold in the kayak marathon event he brought his medal in. 'I was like, "Well, if he can do that, and he's a guy at my club who I train with, I can get one of those."'

Anna recalls her desire to compete in the Olympics pre-dating her knowledge of the event in which that might be. 'We watched the 1984 Olympics at home. My mum was big into watching sport. I was just, "God, the Olympics, this amazing thing!"'

Here was the perfect combination of a high-achieving environment and intrinsic motivation – and she thrived. 'You're training two or three times a day, endurance stuff like you guys. It's hours and hours, and you're getting up early, you do a session at 7.30am, back again at 10am, back again at 4pm. I loved that – in a sadistic kind of way – that feeling of improving. Pushing myself, hurting my body. It's odd for most people to comprehend.'

Not for me, I tell her. The older I've got, the more I've sought out competitive training situations, because I can't get anywhere near the intensity I need by not doing it. That's not to say I don't do a lot of non-competitive training, as it were. You can't go at it hammer and tongs for 35 hours a week. It's just that, for the toughest sessions, I find that I can get the most out of myself when I'm in some way trying to beat the person next to me. Plus, it's what I enjoy most.

Anna's the same. 'Yeah, you get a little boost, don't you, every time you win that effort. I love that every day. You have to love every day; you can't just love the medal in four years' time. That's not enough.'

These days, in her new career, she does a lot of work around intrinsic and extrinsic motivation – the latter being the rewards at the end, the medals or the records, or the salary in a work situation. But if you're doing something every day, often the same thing, you need to have intrinsic motivation otherwise you'll be miserable. The truth, of course, is that all manner of things motivate different people. Author Dean Spitzer identified eight 'desires of motivation', or drivers, for people. It might be recognition, it might be achievement or competence or power. But also on that list is something known as 'affiliation': that is, bonding and interacting with the people you work with.

When motivators aren't aligned or addressed, you don't get the best out of people.

Anna says: 'A lot of times companies focus on the extrinsic stuff, like the pay and the bonuses and celebration of achievement. But a manager or a leader has to recognise that motivations are different for different people. So if I was leading a team and my motivations are achievement and recognition, and I'm constantly creating recognition for my team, but they might be driven by affiliation, and they're all about the people and the team around them, then that's not going to work.'

Anna thought her motivators were exclusively recognition and achievement. And then she got ill.

When people hear about chronic fatigue syndrome (CFS) among sportspeople, they tend to conflate fatigue and tiredness, and assume that it is a question of overtraining. CFS is far more complex, insidious and unexplained than that. An estimated quarter of a million people in the UK, and millions worldwide, have been diagnosed with it – alternative names include myalgic encephalomyelitis (ME) and post-viral fatigue syndrome (PVFS) – and the World Health Organization classifies it as a neurological condition.

Looking back, Anna realises she had signs for about a year and a half, periods when she couldn't train, the worst probably lasting six weeks. Then she'd resume training. Then another two weeks off. The doctors also thought it was because she was overtraining. 'It wasn't,' she says. 'Just before it got really bad, I was training so light, because we were so scared of over-training.' That's when she was diagnosed.

In true athlete tradition, she wasn't going to accept the diagnosis and just give up. 'I was like, "I have to find something to help me get out this illness." I refused to listen to those people who said, "Yeah, you're going to be ill for 20 years, there's no cure." I tried dozens of different treatments to try to recover. Then a friend, one of my sponsors, introduced me to someone who'd tried something called reverse therapy, and I was just like, "Yeah, I just gotta try it." I think that's part of being an athlete – that you try things and ask, "Is this gonna make me better?"'

Reverse therapy, devised by the British psychotherapist Dr John Eaton, focuses on various triggers causing the symptoms. These might be relationships, pressure or your environment more generally. In the time leading up to when she got ill, Anna went from training with a group in Florida to returning to the UK for the racing season and training on her own, without a coach, without any of those training partners. Suddenly the fun was gone. The friendly rivalry was gone. And she began to suffer.

'As much as I wouldn't consider myself to be someone who needed a big team environment, that affiliation, it turns out I did. And that was a big trigger for me – training on my own, not having that support network, that added stress of feeling like you're alone. And then having a coach who was in another country who I'd have to ring up, in a different time zone. Not feeling like I got the support.

'I didn't realise this at the time but I remember having a brilliant training programme and I thought that that was the ultimate thing; it didn't matter about anything else. If I had a good training programme and I worked hard, it would be fine. And it was for a while, and I got my best results – before I got ill, I probably was at my quickest that I'd ever been. But it just wasn't sustainable, because emotionally it wasn't right for me. And I didn't even notice.'

The other problem was that she didn't speak up when she didn't get the support. One of the biggest triggers is non-expression of emotion. 'Looking back on my career, I thought I was very self-motivated, so sure I could train on my own, could push myself, that I didn't need someone there to make me work hard. But actually I needed that environment for my own emotional well-being. So that's a really interesting reflection.'

After she recovered, Anna made it a priority to have a group of people around her, a training partner, a coach in the same country – on the same riverbank, right beside her every day – and a good environment. Not necessarily a massive group, but a group nonetheless. 'Now, when I do my motivation profile, affiliation is much higher on my list than I ever realised it was before.'

She adds: 'When people suffer with depression for example, they isolate themselves and it just makes it worse. They don't speak up and they don't share stuff, and that was something that I didn't do very well, even when I was ill. I didn't share it with people. As an athlete you've got your "I'm tough" poker face on. You'd never show weakness on the start line, even though you're carrying an injury. You're like, "No, I'm fine, I'm hardcore." And so even when I was still ill, I was still hard-core. And that wasn't the time to be like that. And it took reverse therapy treatment, working with this chap, to realise that actually it's okay to show some weakness and to show vulnerability.'

*   *   *

I'm keen to delve deeper into this. As I know all too well, competitive sport is not a particularly empathetic place. Projecting strength is something that becomes ingrained in you. I've certainly done it, and seen it. Probably the best example is when injury strikes. To get help with the injury you have to admit this frustrating 'weakness', first to yourself, then to someone else – a coach, doctor or physiotherapist. It's all too easy to let the projection of strength outweigh the need to admit weakness.

As this book has shown so far, top-flight sport is all about tiptoeing around the very limits of human endurance, both mental and physical. The demands are considerable. Safety nets need to be laid down. Luckily, things are changing.

Professor David Lavallee, the first ever Professor of Duty of Care in Sport whom we met in Chapter 8, has done some key research on the transitions that athletes make through sport and after sport, and has a database of more than 15,000 elite or professional athletes that have retired. A big finding is that – perhaps counter-intuitively – those sportspeople who engage in career-transition planning demonstrate an uplift in performance while still playing. The December 2018 study, focusing on the National Rugby League in Australia and called 'Engagement in Sport Career Transition Planning Enhances Performance', also found that people who were preparing for another career after retiring, or had other projects, stayed within their sport for longer and also within their clubs. 'So a triple win there: a win for the individual, a win for the club and a win for the sport overall,' as he puts it.

Lavallee says he's noticed a real shift in the way that people are looking at this topic. 'The performance gains in world-class systems over the next 20 years will not come from technology or facilities but by providing support in areas such as mental health and career-transition planning. And these gains will not be marginal gains, they will be significantly greater.'

What about those 'other projects' that he speaks of? Surely they're just a distraction? 'If the value that the athlete places on the other things that they're doing is greater than the pressure to just focus solely on sport, it opens up this potential to achieve these gains.' He laughs. 'Sorry for the psychobabble, but the theory around that is called "stress buffering": when someone is able to broaden out their identity. The caveat is that they must want to do whatever it is; they're not being told to do it, or forced to do it.'

So by writing this book I may already be accruing performance gains? 'Could be,' he answers. I must tell my coach.

It's a huge topic, this, and goes to the heart of identity in sport. Retirement is something that haunts pretty much everyone in my profession. Who was it who said sportspeople are the only ones who die twice? I'm past 30 now, which is when any athlete starts looking over their shoulder. 'What are you going to do after sport?' is easily in the top three questions I get asked most frequently. And is easily my least favourite. 'What are you going to be doing in 5 to 10 years?' I often retort. Most people, sportsperson or not, don't have an answer at their fingertips. I'm always aware deep down, however, that it's not quite the same. When I finally hang up the Lycra suit (which I'll be glad to see the back of!), I'll be turning my back on not just my job and hobby but an identity built up over 25 years.

For Ian Botham, this was one of the biggest problems he encountered while president of the Professional Cricket Association – players who'd been cocooned in a cricket environment from 15, 16 years of age, to 37, then dropped back into society with no direction. 'You're living a life that most kids would think is wonderful and would love to do, until you get that letter on your 30th birthday and you're no longer required,' Botham tells me when we meet. 'And that's a real problem in cricket, certainly, but I think it's a problem in all professional sport. We had all kinds of problems: alcoholism, drug problems. All sorts.'

The surprisingly progressive National Rugby League – the Australian version of rugby league's Super League – is leading the way on this now, according to Lavallee. They've stopped referring to 'players' or 'athletes' and just term them 'people who play in the NRL', in part to help alleviate the stress. 'To give them the label of an athlete when they were trying to broaden out their sense of self didn't make sense, so they made lots of changes over several years to be able to create that culture so they were able to break down this dissonance,' Lavallee says.

We talk about track cyclist Callum Skinner, whom I know from the Rio Olympics where he won gold in the team sprint and silver in the individual sprint behind Team GB teammate Jason Kenny. He retired in 2019, aged 26, because he felt that British Cycling did not give him enough support when he told them of his mental-health problems. He said he wanted to work with British Cycling to help 'make the athlete experience more human'.

A few months later British Cycling announced a new mental-health screening programme to improve support for athletes. Dr Nigel Jones, head of medical services for the Great Britain Cycling Team, said: 'We took the decision to revise our approach to athlete mental health and well-being based on the acknowledgement that, as an elite sports team, we operate in a high-challenge, high-support environment.'

I explain to Professor Lavallee about the active decision taken by both myself and Kílian to embrace a sporting life, and the strength we've derived from that. Without being too crude about it, I think it can be quite easy for people to fall into sport. When you look at it from the outside, you wouldn't think that could be possible – that someone could be on a world-class programme or be a professional cricketer or rugby player simply because they were a decent player at a certain age and didn't know what else to do. But it happens all the time.

He answers: 'Self-identity is a really malleable construct and it changes from week to week and day to day, but those intentions people have and the decisions that they make and then the motivations that they have behind that helps strengthen them. I think once you made that decision, your athletic identity became very strong and more exclusive, and you've been able to benefit from that really significantly.'

But, he adds: 'People are really prone to distressful reactions if they lose control of that thing. If you'd got injured soon after making that call, you'd probably have been thinking, "I should have done this, I should have done that."

'I have this theory about the maturity of the system – that the more mature it is, the more likely this sort of stuff is to come out. And I actually think the UK system is mature enough to give people a voice. Callum Skinner is such a good example of someone the system has lost. If I were to give you three words on how duty of care is defined, they'd be "support when needed" – and the temporal bit of that is massive.

'As you know, sports science and coaches take you right to the edge, absolutely to the edge, but they have to put that support around you to be able to allow you to take those risks to be able to achieve everything you want to. To take those risks and then be able to pull you back from that. They can't do it in such a way that that risk isn't managed.'

* * *

Anna Hemmings does a lot of work around heart rate variability (HRV) and managing anxiety – 'that peak state before you start a race', as she calls it. For business and sport, it's based on the work of the HeartMath Institute in Boulder Creek, California. A scan of its website shows it's big on harmony, kindness, compassion, forgiveness. It talks about the quantifiable benefits of 'adding heart' to our daily activities and connections. 'We are at the dawn of recognising love as the new transformational intelligence.' Lord knows what Beefy would make of this, but I'm interested in learning more.

HRV is a measure of the variation in time between each heartbeat – something that's controlled by the autonomic nervous system (ANS). The ANS is subdivided into two large components: the sympathetic and the parasympathetic nervous system. The former activates what is known as the fight-or-flight mechanism. The latter does the opposite and inhibits the sympathetic nervous system.

Such things as stress, poor sleep, unhealthy diet, dysfunctional relationships, isolation or solitude and lack of exercise, experienced over a long period of time, can cause the balance to be disrupted, and your fight-or-flight response can shift into overdrive. Checking your HRV is a good way to identify imbalances. A lower score is associated with depression – or anxiety.

Anna explains: 'It's about getting into a coherent state, as they call it, which can be measured and identified on a computer or on an app. Creating this coherent state allows us to be aligned, mentally, emotionally or physically. So our autonomic nervous system is in balance. When we're in that state, we feel balanced, energised, the mind is in an optimal state.'

Kílian, I think, spends a fair bit of time here.

Anna tells me how positive emotions will create a coherent, balanced heart rhythm, and negative ones, an incoherent rhythm. 'When we are feeling anxious to the point of, you know, super-high sympathetic-system drive, then we're in a very incoherent heart state, which is obvious as an athlete. But when you're feeling calm, when you're feeling excited, when you're feeling content, all of that, then you will get the more coherent heart rhythm.'

There's a lot of work being done around this: when we are in a positive state, when we experience positive emotions – not just positive thoughts but positive emotions – we trigger the production of dehydroepiandrosterone (DHEA) in the adrenal glands. This hormone is a performance enhancer – it generates energy and boosts the immune system – whereas when we feel negative emotions, we're triggering cortisol, the so-called stress hormone. Frustration, anger, fear and anxiety all release cortisol, and when cortisol levels are increased over a long period of time, there are lots of health implications. So we're talking not just performance but health.

'I do a lot of training around resilience in the business world, where everyone's stressed,' says Anna. 'The sympathetic system is being triggered hour after hour, due to a deadline, due to a conflict, due to being shouted at by your boss. And so being able to create balance in that system, in the space of 90 seconds, is so powerful for people in the business world – in the same way that it is for athletes to be able to sit on the start line and use a breathing technique to bring your heart rate down if it's too high, or your hands are shaking. To be able to create calm in the system.'

Balance in an office environment is one thing. I'm not sure it would be desirable on the start line of an Olympic final. Frustration, anger, fear and anxiety have all driven me at different times. It's a balance, isn't it, because anxiety at the right times is evidently really important, I say.

'Absolutely. But there's a level some athletes get to where they're too anxious. In the business world, too. And you're just drained. So someone who is afraid of public speaking has got to do a presentation to the board, and their voice is quivering, their hands are shaking and their heart's pounding – you know, that's not an ideal state to be in. And so being able to use a technique that calms you is great. I completely agree we need a level of anxiety to perform at our best, but there's a balance.'

I wonder whether the best athletes and sportspeople are those who have an innate understanding of such things – the importance of a supportive environment; the balancing of anxiety levels; the broadening of interests to allow for Professor Lavallee's stress buffering; perhaps being open to feedback and knowing when to express vulnerability?

'The people who are doing it really well, we probably don't see so much of, or they've already risen to the higher levels,' says Anna. 'I think people realise that you've got to have a degree of talent, for sure. But the best athletes are the ones that have an innate understanding of these things, a capability to perform, and who can also learn. That's got to be your combination – where they're already up here, but they know they can learn and get even higher.'

Kílian has certainly got higher. In performance. In optimisation of lifestyle. In altitude. So strong are the parallels between this amazing athlete and the thinking and experiences of Anna Hemmings that I'm tempted to introduce the two of them and leave them to put their heads together to solve a few other issues. Like world peace. Much has been written about Kílian's extraordinary physiology. But, for me, his real strengths lie in his mastery of the optimised environment, the management of anxiety, and his knowledge and control of self. When you're involved in life-and-death decision-making in the Himalayan death zone, you wouldn't want it any other way.

11

THE LUCK OF THE BOUNCE AND BEING TOO SMALL TO FAIL

Have you heard the parable of the old Chinese farmer? He lived with his son, and they were very poor. They had one horse on which they relied, but one day the farm gate was left open and it escaped. The villagers commiserated with him. 'That's so bad,' they said. He shrugged. 'Hard to say.'

The next day the horse returned – trailed by a group of wild horses. 'More horses, that's good,' the villagers said. The old man shrugged. 'Hard to say.' A week later, the farmer's son was training one of the wild horses and was thrown, breaking his leg. 'So unlucky.' 'Hard to say.' A messenger arrived in the village the next week to enlist all the young men for an upcoming war. The farmer's son couldn't go. 'That's good,' said the villagers ...

And so it went on.

Listening to the softly spoken Cumbrian in front of me discuss the ups and downs of his career, the twists, the turns, the (apparent) luck and (seeming) crushing misfortune, it's impossible not to think of this parable and the philosophy in which it's rooted.

A talented rugby union player and junior international, he was at his peak in the mid-1990s, when the game went professional, and, in 1998, he took leave from his job as a PE teacher to join Leeds Tykes full-time. Good news? Hard to say. The following year, the impact of another player hitting the tackle bag he was holding tore his hamstring off the bone. He was badly crocked – and out of contract. Huddersfield offered him a player-coaching job, but on the very day he was driving there to sign his contract, his wife went into labour, his daughter was born and pen was never put to paper. Bad news (for his career)? Hard to say.

A job as coach of the academy side at Leeds subsequently came up. He applied, and got it. Five years of success followed, based around the old-school ethos of developing talent from within. Then, in 2005, Phil Davies, the director of rugby at the club, resigned after Leeds were relegated from the Premiership – rugby's top tier in England.

On the very same day, a report on our man, who'd just finished his Elite Coaching Level 5 qualification, landed on Leeds boss Gary Hetherington's desk. Hetherington took a punt and, showing a similar commitment to developing talent from within, gave the unproven 36-year-old the job. Good news? With no fewer than 25 players pouring out the door of the relegated club, most definitely hard to say.

But he somehow masterminded promotion, and from that came a post as Rugby Football Union Elite Rugby Director, and then – with the departure of Martin Johnson, following England's underwhelming performance in the 2011 Rugby World Cup – arguably the biggest job in world rugby: England head coach. And with a home World Cup on the horizon.

Great news? The history books would suggest otherwise.

The man in front of me is Stuart Lancaster. Shaven-headed, rugby-nosed, bright, thoughtful, articulate and incredibly likeable. Many people in his position would be forever defined – and even scarred – by that tournament. But not Lancaster.

Full disclosure: I'm a rugby league lad, at heart. I grew up just a few miles from the Leeds Rhinos ground. I was at school in Bradford in the early 2000s during the Bradford Bulls' golden era, when they won the World Club Challenge title three times in five years, with the Paul brothers (Henry and Robbie) pulling the strings and scoring tries for fun.

Rugby union – often derided as 'kick and clap' in my part of the world – was barely on my radar. When it was, it was as an inconvenience, given that I was forced to play it at school when I'd rather have been running. I got round this by just charging up and down the wing. Largely without the ball. Even England's World Cup win in Australia in 2003, under a glowering Martin Johnson and a nerveless Jonny Wilkinson, didn't make a real impression on me. The first I knew of that victory, in fact, was when I was cycling through Otley near my home on a training ride, and stopped at the traffic lights to see pissed fans pouring out of the pubs chanting 'Swing Low, Sweet Chariot'. My overriding rugby memory of 2003? Bradford Bulls doing the treble.

All that's changed, though, the more time I've spent around the game, its players and its coaches. Since rugby union went professional in 1995, and with the added impetus of that 2003 victory, it has exploded in popularity. The whiff of elitism; whispers of inferior fitness, skill or commitment levels to rugby league – no one mentions that any more. The physicality, the athleticism and the speed of today's game are extraordinary. It's a truly global sport (the Rugby World Cup is often billed as the third-biggest sporting event after the Olympics and World Cup in football), and so the rewards – but also the pressures – have grown enormously. And, as the man I'm having lunch with would no doubt attest, it can be the most precarious of professions.

In my sport of triathlon, luck plays only a fleeting part. It's a structured event, the distances remain consistent. The courses obviously vary – the London Olympics route was largely flat, while Rio had a killer of a climb, and a sea swim off Copacabana beach rather than the comparative calm of Hyde Park's Serpentine. But by and large, we know what we'll be facing. The bike leg offers the greatest potential for misfortune striking, but the chances of a crash or a puncture? Not much higher than a couple of per cent.

In rugby, a high-impact, ultra-dynamic sport played by 30 individuals, governed by multiple, sometimes arcane rules and multiple refs' interpretation of them, and based around an oval-shaped ball, the uncontrollables must be, what, 60 to 70 per cent?

Lancaster smiles. 'More really, actually,' he says. 'The randomness of the events happening in rugby means it's completely out of your control as a coach. You've got to hope that the training and the way in which you've prepared the team will give you the best chance of winning, but you can never guarantee it. I definitely lost international games on the back of decisions that, subsequently, the assessor of referees has said, "Yes, he's got that wrong."'

The luck of the bounce is the biggest cliché in sport. But it's grounded in real life, and few balls are as unpredictable as an oval one. Take the 2019 Pro14 Grand Final. Leinster – the Irish provincial team Lancaster now coaches – taking on Glasgow, in the Scottish city's Celtic Park stadium, an incredibly tough fixture. The Leinster scrum-half charged down a kick from Stuart Hogg, the full-back, and the ball ricocheted into Glasgow's narrow dead-ball area. It spun on its axis, somehow stopped just short of the dead-ball line and Leinster centre Garry Ringrose pounced on the ball to score what would prove a decisive try. The match was won 18–15. 'Nine times out of 10 that ball would have gone dead,' says Lancaster, with a wry shake of his head.

It's a common theme in rugby these days. For every All Blacks-style trouncing, far more matches, particularly international ones, are won or lost by the slenderest of margins: a single missed tackle, a collapsed scrum, a contentious penalty in a kickable position.

I'm keen to hear how he, as a coach, prepares himself – and his players – for such swings of fortune. Building the instinct of the squad to ensure that they're equipped through training to cope with any situation under pressure – 'unconscious competence', he calls it – is something he has focused on at Leinster, and with palpable results. 'Obviously you can't legislate for every different scenario,' he explains. 'But you can go a long way to doing that by the way in which you train, the way in which you build the minds of the players, the way in which you get their instincts through high-intensity accurate training with a good review process.

'The more successfully you've done that in training, the more settled you feel in the lead-up to a big game. You still know something will happen that could affect the outcome that you're not in control of. But if I take Leinster, for example, the way in which we prepare, there's no stone left unturned – they are 100 per cent aligned to the philosophy that I believe in. They can deliver that under pressure. There have been times at Leinster where there's a flow to our game and there's an unconsciousness about what we're doing. We are very hard to beat when we're in that flow.'

But what about when they're not? He nods and smiles. 'We've still got to learn to win. I would describe it as "Leinster rugby", when everyone is in synch; and "pressure rugby", when you have to dig it out, find a way.'

It's a coaching ethos that aligns him with some of the very

best in any sport. In his book *Leading,* Manchester United manager Sir Alex Ferguson said the key to excellence was in 'eliminating as many surprises as possible because life is full of the unexpected. That's what our [...] innumerable training sessions were all about.' Lancaster uses the example of the New England Patriots, who won the Super Bowl in 2019 for the sixth time this millennium (making them the joint most 'winningest', to use that painful term, in Super Bowl history). All the victories were masterminded by quarterback Tom Brady, working alongside head coach Bill Belichick, and not all of them were a procession.

'Sometimes they won by playing a power, attritional game, because their passing game wasn't working the way they wanted it to. They were just competitive, they were physical, they stuck in the game, even as everyone was writing them off,' says Lancaster. 'Their mantra is "Everyone knows the rules and everyone does their job." So even if you're not in the flow, you're going to be competitive.'

I know that feeling. Those victories that I've had to dig out, I tell him, I'm often prouder of than the 'flow' ones. I remember winning a race in Stockholm by getting a small lead on the bike and holding on for dear life during the run. An injury had stopped me run-training so I knew on the start line I needed to find a different way to win. I was incredibly proud of my performance. But, in rugby, the correlation between performance and result is far weaker.

'The longer you've coached, the more you just have to accept it as part of the profession that you've signed up to, but it's a very, very uncomfortable feeling to be sat as head coach of a national team in any international thinking, "I hope this goes well – but I've got no guarantee it will because of the randomness of the sport." You're nervous because you know the margins between success and failure are tiny, but the consequences are huge, particularly at international level.'

He adds: 'You look at the England one-day cricket team in 2019. They won the World Cup in that final super over, with the ball coming off the back of the bat of a diving Ben Stokes and going for four! But you know the way that the narrative will then play out, on the defeat or victory. They'll narrow it down to one person and one thing; if things go well and things go badly, and that's the really difficult thing to cope with.'

Which brings us to the elephant in the corner of the room – the one wearing an England rugby shirt with a Rugby World Cup 2015 motif on it. This was where Lancaster's luck deserted him spectacularly. He'd prepared the England team for their home tournament in a characteristically painstaking and diligent way, instilling the squad with an ethos that could only be described as Lancastrian: no egos, collective responsibility, openness with the fans and the media, value-orientated. All of which sounds, and looks, great when you're winning. Not so much when you lose to Wales, get thrashed by Australia and become the first ever host nation not to make it out of the group phase of your own Rugby World Cup.

What are his memories of the tournament? He looks serious for a moment. 'There was this big crescendo leading up to the World Cup, and then the one thing that I didn't need to happen was what happened: we lost a game we should've won. We were 22–12 up against Wales and we lost it 28–25. We lost it by the smallest of margins. It was on my watch, therefore it was my responsibility. As a coach in rugby you can easily turn round and say, well, it was this, this and this, but at the time I just felt that I had to take responsibility because I was in charge.'

There were indeed multiple contributing, not to mention mitigating, factors. A number of star players were missing, through suspensions, non-availability due to England Rugby's 'no overseas rule' or, in centre Manu Tuilagi's case, after he pleaded guilty to assault. The draw for the tournament was made in December 2012, nearly three years before the event, something Wales coach Warren Gatland said was 'ridiculous'. At that time, Australia, England and Wales were ranked third, fifth and ninth in the world, placing them in three different tiers and ensuring they could be drawn against one another. By the time the tournament kicked off, they were second, third and fourth. Add in the fierce rivalry that England enjoyed with both teams and it was easy to see why this was labelled the 'group of death'.

All of this was quickly forgotten. The blame was placed firmly at Lancaster's door, with much made of his decision to bring rugby league convert Sam Burgess into the squad. I've met Sam a few times; we were born in the same hospital in Dewsbury, West Yorkshire, just a few months apart. We've joked that there was obviously something kicking around in the Dewsbury water in the late 1980s. I really wanted him to be successful after his astonishing performances in league for the Bradford Bulls and then the South Sydney Rabbitohs in Australia, to whom he transferred after being wooed by club owner Russell Crowe. For pure athleticism he was at the top of the tree, in both codes of the game.

Bringing him to Bath rugby club, fast-tracking him into the England team for the World Cup at the expense of proven internationals, was a massive, career-defining selection for Lancaster. And it backfired. Lancaster takes a sip of his coffee, then tells me that what followed was a 'firestorm'.

'My personal reputation got hammered. There's no PR company defending your reputation – it's like you're fighting an army with a peashooter. Your thoughts are to do the best you can, and look after your family. You've got to suck up a bit of it, there's no doubt. It was a very tough time for me, my family and my friends.'

It's a vivid example of the binary nature of victory and defeat in sport – how success and merit are often confused. Is every England manager who doesn't win a tournament a failure? Is every World Cup-winning manager a great? Success seems to legitimise every tiny element of preparation, while failure undermines often valuable insight or innovations. Jonny Wilkinson drops a goal to win the World Cup in Australia in injury time, and 38 days later coach Clive Woodward is knighted. England captain Chris Robshaw opts not to kick for goal to tie a game against Wales, instead kicking for the corner to try to force a try, and within weeks Lancaster is out of a job.

Results can be transformative for both coaches and players. But so too can failure. As José Mourinho said when he returned to Manchester United (as coach of Tottenham Hotspur) in December 2019 for the first time since his sacking, 'You never lose – you win or you learn.' It's a great saying – Nelson Mandela's originally – and one that I believe all successful people in sport subscribe to. Because failure in our careers is not an 'if', it's a 'when'. So if you can deploy it to your advantage, then that's exactly what you'll have.

Lancaster braved the firestorm, kept his counsel, stayed out of the spotlight and was complimentary about his successor, Eddie Jones, when Jones won the Six Nations Grand Slam the following season in his first year in charge, England's first since 2003 (how that must have stung, with a largely unchanged team). The former schoolteacher quietly went back to doing what he does best – voraciously searching for every conceivable edge in sporting performance.

For years, Lancaster has been an advocate of cross-sport idea sharing, including as a member of the P8, a think-tank of key sporting coaches and thinkers, set up by the Leaders in Sport brand and loosely modelled on the geo-political G8 (now the G7). Cycling supremo Sir David Brailsford, football innovator-in-chief Arsène Wenger and triple-Ashes-winning cricket coach Andy Flower have all attended. Lancaster once said of the gatherings: 'With my rugby head-coach hat on, it's invaluable. With my pure interest in sport and leadership, it's gold dust.'

He tells me about meeting Gareth Southgate in this forum around six months before the England football team, under Southgate's stewardship, overperformed in the 2018 World Cup, reaching the semi-finals. I assume they found plenty in common; Southgate's much-trumpeted return to core values – to decency, to approachability, to mutual respect, even to smartness of turnout (remember the waistcoat?) – mirrors the ethos that Lancaster has looked to introduce in pretty much every squad he has ever coached. He remembers Southgate as an 'open-minded coach who's prepared to learn from other sports'.

Certainly true, but not to the extent of Lancaster: in the years following his World Cup ignominy, he travelled around the world, exposing himself to as many sporting environments as he could. He worked with the Football Association, British Cycling, NFL franchise the Atlanta Falcons and even spent a couple of weeks with New Zealand provincial rugby side Counties Manakau, helping out new coach Darryl Suasua and staying at his house. Remember, this was someone who'd coached England, one of world rugby's superpowers, in 46 Test matches. The Leinster job came on his return, and with it two semi-finals in the first year, two titles in the second – and personal redemption.

The waitress stops by and we order another tea. We're in a hotel in north Leeds, just minutes away from Lancaster's house. I've just returned from racing in the 70.3 World

Championship in Nice. I'm home for three days and delighted to be able to spend a few hours with him. It's a beautiful autumn morning, with sun streaming through the restaurant windows. There's hardly anyone around. As we speak, I begin to get a sense of why the current Leinster team, packed with some of the greatest players to ever pick up a ball, speak of him in almost messianic terms.

I'm keen to ask him about some of these players. Lancaster has worked closely with two of the best fly-halves to come out of the northern hemisphere in the past 25 years: Ireland's Johnny Sexton (a Leinster player) and England's Owen Farrell. I watched the former in the 2018 Six Nations single-handedly win a game against France in Paris (the first step towards a grand slam, as it turned out). In the style of one of the great quarterbacks, something that wouldn't have been lost on Lancaster, he orchestrated 41 phases of play, inching his Ireland side up the pitch in the face of frenzied French defence until they were just close enough for him to kick an enormous 42m drop-goal three minutes into injury time to snatch victory. It's one of the great examples of sporting mastery, of composure and executing skills under pressure. Farrell has been equally critical to England in the past few years – and who was the first to cap him, as a precociously talented 20-year-old in 2012? Stuart Lancaster.

So what does he think sets such players apart? He doesn't need to think. 'The ability to see things in a game before others have seen them,' he answers. 'They've just got this ... someone described it to me as like a chess master who can see four moves ahead and knows what's going to happen before it has happened. Andrew Johns in rugby league; elite netball players. Owen has it, Johnny has it. They've seen the picture so many times, either through video, through analysis or through playing the sport for so long.'

This reminds me of Josh Waitzkin's thoughts on 'chunking' – the brain's ability to collect individual pieces of information and organise them into larger groups. A chess player will recognise the pattern of pieces on a board and instinctively know the possible developments that will take place, just as a rugby player recognises something in a formation and has an inkling of what's going to come. It's probably a combination of experience, the ability to learn from it and how quickly you can access the relevant information when it's needed – in international rugby's case, in the arena of competition amid 80,000 screaming fans.

Lancaster continues with his characterisation of elite players: 'They have the technical ability to deliver. The physical gifts as well: pace, power. And then the third area is the mental attributes – so the resilience, the mental toughness, the confidence, the self-belief, the integrity as a person. The best way to describe it is in terms of three circles: physical gifts; technical and tactical gifts; and mental gifts. And a lot of the players I've coached have two of the three. They might be brilliant technically and tactically; mentally they've got all the component pieces. But they're not genetically gifted or whatever. There are very few that I've coached that possess all those three things.'

He's getting into his stride now. 'Let's score each one out of ten. I think the very best are on sort of 9, 9, 10 in all three areas. Farrell, Sexton are 9 or 10 out of 10 in all three. But there are still players who can become international players who are maybe 8, 8, 7 or 8, 7, 7, and you know you need those players on your team.

'Some of the players I've coached for England I'd maybe call B+ on talent but A+ on character [typical teacher!], because rugby's an emotive game that requires commitment and a desire to want to play for each other, and some players are great connectors and great energisers. And perhaps they haven't got all the skills and attributes to be the very, very top, but you'd want them on your team anyway.'

Wow. Players representing their country in rugby, on the highest stage, and they're little more than solid in terms of talent. How's that for encouraging?

'Ultimately I respect anyone who is prepared to stand in a tunnel before an international game in a colosseum of 80,000 people against New Zealand or South Africa or whoever it is, and you stand in line with those 15 players, walking out into that arena, for the physical confrontation that's gonna happen, and also in the knowledge that you might lose the game on an error that you make. I mean, that takes incredible, incredible toughness.'

That 'colosseum effect' is something I've never experienced – and am hugely envious of. Rugby players, football players, the track and field athletes. Beefy and Alastair Cook. Michael Owen and Denis Irwin. All contend – or used to contend – with the stadium factor, whereas even the biggest crowds in triathlon will be more dispersed along a course. So what's it like to be in that tunnel Lancaster speaks of? To hear and feel those tens of thousands of fans above you baying for victory, and to have to step out and perform – particularly in a sport as gladiatorial as rugby?

Wales's record try-scorer, Shane Williams, certainly knows. During a spectacular career he won 91 international caps (87 for Wales and four for the British & Irish Lions). Now, there are 87 caps for your average country, and then there are 87 caps for a nation that takes the sport you play more seriously than almost anything else in life. A match at the Principality (formerly Millennium) Stadium will make even the most emotionally stunted neutral's hairs stand up on the back of their neck. The singing, the passion, the knowledge of the game, that anthem. It must make the players feel like they're 10ft tall.

'Yeah, I thrived on it,' says Williams, with a broad smile, when we catch up. 'There was no better feeling for me as a rugby player. Warming up, then going back into the changing room and hearing all the people above you, and then going down the tunnel and the crowd going absolutely nuts. I could feel the expectation and I loved it.

'Every time I ran out into the Millennium Stadium I knew there were 75,000 people there watching me, and millions watching on telly. I used to love it. Playing on the wing, I could hear people chanting my name, even speaking to each other or trying to talk to me. I used to get caught up in it. I had to win the match for these people – and to entertain. I wanted to put on a show. When I had that mindset I played my best rugby.'

With apologies to Robbie Paul, Williams is pound-for-pound my favourite rugby player. He was so elusive, so lightning fast, so unorthodox – popping up all over the pitch, and conjuring tries from nothing with footwork, pace or sheer audacity. He scored 58 tries for Wales. No other player, stretching back through 130 years of international rugby in the principality, has come close to that mark.

It was in 2007–08 that Wales's most-capped winger was at his best. He was World Player of the Year in 2008, scoring six tries in that year's Six Nations as Wales claimed the Grand Slam and being named player of the tournament. During that period, he was unplayable. Messi, but with bigger thighs.

What a rush that must have been. He agrees. 'I was scoring tries, and it all just seemed to snowball. The bounce of the ball would go my way, I was trying new things and taking on defenders. I felt invincible; I would be devastated when games finished. It got to the point from 2007 to 2008 where I basically just thought I was the best rugby player on the field. And ball in hand, almost arrogant. I wasn't going to come second best.'

We're back to confidence. Swansea-born Williams wasn't over-endowed with confidence; indeed, as we'll hear, for much of his career, he struggled with it. When it's there, it can do great things for a sportsperson, but it can't be contrived. This tallies exactly with what I believe about, well, belief. That you can't manufacture it. 'I'm going to win' has no real resonance in your mind unless you think that on an intrinsic level. I remember sitting in classrooms and being talked at by psychologists, and them saying, 'You're never going to win at the highest level until you believe you will.' And I would think, 'That's rubbish.' The first few big races I won I had no expectation of victory at all – I just trained hard, turned up and hoped it all clicked. Only with a few key wins under my belt did I begin to think I was a genuine contender.

Williams says: 'I wish I'd had that mentality [that I was the best player on the pitch] when I started out. But you don't. When you're doing something at such a high standard you tend to think, "Oh my god, how am I here?"' Remarkably, this imposter complex endured even into his glory years. 'I was playing in a semi-final of a World Cup [2011] and you have to pinch yourself. In 2008, I was named World Player of the Year, and even now I think, "How the hell did that happen?!" It is quite surreal. Sometimes I go back and look at games we won or tries I scored and I can't believe that was me. I don't know if it's the same for everyone. I was very privileged in what I've done. It still hasn't sunk in.'

In his autobiography *Open Side*, Williams's teammate and former captain Sam Warburton spoke about sizing up his opponent before a game in the following terms: 'I knew genetically I was quite blessed, a good athlete, quick, powerful, strong, agile. I would look at opponents and think, "He's not got my genetic make-up and he doesn't work as hard as I do, eat as healthy, train as much, rest as well, have my belief, my mental strength. He can't be as good as me."'

Williams took the same approach. He tells me how he used to train until he dropped, then analyse the data from the GPS trackers fitted to the players' jerseys to check how many miles he'd covered. 'If any of the other wingers had covered more I'd be so frustrated,' he says. 'I didn't want to leave any stone unturned or give these guys an excuse to take my jersey. That jersey was mine. And it was mine to lose. And I always had the mindset that not performing in training is a good way to lose it.

'Look, I wasn't a natural sportsman growing up. I was pretty quick, but I never excelled. For me it wasn't natural. I knew I had a few good attributes, but I didn't have the best attributes. I got a lucky break and became a professional rugby player, and I just realised I had to work hard – and would always have to work hard – because I was up against the odds. I knew I'd been given an opportunity that any kid in Wales would have chewed their right arm off for, and I was willing to make that work.'

His size lay at the heart of those challenging odds. If you were applying Lancaster's model of the three interconnecting circles, you'd give Williams 10 for attitude (as we've seen), probably a 9 on the technical and tactical side. Physical gifts? A 6 or a 7 – at best. Just 5ft 7in and '11 stone soaking wet', as he puts it, when he was first capped, Williams would have been small in the 1970s heyday of Welsh rugby, let alone when he was playing 30 or 35 years later, when the premium placed on size and power made him a conspicuous outlier.

Legendary All Black Jonah Lomu was 6ft 6in and 19 stone. Williams's teammate George North is 6ft 4in and 17 stone. Both played the same position as him. Prop Uini Atonio, who plays for France, is 24st 8lb – the heaviest player ever to 'grace' the Six Nations. That's more than twice Williams's weight! Given rugby is an overwhelmingly physical sport, he was at a huge disadvantage from the off.

'Going through school I was the smallest in the class, smallest in the year, and teachers used to put me in the second team so that I wouldn't get hurt. I thought I'd got rid of that stigma when I became an adult and started playing senior rugby, but as soon as I became a professional that question again started to come. Is he big enough? I was reading it every week.'

Even after he'd broken into the Wales team and was scoring tries, it still haunted him. When Steve Hansen came in as Wales coach in 2001, Williams was told he wasn't big or strong enough and that he was going to be dropped. He started taking supplements and bulked up, but in the process he lost some of his agility, pace and scoring prowess. He started picking up injuries, then he lost form because he wasn't fit. He now fitted the mould of the destructively built modern rugby player, but it clearly wasn't right for him – and Hansen still wasn't picking him.

'For a good 12 to 16 months I was trying to please this guy who didn't really know me, didn't know my game. I felt sorry for myself initially, down in the doldrums. But, looking back, that period where he dropped me from the team was probably the period that made me as a rugby player.'

Williams eventually changed tack. He went back to focusing on the player he was, rather than the one he wasn't. He did more speed work, more plyometrics, shed some bulk. His form returned – and so did the Wales jersey.

There's a lesson here: the pitfalls of working on weaknesses to the detriment of strengths, of becoming a strong all-rounder but average, rather than a champion with some manageable flaws. It's an easy mistake to make in my world of triathlon.

Try to improve your cycling at the expense of running, and you might be a better all-round triathlete. But suddenly you can't win races any more on the running leg. Instead there is a lot to be said for maximising your strengths and strategising accordingly.

We've already seen how Stuart Lancaster dealt with criticism – lying low, and returning when it felt like the right time to silence the doubters. It's an effective approach, but not everyone has the luxury – if we can call it that – of an extended and enforced period of absence. For any international sportsperson, scrutiny is constant and detractors are never far away, particularly in the internet age. Now multiply that by a factor of 100 for a Wales rugby international.

'Being a rugby player in Wales, you're always under pressure,' says Williams. 'Rugby down this way is pretty much a religion, and every match is a big match, as you're reminded when you open any paper or speak to anyone in the street. You're kind of put into this goldfish bowl. When you get into a team, and you're quite young and naïve, the pressure is massive.

'I just got on with it – and the older I got, the more experienced I got. From mid-career I kind of shut everything out and concentrated on my game. If people came up to me and were negative, I'd completely shut that out. But there's no training for that. No one prepares you for it.'

Williams's life is largely pressure-free these days. He's a sought-after and insightful rugby pundit and commentator. We speak a number of times in the build-up to Ironman Wales, in Tenby, in which he is competing for the fourth time (he seems even more enthusiastic about triathlon than I am). He's taking part with his old teammate Gareth Thomas, who bravely reveals his HIV diagnosis on Twitter just before the race, hoping to break some of the stigma around the disease.

Like many former sportspeople, Williams, who'd never attempted a marathon prior to retirement, least of all one preceded by a 2.4-mile swim and 112-mile bike ride, finds a natural home in endurance sport.

'Before that first one, someone told me the distances and I thought, "Oh shit." It was the hardest day of my life, but pushing myself, finding myself in dark places, thinking I can't do this and eventually finishing it … these are things I thought I'd never have again. I'm never going to be anywhere near the standard of you guys, but I just enjoy doing something I'm completely not comfortable with. And it's a lot healthier than the pub.'

Gareth Thomas's announcement puts everything in perspective. And perspective of the world outside and beyond sport is not something Williams, or AP McCoy, or Alastair Cook, or any of us within sport have enormous experience of. Williams likens his international career to a period of temporary insanity.

'When I was playing I'd go days when I wouldn't think of anything apart from playing, or training. My life was rugby. I was completely focused on being the best. I wanted to win every time I played. I was obsessed. I think, if you speak to any player, they were the same.

'Since I've retired, I've realised that there are more important things – I have my family and my children, and they are my priority. But I always look back and think, "Jesus, I must have been hard work to live with at times," because that game on a Saturday afternoon was all I cared about, winning and doing whatever it took to win it, and doing whatever it took in training to make sure I was ready.'

How did he maintain that motivation for so long? Three things, it turns out. The thrill of performing on the biggest stage – something that often gets overlooked amid the pressure, performance anxiety and painstaking preparation of a sporting life. 'When I beat a player in a game, that would just give me such a massive buzz that I wanted it again and again,' Williams tells me. 'I just loved performing and entertaining. Scoring tries and just having the whole crowd go ballistic. It was unbelievable.' Olympic, world and Commonwealth champion Victoria Pendleton once described it like this: 'You've experienced what it's like when it's good so why on earth would you ever want to let that go?' Strong motivation indeed.

Then there was fear of failure, remarkably. Williams – demonstrably one of the greatest rugby players of all time – felt he was only ever 80 minutes away from a bad review. Right up to the end, this fear drove him on, he tells me. 'I was playing very good rugby almost because of the fear that I didn't want to see that negativity from earlier in my career again. I think sometimes being scared makes you stronger.'

There's a great example of this. After retiring from international rugby, he continued to play for the Ospreys regional franchise, culminating in the Grand Final of the Pro12 league in 2012 against Lancaster's current team, Leinster, in Dublin. It was to be Williams's last game. He scored two tries, the second to win the game (31–30) in the 78th minute with his final touch of a ball in competitive rugby – 'Shane Williams's script writer surely hails from Hollywood,' a report in the *Guardian* duly noted.

That's not how he recalls the day, though. 'There was the fear even then,' he tells me. 'I didn't want to go into that final, play terribly, lose the match and have people say, "He should have retired last year." Every time I played I wanted to play out of my skin.'

The final motivation, the thing that kept that fire burning? The size factor. 'After I was criticised for being small and not physical enough when I started playing for Wales, it was like my focus quadrupled. I was obsessed with proving people wrong. I had to work harder in the gym; defensively I had to change my game. My whole focus was, "You're playing against this guy at the weekend, you're giving away three or four stone – this is what you're going to have to do."' Being small was my biggest motivation. The fact that I had to prove everyone wrong, all the time, probably made me the player I was eventually.'

So, ironically, if you'd been four inches taller, you might have been half the player?

'I honestly think that would have been the case,' he says, with a chuckle. 'If it had been put on a plate for me and not been so difficult at the start, I wouldn't have had to work so hard and I wouldn't have become the player I was. So I'm quite happy – and quite relieved – that I'm a short arse.'

The extraordinary good fortune of being too small to play international rugby, as the old Chinese farmer might put it.

12

UNTOUCHABLE

'I put myself through hell every single day so
I can have the reward of beating people by
as much as I do.'

Sydney 2000 will always be one of my favourite Olympics. It had energy and excitement, and it had the Olympic début of my sport, triathlon. It came at the sweet spot for me between rising awareness and peak impressionability. And it was notable for the overlapping of the career trajectories of two generation-defining athletes: one making their first global splash, the other drawing on all their experience to clinch one last gold.

With a symmetry that would please any of my fellow sporting obsessives, both were 400m specialists (though you'd barely know it for the ease with which they transcended their events). One was so unorthodox he was once described as running 'like a policeman in a silent film'. Early mutterings about his technique didn't last long. He was simply too dominant. The other displayed such technical mastery in the pool, it was like watching an aquatic version of Federer stroking forehand after forehand down the line. One was a Texan, the other from Sydney itself. One 33, the other 17. Michael Johnson and Ian Thorpe.

Aura, that elusive quality, is often associated with longevity. One of the things that made Thorpe such a sensation was that he had bucketloads of the stuff before he'd even swum his first Olympic heat. His monumental physique – a wingspan of almost two metres and those soon-to-be-famous size-17 feet. That amazingly fluid stroke. And, of course, the bodysuit.

In the 21 years since, we've become accustomed to seeing elite swimmers take to the water in all sorts of gear. This reached its height, or nadir, around the Beijing Olympics, with the so-called 'supersuits' made from non-textile and non-woven material that were a country mile away from Thorpe's early prototype, and so performance-enhancing that the records set in them now carry asterisks.

But back then no one was wearing them, until this boy-giant stepped out in front of a pumped-up, partisan crowd, covered in black from neck to wrists to ankles and topped off with the golden Aussie swim cap. The effect in the water as he began powering back and forth was shark-like: supreme power and efficiency, with plenty of menace.

That aura had been rapidly building in the years preceding the Sydney Games. Aged 14, Thorpe became the youngest man to represent Australia. At the 1999 Pan Pacific Swimming Championships, also in his home city, he broke four world records in four days.

The year before, his victory in the 400m freestyle at the 1998 Perth World Championships made him, at 15, the youngest male world champion in history. Dig out footage of the race if you can. Grant Hackett was in the process of 'blowing the race away' ('It's going to be a rippa,' says the commentator as Hackett, who went on to win the 1,500m freestyle at both the Sydney and Athens Games, carves out a huge lead). But in a demonstration of tactical perfection, a teenage Thorpe inches his way back into contention, reeling Hackett in length by length. Thorpe leads for just one stroke of the race: the final one.

This immaculate timing was to be a feature of one of the great moments of Australian sport on the first night of competition at the Sydney Games. But first Thorpe had to deliver on that promise in front of an Australian population, and media, who went way beyond expectant. Sydney's *Daily Telegraph* front-page picture of Thorpe that day was headlined with one word: 'Invincible'.

It's the media that Thorpe and I discuss first when we hook up, from opposite ends of the world, during the lockdown summer of 2020. We've met before, and exchange WhatsApp messages to set up the interview. As is typical of those who make their living in sport, we miss a good few calls from one another (there's always some training session or other that gets in the way) before we succeed in speaking.

It's late evening for him, mid-morning for me. The now 37-year-old is chatty and genuinely interested in this project and the other stars I've spoken to. But a wariness is there too; or at least a thoughtfulness and precision to what he says. He doesn't want any ambiguity or room for reinterpretation. It's something I recognise in many top-flight sportspeople, myself – from time to time – included.

This comes as no surprise given the media scrutiny – some would say hounding – he was subjected to both in and out of the pool throughout his career and into retirement. 'Everyone speaks about the British press and the tabloids, but I constantly remind people that Australia invented that and we exported it to you guys,' he says with a laugh.

What happened on that first night in Sydney was *Boy's Own* stuff (while still in boyhood), but these things are never the formality they look with hindsight and the passing of time. The paralysing pressure and mental toll of translating Olympic gold medal-winning form to an Olympic gold medal have claimed countless victims over the years – people who get on the start line and can't deal with the fact that there's no reason on earth why they can't perform to the best of their ability on this one day.

Thorpe, for all his pedigree, agrees. 'I do talks and I say to people, "If I said today that in 1,520 days you had to be at your absolute best no matter what it is and no matter what you're going through …" Well, that's the reality for an Olympic athlete, and it doesn't matter how good you are in training. It matters how good you are when it comes to racing. You're never judged on what you do in training.'

He tells me about his début Olympic night. 'It was unique. My event was the first day of competition. When I went into my 400m final, Australia hadn't won a gold medal – so the pressure did mount and everyone just assumed that I'd win, and it was because of the success I'd had leading into it, without considering that I may not have prepared for this mentally or whatever else. But it's not like I'm the perfect athlete.'

Thorpe, of course, performed like he was born for this stage. He led throughout, with Italy's Massimiliano Rosolino the only rival able to stay anywhere close, a churning wake his reward for this proximity. With the crowd chanting 'Thorpey, Thorpey' (an Aussie crowd will stick a -y on anything; good job I wasn't born Down Under), the young Australian stretched away in the final 50m, winning by three full seconds in a world record of 3 minutes, 40.59 seconds.

I've done plenty of competitive swimming over the years. It pays a third of my mortgage. It makes me well placed to state the following: I've never seen a more accomplished swimmer than Thorpe. It wasn't just the speed. It was the fluidity of his technique and the way that nothing – not the occasion, not the venue, not the excruciating lactic acid build-up in the closing stages of a race as demanding as the 400m – compromised that.

The Times correspondent Simon Barnes, writing about Thorpe's performance four years later in Athens when he won what was billed as the 'race of the century' against a young Michael Phelps and his long-time rival, Dutchman Pieter van den Hoogenband, put it best. He called Thorpe 'the only man on Earth with gills', adding: 'It was a performance that held power and serenity in the most extraordinary state of balance.'

I ask Thorpe about the suit. As a sportsperson you try to maximise everything: your training, your home life, your nutrition, your sleep schedule. Even your thought patterns. Was this the same, or was it about making a statement?

'It was innovating, yes,' he says gently. 'But I broke world records where I was wearing next to nothing and where I was covering up every bit of my body. Had I thought it was the swimsuit that did it I wouldn't have been swimming. We're talking about hundreds of tenths of a second, and that's it. It was the hard work when I was training that created the performance.'

He tells me about how the new look came about. 'I tested it and also looked at, you know, it's Adidas ... If Nike comes into swimming, then that actually elevates the sport as well. So I thought about it on multiple levels. But I never had to wear that swimsuit; I could have worn whatever I wanted to wear, which was what was quite unique about my swim deal.'

After his 400m win, Thorpe barely celebrated: his face seemed to mirror the relief of his compatriot Cathy Freeman in the same Games. But unlike Freeman, he knew he still had to perform. 'The next race had become so important for the nation,' he told Michael Parkinson in that famous TV interview all those years later.

That race was the 4x100m relay, aka the 'air guitar' race. For me, it's the closest parallel to the last-leg excitement of Britain's victory in the 4x400m in the 1991 World Championships, with Kriss Akabusi on anchor, if you can remember that. But that was in Tokyo – not in front of a sports-mad home crowd. And it was also without the extra spice of a memorable slight from their closest rivals. US sprinter Gary Hall Jr said his team was going to smash the Australians 'like guitars'. He could be forgiven some confidence; the US had never lost the event in the history of the Games.

Thorpe describes what followed in the Sydney International Aquatic Centre as 'electrifying'. If it was, then he made it so. Swimming the crucial final leg, he hit the water a fraction ahead of Hall, only to see the sprint specialist surge ahead. Coming into the turn at 50m he was half a body length down, seemingly overawed, and the deafening screams of the home crowd were starting to morph into groans.

Pretty much every teenager on earth would have crumbled at this moment. Yet Thorpe nailed his turn and made up some water. He was still behind, but closing with each stroke. It was going to come down to the finest of margins and a Froome-esque ability to withstand pain. Thorpe would later say, 'I realised at 25m to go, it's going to be really close. But I knew he [Hall] would be hurting more than me. I'd replicated that level of pain so many times in training and been able to get through it, and do it again, and push it even further.'

The mouthy Hall was overhauled. Thorpe won the touch by a tiny margin, the Aussies clocking 3 minutes, 13.67 seconds (taking nearly two seconds off the world record). The aquatic centre went crazy and the foursome celebrated by pumping the sky with their fists and, in a two fingers up to the Americans, playing air guitar. It was swimming's rock star moment.

What a night. But the focus of Thorpe – who in subsequent years would emerge as brittle as well as brilliant, and incredibly private, obsessed with the minutiae of technical perfection rather than the crucible of competition – was already shifting.

'In Sydney at the closing ceremony I considered walking away from sport,' he tells me. 'I'd accomplished all of my childhood dreams. Not goals but dreams. And dreams are embarrassing because you don't know if you're allowed to dream that big.'

Eventually in 2006, afflicted by 'crippling depression' and 'intense loneliness', he did in fact quit – still only 24. He said he'd become like a performing seal. But as with all the greats, he had one eye on a return. In an interview in November 2012, after missing out on qualification for London, he said, 'In 2016, at the Rio Olympics, I'll be 33,' adding that he felt it was 'completely feasible' that he could compete there at that age.

Damn right, and proof of that could be found in that same Sydney Games: Michael Johnson, aged 33 years and 12 days. 'You used to have to be a young man to do the 400m flat,' noted the commentator when the question of age was raised as Johnson crouched in his blocks in the lull that followed Cathy Freeman's stunning display of performance under pressure.

Johnson, better than almost anyone, would have known what Freeman had just been through. Four years earlier, in his home Games in Atlanta, he'd attempted the never-before-achieved 200m and 400m double, piling up the pressure on himself by wearing custom-made gold spikes. He didn't just deliver. He dismantled the world record by 0.34 seconds in the 200m (0.34!), while running the nearest to perfection he feels he got in his career. He also took gold in the 400m, with an imperious 43.49, a new Olympic record. Those were the Games where his aura was forged. He would go on to set a new 400m world record of 43.18 in 1999.

As with Thorpe, interviewing MJ is an odd process. Echoes of previous interviews come through in that distinctive Southern accent and his calm, intelligent delivery. I wouldn't be surprised if Johnson had been the coolest head in the stadium on those ferociously pressured nights in Atlanta. If so, I can't help but feel, how unfair is that? A temperamental dominance almost as complete as the physical and physiological one.

The sprinter needed all of his mental strength when, years later in 2018, he suffered a stroke. He's recovered now, and when we speak he's in lockdown in Malibu, just outside Los Angeles, where he hikes, hangs out, rides his bike and, he tells me, still exercises four to five times a week. You can just picture the double-takes when he trots past fellow joggers.

The glory years and towering highs of Johnson's career are so well documented, I wonder whether I'll learn more focusing on the rare low points. Barcelona in 1992 was one. Johnson was the favourite for the 200m, but at a warm-up meeting in Salamanca two weeks before the Games, he and his coach ate in a local restaurant and picked up a dose of food poisoning. It's happened to me a couple of times in my career in the lead-up to major races. Peak condition honed over months of graft disappears in a matter of hours. Weakened, and with his run-in to the Olympics derailed, Johnson lost in the semis.

'Other than Barcelona, pretty much every other race in major championships I went into feeling in optimal condition,' he tells me. The other exception? 'Sydney. I went into that after recovering from an injury and having not had any races for almost two months. Those were the situations where I thought,

"I could execute to perfection here, but given I'm not in the greatest shape I'm going to have a real fight on my hands."'

Of course, he still triumphed in Sydney – ending his career with a dozen major golds (four Olympic and eight World Championship). No silver. No bronze. Just extraordinary. 'He had that totally under control, every step of the way,' said the commentator, unknowingly.

Greatness carries its own burden, as Johnson explains. When you're on the starting line, no one cares about, 'Oh he's injured, or he's not in the best shape because he couldn't get in preparation races, so if he doesn't win, no problem.' As Johnson puts it: 'When you're at the top, you show up on the start line and people expect you to win, and that's what I expected of myself. The approaches may be different, but the expectation is always the same.'

That expectation is not just the crowd's. Dominance – certainly of the level achieved by Johnson (up to June 1997, he had an eight-year, 58-race winning streak in 400m finals) – messes with competitors' minds, too. Britain's Roger Black, who won silver behind Johnson in the 400m in Atlanta, nearly a full second back, once said, 'The rest of us are just running for second, right?' Black wasn't being entirely serious. But nor was he joking. When the other seven finalists in Sydney saw Johnson rolling his shoulders and stretching his neck, calm eyes fixed on the track ahead and those bloody gold spikes on his feet again, hearts must have sunk – giving Johnson a vital, unseen advantage that helped him overcome his lack of form.

No amount of external pressure on Johnson could compete with what he applied to himself. It's a mentality we've seen time and again in these chapters – and it perhaps explains why Johnson chose to wear those conspicuous spikes.

'I want to win more than I'm afraid of the consequences of losing,' he tells me, simply. 'For me it's always been like that.

That desire to win is overwhelming and I put a tremendous amount of pressure on myself to deliver. I knew that, given my talent and given all the work that I've done, there's no reason why I can't win. It's going to come down to how well I can execute this race over the next 19 or 43 seconds. In that situation, that outweighs any pressure anyone could put on me. I don't really care about the pressure that's external. I truly don't.'

We've talked plenty about coping mechanisms for pressure. Johnson, a known obsessive, certainly didn't leave this to chance. 'My position was always that it would be ridiculous to go out every single day for years training for this moment physically but not have any strategy for how I'm going to deal with the pressure that I'm going to be feeling, which is going to be building with every moment I get closer and closer to the gun going off.'

It sounds so simple and obvious, but so many athletes and sportspeople overlook that. 'They think the pressure is what it is, there's nothing I can do about it, so I'm not going to really focus on that,' says Johnson. 'That's a mistake and a mistake that many athletes make.' I'm sure that the golfer Jean van de Velde – who memorably took seven shots on the final hole at the Open at Carnoustie in 1999 when even a double-bogey six would have made him the first Frenchman in a century to win a major – would have some views on this.

So what was Michael Johnson's coping strategy? What on earth was going through his head as he packed those spikes in his kit bag at the hotel to depart for the transfer to the 85,000-seat Centennial Olympic Stadium in Atlanta?

'It was understanding and recognising distractions and knowing what to do,' he answers. 'Things inevitably will come into your mind just before you're going to go out there and race: the competition and how prepared they might be; what the media are going to say if I lose this race. But those things are unproductive at those moments.

'So it's about, number one, recognising those thoughts when they come into your mind; and then being able to respond immediately by replacing them with things you can control, like visualising yourself running the race and focusing on the execution.'

He tells me about the importance of having the right people in your corner at the right times, those who understand what you need – and what you don't. We've all encountered misfiring coaches who work themselves (and you) up unnecessarily or confuse you with last-minute, self-justificatory advice. Parents, too, who feel the urge to dispense advice that, however well intentioned, strikes precisely the wrong chord at that crucial pre-race moment: 'Just enjoy it. It doesn't matter if it's not your day. We'll still think the same of you, whatever happens.'

'I had strategies around who was in my inner circle, who was with me in those moments when I was preparing for the race,' says Johnson. 'I had to make sure they understood what sort of atmosphere I liked, the environment I needed around me in order to be in the right mindset before I go out and race.'

Johnson was often accused of being arrogant. That's bollocks, in my view. Superhumanly confident, yes. Incredibly sure of his talents, definitely. But also humble enough to recognise he needed to maximise his gifts, and to accept – looking back – that good fortune played its part.

As he tells me, 'Those athletes who have the sort of consistency and longevity that I was able to accomplish in my career … you don't get there without a bit of luck. It certainly takes a tremendous amount of hard work, and an understanding of how you deliver under pressure. But you need a little luck, and I had that throughout my career.

'Of course you can create your own luck,' he continues. 'Being consistent in the 10 years of my career building up to the 2000 Olympics, which was my last race … I wasn't in the best shape, and there were certainly people in better shape in that race than I was because they had two months of build-up and preparation.

'But having not lost to any of those people over the previous 10 years, and having shown that dominance, I'd created a situation where I had an advantage. They had never beaten me before and felt like, "I'm probably not going to beat him today either." So to some degree you can create your own luck.'

There's one other name I'd like to include with the illustrious figures in this final chapter. Someone who has a decent claim for currently being the most dominant athlete in any event in the world.

There are many perks that come with winning Olympic medals. A big one, for those in the GB team, is that British Airways sends a plane to the Olympic city the day after the closing ceremony to take the team home. Most of the few hundred athletes and support staff file onto the jet nursing some kind of hangover. If you've been successful you're rewarded with better seats. Gold medals mean first class. A few silvers, business. You get the picture.

On the way home from my first Olympics in Beijing I was out back, two rows from the toilets. Returning from Rio I climbed the stairs, was directed to turn left and found a spacious seat waiting for me in first. In the seat next to me: Adam Peaty.

Peaty was one of the big success stories of that Games. He took GB's opening gold, in the 100m breaststroke. Although perhaps not a youngster in Thorpe's terms, he was still only 21.

Comparing athletes across the ages is a dangerous game, as there's simply too much context that needs to be considered. But as both Thorpe and Johnson showed, the measure of greatness can often be seen in the margin of victory. Peaty was the first British man to win an Olympic swimming gold since Adrian Moorhouse won the same event in Seoul in 1988. Moorhouse won by a hundredth of a second with a time of 62.04. Peaty triumphed by 156 times that margin with a world record 57.13.

Moorhouse, understandably, wasn't short of praise – 'He's got everything' – and Thorpe calls him the best breaststroker he's ever seen. Four and a half years after our pampered flight home together (we speak in January 2021), he's broken the world record 13 times, and holds three world bests: in the 100m breaststroke, long and short course – 'short course' means in a 25m pool, so three turns instead of one – and the 50m breaststroke. He's the first man to swim under 26 seconds for the 50m and the first to break 57 seconds in the 100m, in which he's swum 19 of the fastest 20 times in history.

When we catch up, it's impossible not to reminisce a bit about Rio. I tell him that coming home on that plane was the first sober day we'd had in about a week. 'Why were you sober?' he responds, with a laugh. With the enforced distance of lockdown and the improvised training – Peaty has had a so-called 'endless pool' installed in his garden in which he trains, remotely connected to his coach Mel Marshall on FaceTime – those Games feel like a different world.

I ask him how he keeps the intensity up, particularly when he's already achieved so much. 'It's about winning, of course,' he says. 'But more than that, I just want to dominate. It's that simple.

'It's about mindset. As an athlete, we train our bodies pretty much every single hour, because when we're not training, we're resting, right? But if you're going to be the best in the world, you've got to train in a way that sets you apart from the rest of the world. And if it isn't there, you've got to put your foot down and go, "I ain't accepting this shit, no way."

'Because I know that when I get to the Olympics, that isn't going to be good enough. Because you only get one chance every four years. Literally one chance, that's it. One thing goes wrong, you've blown the whole thing. So you've got to not allow yourself to be complacent, haven't you?'

It's that supreme work ethic, even in a sport packed with masochists, that I love. Peaty has the tightest of bonds with Marshall, a super-pragmatic, highly respected former pro swimmer. In an interview with swimming veteran Brett Hawke, she summed up her prodigy perfectly. 'What separates Adam is you won't find anyone who works harder. To the ends of the earth. He's always the last man standing … [To excel in swimming] you need to be physically capable, psychologically capable, technically capable, tactically capable and your character needs to be capable. All of his capacities in those areas are huge.'

If we're putting Peaty on the same level as Johnson and Thorpe, and I don't think he's there – yet – a comparison of temperament is interesting. It's a reminder that dominance can take many forms. Johnson: obsessive, with amazing mental strength. Thorpe: pure talent and the stubbornness to drive himself on. But neither had what is a key weapon in Peaty's armoury: competitive rage. Thorpe and Johnson's battles were with perfection and with themselves. Peaty is much more gladiatorial. He lives for the crowd, and to face down his competitors.

There's something of the prize fighter about the man from Uttoxeter in Staffordshire, even when he's sitting in his living room on a Zoom call. He's got the physique: 6ft 3in, 6kg heavier than in Rio. The look: shaved head, tattooed arms. The quick, massive hands (Marshall likens them to 'buckets') that give him such a high tempo in the pool. And that combative nature.

He doesn't deny it. 'It's quite aggressive in my head, the way I perceive sport,' he tells me. 'So it's like if you're walking out to an Olympic final and there's seven other guys there – in your head you've got to be willing to knock them out. You've got to find something in your brain that is going to find that fight or flight. And finding that fight or flight and manipulating it, because we've had this for thousands of years and it's made us the apex predator on earth, right?

'There's something about that human instinct of fighting and me manipulating that into a performance. That's where I get the edge. It's like I look at anyone at the start line or look at anyone coming out and think, "You don't deserve this." I love boxing and I love that quote they throw around, I think it was Ali: "If you even dream of beating me you better wake up and apologise."'

Lord help anyone who does triumph against him. How does he think he would respond? 'I can take a loss and I can spin it back round, but when I take a few losses it just really starts to piss me off. At the ISL [the International Swimming League, established in 2019] a few months back, I knew I was going to lose because those guys had been fresh, they hadn't had to quarantine, they had access to pools and had been competing. So I went there and I was like, "You know what, I'm going to take a few losses here, but I'm going to focus on my process and I'm going to break the world record in the semi-final and the final." And that's exactly what I did.

'I believe losing every once in a while is just as healthy, if not healthier, than winning all the time. Because you don't have any perspective when you win all the time. It's good to have a bit of fire in you, a fire that isn't just the motivation of winning gold. It's a fire of "I'm angry now."

'I believe that competition is extremely healthy and it brings out the best in people. I hate losing. I hate it. As a kid I'd sweep the Monopoly board [not another one!]. I've swiped the draughts board. I just hated the idea that someone could be better. Which is very toxic, I know, but I've learned to live with that now. I've learned to kind of control it. But when it comes to swimming? Yeah, you've got to have a very aggressive approach.'

The competition thing is very relevant to me, I tell him, having a brother I've grown up competing with. Ten or fifteen years ago, Jonny and I couldn't play Monopoly; we'd play crazy golf and be swinging clubs at each other's heads. Table tennis in the garden would end up with bats thrown at each other. But now it feels like we channel our competitiveness into things that are really important to us. Like winning races. I don't know whether it's learning to live with it or learning to use it.

Emotion aside, Peaty is a big believer in process. He and Marshall work on it tirelessly. Famously, she'd make him listen to the crowd noise of him coming out at a big meet, his name being announced and all the other build-up in the arena on headphones ahead of each race-pace rep she had him doing in the run-up to Rio. The idea was to desensitise him. Those reps were meticulously honed, with a set stroke count and rate over each 50m rep and a (gradually reducing) time Peaty was expected to hit exactly at the turn. In Rio, Peaty swam to within a tenth of a second of his target time for the first 50m which is, frankly, amazing. With so much talent and adrenaline, the second half looked after itself.

This, for me, is what differentiates a good coach from a great coach. This type of session combines physical performance with mental precision and adaptation to the competition environment. Any short-timeframe event (sprinting included) is about execution; tying together all the strands of performance that have been honed in training over the years. He was training under close to race conditions, again and again and again. Executing for Adam Peaty is a combination of performing to the level he has achieved a hundred times in training, with a little bit of an oomph from competition. Actually, make that a very large oomph.

'We always say, me and Mel, we've got to be at peace with ourselves. So before we go out to the Olympics, or the Worlds or Europeans, everything is done, everything's sorted. So I can store it away, don't have to think about it. That's my peace. Then I can race and go, "You know what, this is the only thing in my mind, this is my flow, this is my energy." I can put everything into this thought process right now.'

I've heard many athletes say this and can relate to it myself. For me it's about having everything in order so there are no nagging worries in the back of my mind. I don't want to be standing in the pre-race holding zone worrying about highly relevant things ('Will my bike gears work OK?') or completely irrelevant ones ('Did I lock the back door?').

After he and Marshall achieved Project 56 in Gwangju, South Korea, in July 2019 – Peaty's time was 56.88 – a new target was needed. That has become Project Immortal, aiming for a flawless performance with a time that can never be beaten. 'Gwangju wasn't even my best race,' he explains. 'We broke it down, we went, "OK, our perfect race is 56 low," around that. But everything has to go perfect – the preparation, the race and all the variables.'

He sees post-Covid performances rising sharply, aided by rest and freshness – time off the sporting treadmill. 'Over time, athletes need to know when to rest and when to recover. I think that's why Covid has been interesting. A lot of people have had a break, have used the psychologists, or kind of used their own mental tricks or developed mental ways to perform even better. I think we will see a lot of outstanding performances.'

You sense he's almost looking forward to a defeat. For the ammo it would give him – and maybe for the added richness to the Adam Peaty narrative. 'People in this country love someone who gets beaten but gets back up again. It's a bit of drama. I can almost see what would happen: taking a big knock at a championship would put me into an afterburner for a long time. It would annoy me so much. I don't really hold grudges, but when I get beaten I hold that very, very close to me.'

I'm curious as to whether he sees sport as entertainment. His answer is surprising.

'One hundred per cent. I think that's why people love the Olympics. You never know what's going to happen. You want sport to be entertaining because that means people buy into what you do and more people will appreciate what you do. I think that's why it's so important that we see ourselves as entertainers because that's what we are. And what are we, if we're not? I don't really know what category we'd fit into.'

I have no doubt that he'd respond to a high-profile defeat in devastating fashion. Yet I can't see it happening. To be honest, I don't think he can either. Peaty is simply too strong in all the key areas: the track record, the experience, the hunger to learn and improve, the desire, the anger, the self-belief, the team around him, the focus, the self-punishment, the precision, the performance psychology. Oh, and he can swim a bit.

If I were a 100m breaststroker right now, I'd chuck it all in and become a lifeguard.

Peaty is combative to the last. 'People can think that they can beat me, and people can say that they can do this and that and whatever. We call it the "bullshit circle", and you see it every season, every Olympic cycle: people popping these times out in their home country, in their home pool, with a home crowd, where they're comfortable. Try doing that in an Olympic Games in a final that comes around every four years. You can't compare.

'In the 100m, I think there are a few swimmers that can go possibly 57 high but I just don't see them on the last 25m getting anywhere near. It's not an arrogant thing, it's not a cocky thing. It's an underlying confidence. No matter what goes wrong, I can catch up.

'I've proven that. I've touched the wall a second behind at 50m and caught up and won. I enjoy it. I train harder than anyone else, I believe. I put myself through hell every single day so I can have that reward of beating people by as much as I do.'

EPILOGUE

Nearly four years ago I set out on a quest. Unusually for me, it wasn't a journey with a clearly defined goal. As you read this, I'll be coming to the end of my fourth four-year Olympic cycle (well, three four-year ones and one five). Each has been different, this last one strikingly so, but they've all followed a broad pattern. With this project, everything has been a little more ... up in the air.

Would those I hoped to speak to prove obliging? Would they be happy to share the methodologies that have brought them such sustained success? Crucially, would those common themes I believed and hoped existed emerge – or would I be left with a collection of insights from a deeply inspiring yet entirely disparate group of one-offs?

The preceding pages provide emphatic answers to these questions. I've accumulated a mountain of material, more than I dared hope for, from a group of academics, coaches and current and former sporting stars who have proven exceedingly generous with their time. Let's see if I can make some sense of it all.

The first surprise was just how much winning seems to be about failure. Living with failure. Fear of failure. Atonement for failure. The word litters these pages and looms over many of the characters in this book in some way.

Welsh rugby star Shane Williams was dropped from the national team early in his career. This defined him, while fear of underperforming seemed to pursue him down the wing pretty much until his final touch of the ball in professional sport. Alex Danson and her Great Britain hockey team mates experienced defeat in Beijing in 2008 and failure in London four years later. Those tears shed after their semi-final exit at their home Olympics hardened into a tremendous resolve.

Ronnie O'Sullivan, for all his prodigious (and hard-won) talent, has had a career littered with high-profile failure, with a stream of first-round exits punctuating those all-conquering campaigns. Stuart Lancaster oversaw England's disastrous Rugby World Cup campaign on home soil in 2015, yet used it to deepen his drive and sense of purpose.

For AP McCoy and Ian Poulter, failure has been about plying their trade in sports, where, on a purely statistical basis, you lose far more often than you win. Even for someone as prolific as AP, who rode a scarcely believable 4,357 winners, it was an uncomfortable fact of life. Analytics has, latterly, become a big thing in tennis. I recall Craig O'Shannessy, of Brain Game Tennis – who has worked with multiple-grand-slam-winner Novak Djokovic – pointing out that even the top player in the world each year only wins 55 per cent of the points they play. The best are able to reconcile themselves to this, and reset accordingly.

Mark Cavendish spoke eloquently of how little a legacy – even one as stellar as his – counts in the fast-moving world of international sport. Forty-eight grand tour stage wins and he's got, in his own words, 'fucking Continental riders laughing at you'. No one misses you, he says. Michael Owen described similar emotions in the career cycle of a football striker: the thrill of scoring World Cup 'worldies', or winning the Ballon d'Or, being replaced by apprehension that these trophies, these records, your place in the team, your entire reputation could be taken from you. And that fear then driving the latter years of achievement as effectively as precocious skill or excitement drove you to the world stage in the first place.

'Enjoyment didn't spur me on,' he said, of this latter period. 'It was fear of someone being better than me.'

One always assumes that those in the sporting world must be insatiable optimists – having an in-built conviction that they can make things better. But the dominant characters we've met don't all seem sunny and optimistic to me. They're not content, in the normal sense. And I don't think the two things are unrelated. AP McCoy told me that it wasn't until he'd ridden 4,000 winners that he got a sense of achievement and began to think, 'Do you know what, this is actually going OK.' It almost feels like innate pessimism.

Two failures have shaped my career. The first time I went to a world championships, as a junior in 2005, they were held in Gamagori, Japan. I was delighted to qualify. And overawed. I ended up 41st and actually think I may have shed a few tears on the way round. On returning to Leeds, my coach Malcolm Brown said to me: 'You must never travel so far to be so poor ever again.' I was never happy with just qualifying again.

In the World Triathlon Series in 2013, I was leading going into the final race. The event was at home and in the same spot, Hyde Park, where I'd won Olympic gold the year before. But my Achilles was a mess. I knew deep down that I wouldn't be able to complete the 10km run finale. The cold, drizzly London day reflected my mood.

I got through the ride, jumped off the bike and the first stride on the blue carpet caused pain to shoot through my leg. I was gutted – but I couldn't pull out of the race because I have always had some weird thing about not finishing. I've only not finished three races in my entire career, in fact – one was a mountain race where I got lost; the second a long-distance tri where I physically couldn't move a step further; and in December 2020 I pulled a calf at Challenge Daytona.

I ended up limping round the 10km course and had to watch from afar as Jonny attempted to outsprint Javier Gómez from 200m out and lost the race, and the world title – prompting my 'tactical numpty' criticism in a live BBC TV interview afterwards (he should have just sat on the Spaniard's shoulder). Both of these failures are, in their very different ways, as sharp in my memory today when I reflect on my career as the highs.

What are some of the other big findings? Selfishness is a recurring element. Beryl Burton's was particularly overt. That of the two jockeys, AP McCoy and Richard Dunwoody, as well. But it's an unspoken undercurrent, too, among all those who've told me about their devotion to hard work (and it's most of them) and pushing themselves harder than any of their contemporaries. I know that this simply isn't possible without a staggering degree of self-absorption. It's only as friends and family have begun to relay stories to me about my own behaviour over the years – tales of which I have no recollection, given my extreme focus at the time – that I've begun to appreciate my own weakness in this regard. Or was it strength?

I've been heartened by just what a significant role innovation plays in the careers of all the sporting greats we've met. Not necessarily quick-and-easy equipment or physiological developments, such as Ian Botham wearing his adapted sunglasses on the cricket pitch to bag more catches. More the innovation in approach, in thinking.

'The great menace to progress is not ignorance but the illusion of knowledge,' said American history professor and author Daniel Boorstin. So-called 'overlearned' behaviour can be the enemy in so many areas. But somehow sport seems particularly susceptible. I've met so many supposed experts on my path whose rigid mindsets, masked by an evangelical zeal, aren't just limiting, they're dangerous to those of us looking for that crucial edge.

There's a central conflict at play here, then, among the top performers: they need to have supreme confidence in what they're doing in training and on the field of play, while simultaneously acknowledging that they're not as good as they could be.

Taking the widely accepted blueprints, structures and systems of their respective sports and constantly challenging them is something all our subjects share. Formula One driver Mark Webber put it best: 'If you're a one-trick pony, you're fucked.' Ronnie O'Sullivan told me he has reinvented himself 'four or five times' over the course of his illustrious career. AP learned from his mentor, Richard Dunwoody – slogging up and down those motorways to race meets – how *not* to run his professional life, and made himself all the more effective for it. 'Madness', Dunwoody called it. AP innovated, got a driver, a secretary. Never has personal admin played a more effective role in sporting greatness.

These are simple things, you'd think. In a work or office environment, they're addressed all the time with little fanfare. But I can attest to the craziness of tempo of a professional sporting career, the 'keep moving or die' ethos that stems from the precariousness of what we do, and how this drives institutionalised thinking. Taking time out to assess and improve can sometimes feel impossible. But the sporting elite in this book have found time to do so.

Webber forced himself to embrace the technical complexities of F1, even though it didn't come naturally. 'I needed to start sleeping with those cats,' he told me, memorably, referring to the pit-lane magicians responsible for the multi-million-pound cars F1 drivers operate in. Why? Minuscule performance gains.

Alex Danson and her teammates went beyond innovation, almost to revolution: they lobbied for central contracts, they forced these through and then they completely rethought the nature of squad preparation – not just paying lip service to the themes of inclusivity and collaboration but restructuring their squad like some sort of utopian island community. Total buy-in. How? Why? The same answer: because Olympic glory was in reach.

Perhaps my favourite innovator is Kílian Jornet. We're cut from the same cloth, me and the Catalan endurance giant; endurance sport is our livelihood. We understand the pain and the rewards. I've always considered myself a free thinker, but getting to know Kílian vividly illustrated my limitations. He hasn't just tinkered with innovation; he's turned the whole process on its head – prioritising fun and engagement, optimising his environment so totally, keeping his legs and motivation fresh by a constantly changing roster of challenges, and making himself all the more dominant for it. Switching to Ironman (still within the scope of my sport, triathlon) is my big change-of-direction goal; with Kílian, you wouldn't be surprised to learn he'd tried to join FC Barcelona.

One of the privileges of meeting a number of sportspeople who've dominated over so many years (in some instances, for nearly a quarter of a century) is hearing about the changes within their sports during that time. I had a laugh with Richard Dunwoody about the crap mechanical horse simulators he was faced with at the start of his career and how they've evolved. Michael Johnson's decade of dominance saw huge changes in athletics. Cav was the first to study – really study – route maps and online images of run-ins to bunch sprint finishes, with appreciable results.

In cricket and football, the innovation has been more about ethos. Beefy Botham – and to a lesser extent Denis Irwin – performed in an era when their sports were characterised by appalling diets, mediocre fitness and institutionalised drinking. Think of the relative performance gains available to a player in either sport back in those days if they'd adopted the more monastic culture of the current crop. Ben Stokes is devastatingly effective now. What sort of record-breaking carnage would the England all-rounder have wreaked in the 1980s (though context is clearly everything)?

Then consider, what are the things in sport that we take for granted now that we'll look back on in 10, 15 years and shake our heads at? Staying ahead of that innovation curve is something all the sporting greats here have done. What are the psychological or behavioural limitations of today? That's what athletes need to be asking themselves, then challenging. It's pretty bloody exciting.

But to challenge accepted wisdom and convention you need big reserves of something else that features prominently in these pages: self-belief. Michael Owen nailed this. Anyone can pep up your confidence, he said. A nice comment here or there. Some praise. Great. Then you bomb out of a race or lose in the first round and it drains away.

Those who've dominated don't worry about the vagaries of form. When bad luck strikes (which it will), when injury hits (likewise), when there's a potentially fatal crash on the track that requires a helicopter evacuation an hour before you have to go back out and try to find those extra two-tenths of a second ... those with the self-belief don't waver for a second.

Where does it come from, this bullet-proof self-belief? From multiple sources, including environment, upbringing and support structures. But also from two key areas we've highlighted here: buy-in and hard work. Kílian Jornet shared some of his wisdom around this with me: 'I know that if you want to do something great, you can't do a lot of other things. If you want to open a door, you need to close another. It needs to be a conscious choice. I think the problem is when you just follow the mood, and then you just hit the wall because you haven't been thinking about it.' None of the subjects in this book, none of the great champions in history, I'd wager, 'just followed the mood'. AP put it best: 'I never wanted to be dependent on others; I wanted for me to make the decisions.'

And then there's that hard work, never the sexiest of topics but generating substantial gains in so many ways. The obvious ones – you're fitter, you're optimising your physiology, you're enabling yourself to practise more – as well as the less obvious psychological benefits: knowing (or even just believing) that very few people, if anyone at all, have prepared better than you, and the strength that flows from that.

'The one thing I do know is that I did work as hard as anyone, if not harder, from an early age.' That from arguably England's greatest ever batsman: nerveless, sweat-free, elegant opener Alastair Cook. Not the most obvious gym junkie.

We heard from (and about) other perceived 'artists' with a ferocious work ethic. Denis Irwin recalled Eric Cantona's tireless devotion to practice. Cristiano Ronaldo's, too. Froome's is better documented, and reiterated here by both the multiple Tour de France winner himself and his former teammate Cav. Ian Thorpe references it when talking about his crucial last leg in the relay that sent Australia into orbit on that first night of competition in 2000. As I know only too well, it's the day-to-day training from which you draw your strength. Josh Waitzkin speaks of a lifestyle of reinforcement in pursuit of excellence. High performers aren't defined by what they do in those rare big moments, he said, but what they do day in, day out. 'If you're going to be the best in the world, you've got to train in a way that sets you apart from the rest of the world,' Peaty told me. 'And if it isn't there, you've got to put your foot down and go, "I ain't accepting this shit, no way."'

Alex Danson spoke articulately on the subject too, saying: 'I've always believed that the most talented people aren't the most successful. It's the workers.' This was wonderful to hear; so candid and refreshing. And it feeds into a central premise of this book: just how bloody ordinary we all are. As discussed, too many people (myself included) succumb to pedestal syndrome.

Perhaps with the exception of Beefy, everyone I spoke to shared, to some degree, my imposter syndrome. Gold medals, epic goals, titles, awards, fame, money – they may enjoy the trappings, but it's rare that they feel proportionate to the recipient, it seems. No sportsperson rests on their laurels, of course; they'd simply get trampled. But not feeling entirely at home, or too comfortable, appears to drive on the very best.

The other big positive is that – assuming you're prepared to work your arse off – so many gains are available. It was revealing to talk to Professor Samuele Marcora and Dr Michael Joyner about the science of suffering. How to train the brain, adapting not just physiologically but psychologically to the extremes of endurance sport in particular. Joyner spoke of the 'relax and win' principle, honed through voluntary immersion in 'boiling water' levels of interval work. Eventually, the mind begins to adapt, such that, when asked to overcome the suffering in a race environment, it can do so with less mental strain. Perception of effort is reduced, which in turn boosts performance. Racing someone with the exact same physiological capabilities, you suddenly have a small but significant edge.

It's been the bedrock of Froome's career. Suffering, so as not to suffer. And there's very little mystique involved. It's like a pact of mutual benefit – or at least mutually assured destruction – between body and brain. And the best bit? That it's 'highly learnable', concludes Joyner.

That normality can apply to physiology, too. We've met a jockey and racing driver who were too tall, a rugby player and footballer who were too small, a cyclist and sprinter who were ungainly. My friend and fellow London 2012 gold medal winner Jess Ennis was nicknamed 'the Tadpole' as an emerging athlete, such was her diminutive physique.

Three things strike me about this. One, you should never rule yourself out of a sport because you believe your physique is suboptimal. Two, that suboptimal physique can actually prove advantageous. And three, there are enormous motivational gains that can come from this.

Martina Hingis is one of the greatest tennis players in history. Including doubles victories, she won 25 majors over the course of her 23-year-long career. In an unpublished interview from 2018, she was asked about her extraordinary longevity and success. She attributed this firstly to her mum, a great coach who taught her when she was very young and who encouraged her to follow an active lifestyle. 'Plus maybe a little bit of talent; things came to me easier than other people,' she said. 'But definitely lots of luck – and many, many hours of hard work. Physically I was unremarkable, which was why I needed to continue to be good at what I did. I couldn't just muscle through. I had to constantly be doing things so I didn't lose the eye for it. In today's tennis, it helps to be tall – but a little bit of cleverness and intelligence also goes a long way.'

One shared factor among all the high achievers I spoke to was the clear and constant presence of *other people*. The temptation at the top – and it's one I've succumbed to at times in the past – is to self-isolate (even when not in lockdown). No one is going through what I'm going through. I'm an outlier. I'm strong and can do this by myself.

Yet, if the examples we've met are anything to go by, sustained success cannot be achieved alone, even if you think, as world champion kayaker Anna Hemmings did, that it can. She needed serious illness to realise that affiliation – bonds with other athletes, coaches or a team – was a central motivation for her. 'No, I'm fine, I'm hardcore' is the image you find yourself projecting in sport, she told me. Yet the strongest thing she did – and one of the most effective – was showing that weakness.

These *other people* can assume all sorts of guises: coaches, psychologists, partners, rivals. Proximity to inspiring figures is remarkably common among the dominant, I found. Donna Fraser told me about her extraordinary summer with Cathy Freeman ahead of that defining race in the Sydney Olympics. 'I realised, "This is how champions train. I need to raise my game,"' she recalled. Ronnie O'Sullivan felt the same when modelling himself on Steve Davis and, later, playing Stephen Hendry. The young AP was entranced by Richard Dunwoody, telling me: 'I saw him when I was a young jockey coming in after a really, really bad fall, and going back out [to race] again. If that's what you need to be a champion, I thought, then I'd better get used to it.'

The extension of this, frighteningly for anyone leading their field, is how many stars of the future they're helping to mould through their dominance now. And so they in turn are pushed, and the whole thing repeats itself.

One of the best-known examples of bar-raising, with almost instant results in its wake, is Roger Bannister's epoch-defining performance when he broke the four-minute mile in 1954. Just over six weeks later, Australian John Landy shaved another second off. The following year, three athletes broke four minutes. Now that Kipchoge has cracked two hours for the marathon (despite the run not being officially recognised), will that level become more common? Are we looking at a generation of sub-57-second 100m breaststrokers coming in the wake of Adam Peaty?

Would Richard Johnson, 16 times runner-up to McCoy as Champion Jockey, have toiled away well into his 40s, with thousands of winners under his belt, had AP not raised the bar so stratospherically high? Champions beget champions, and exposure to them is what's needed. Other people are the key. What was it that Socrates said? The stupid already have all the answers. Average people learn from their experiences. Intelligent individuals learn from everything – and everyone.

Which brings us neatly to the theme of intelligence. You could argue that taking up a career that resulted in 682 high-speed, bone-crunching falls, as it did for Richard Dunwoody, isn't suggestive of the highest levels of brain power. But, researching this book, I was struck again and again by the mental attributes and mental dexterity of the subjects. There's sport-specific intelligence – Michael Owen describes his amazement at the vision and command of space of former teammates such as Wayne Rooney and Steven Gerrard. But also having the cognitive skills to master and maximise your psychology and challenge accepted wisdom, to shift focus and to manage motivation.

So many dominant characters seem to think – an awful lot – about thinking. They are, either innately or through sustained mental application, experts at metacognition. This feeds into a whole range of conscious processes such as planning, monitoring, evaluating and even imagining: it's one thing for Ronnie O'Sullivan to execute the impossible snooker shot, quite another for him to conceive of it in the first place. Mark Webber talked eloquently about the 'frame rate' that an F1 driver has to adapt to absorbing: click, click, click. What you see, what you focus on, what you disregard – all done at hyperspeed in a real-time competitive environment. Chris Froome told me that he had devised a process of visualisation so effective that it served like an extra gear.

Take a scan of Cathy Freeman's brain in the couple of hours leading up to her achieving what an entire country and race were longing for in that 2000 Sydney Olympics 400m final. Seven others were hellbent on that not happening. The event was so technical that her massively experienced training partner, full of confidence and in the shape of her life, botched it. Freeman's brain activity, drawing on every ounce of experience, the silencing of internal voices, the self-talk, the management of crushing pressure, must have been immense, before you even got to the athletic performance itself. Johnson's too.

'It's all between the ears' is the cliché. But it really is, in so many ways. Self-control. Self-awareness. These are the hallmarks of dominance, and they're applicable to everyone. Kílian Jornet put it best: 'I think what separates those who are really at the top is knowledge of yourself.'

And what about goals – or lack of them? All the sportspeople featured have targeted specific victories, or titles, or milestones. But the best have allowed themselves and their ambition to transcend that. Playing for Wales, running for Great Britain, winning the Tour de France. If that's your ultimate goal, then what happens when you attain it?

AP McCoy told me he'd often forgotten about the victory by the time he took the saddle off. Ronnie O'Sullivan revealed the immense frustration of winning when playing poorly. Beryl Burton just went on, and on, and on. Those at the top thrive on the process not the result, which is remarkable given we're in a results-based business to a ridiculous degree. American human-performance expert Brad Stulberg addresses this in his book *The Passion Paradox*, published in 2019. Dopamine, the hormone that regulates perseverance, is released during the path towards an outcome rather than upon achievement. This is an evolutionary response to keep us striving as hunter-gatherers. But in people with a high degree of persistence, their dopamine receptors are less sensitive, which means more dopamine is needed for the same response.

Kevin de Bruyne, the Belgian midfield star of Manchester City's back-to-back Premier League titles in 2017–18 and 2018–19, once said that his fastidious Spanish coach Pep Guardiola was not just interested in winning. He wanted perfection. 'He sets goals that are so high, they're almost impossible to reach.' Alex Danson seemed to understand this, when she told me: 'I love the thrill of *trying* to win. Actually, the winning is just not as great, is it?'

This is about being process-orientated rather than goal-orientated, and having a growth mentality rather than a set one. Recognising that it's the day-to-day discipline rather than the Saturday-afternoon glory that counts most. 'The secret is that everything is always on the line,' wrote Josh Waitzkin.

I've enjoyed hearing about the self-perpetuating nature of dominance. Yes, you've got 'kids' coming at you, fearless and cocksure, with 10, possibly even 20 years on you. But sustained success in a sporting arena has its compensations. 'You look around and you're like, "The guys I'm racing aren't even shaving yet,"' Mark Webber told me, sitting at my dining-room table. 'But you know what? You're wiser. You've got composure, right. "Composure" is a huge word in sport – having belief in yourself at key times, when it's hotting up.'

Paula Radcliffe raced hundreds of times in her career. Denis Irwin made 682 top-flight appearances as a footballer. Alastair Cook faced 26,562 balls. Ronnie O'Sullivan has played nearly 12,000 frames. Yes, the younger players and athletes have fewer scars. But they don't have that stockpile of experience. 'Like everything, you get better,' I recall AP McCoy telling me.

'You get better at winning, you get better at falling, you get better at coping with pain and injury. You have to.'

And this is the final finding. Everyone in this book has said as much. You've got to love what you do. Strip away the gongs, the trophies, the external acclaim, the adulation, the money. Would you still be doing it? For the very best, absolutely. If there was no one to watch you drive past, would you still buy a Ferrari, the old saying goes. Well, if there was no one to watch me run past, I'd still be running. Cycling and swimming, too. And that goes for everyone in this book in their sports. You hate it from time to time, but only the appalling pressure, or the logistical obligations, or the peripheral crap. Never the thing itself.

That doesn't mean they can't love the success. Some of the most fun I've had with this book has been teasing out what it feels like to be right at the top. Ronnie talking about 'fucking flying' in a major tournament, knowing with a sense of delight that 'there's no amount of money that can put anyone in this situation'. The euphoria of Shane Williams scoring a match-winning try to send the whole of Wales 'absolutely ballistic'. I've never known that, but I have experienced the pressure of an Olympic final moments from starting, me as the favourite, the home crowd pumped up, and my heart beating so hard that I could feel the blood pulsing through my neck and straining against the Velcroed collar of my wetsuit. You feel alive.

Mark Webber again: 'Those last moments of a race, when you've got it won, when it's just all so beautiful, and it's just coming together and all the prep, the thousands of hours, and you're … executing, executing on what you've planned. Mate, it's out there.'

So on I go, into the final years of my career. I'm petrified by what awaits. Not potential failure – just retirement. But I'm not done yet, and this process, this project, has – as I hoped it would – reinvigorated my passion for what I do, and given me the insight to hopefully wring the last drops of success out of my career. I've paused, I've taken that deep breath, had a good look around, and now I'm ready to plunge back in, excited about what lies ahead for me, and for elite sport.

What was it that Chris Froome's coach, Tim Kerrison, said? We are nowhere near the limits of human capability.

ACKNOWLEDGEMENTS

My heartfelt gratitude goes out, first, to the inspiring individuals featured in this book who gave so willingly of their time in interview. It really was humbling – and a rare privilege – to be afforded such insight. I look forward to staying in touch and possibly even working together again on future projects.

I can say with absolute certainty that this book would not be in existence without Duncan Craig. His guidance, skill and energy were crucial. Thanks, too, to the team at HarperCollins, particularly Oliver Malcolm and Simon Gerratt.

This book is really a study of the how, the why and the what of performance. I was encouraged from an early age to ask questions and to be curious. There are two people to whom I will be eternally grateful for the source of this inquisitiveness, and for so much more besides: Mum and Dad.

Thank you to all those who have put up with me talking about this project over the past four years, whether on a bike ride, over a cuppa or on the physio bed. Your patience, interest and advice have been brilliant. Special mentions to Coach Malcolm for his encouragement, Edward for printing the whole book out multiple times and making red-pen corrections, Dad for his fatherly perspective and Ruth for reading the whole thing in two sittings.

Last but not least, an apology to the people I see and work with every day. There have been times when this project has made me late for training, made me tired after a long night or just generally put me in a grump. To Jonny, Richard, Ian, Coz, Bucko, Gordon and Harry, thank you for your (continued) understanding, support and friendship. I don't say it enough just how grateful I am to all of you.